D0945242

Modern Critical Views

These and other titles in preparation

Modern Critical Views

WALTER PATER

Modern Critical Views

WALTER PATER

Edited with an introduction by

Harold Bloom

Sterling Professor of the Humanities
Yale University

1985
CHELSEA HOUSE PUBLISHERS
New York

THE COVER:

The cover depicts Pater's Aesthetic vision of the Mona Lisa as the ageless, vampiric consciousness of Western imagination, the Muse of belatedness, possessing more knowledge than is good for her, or for us.—H.B.

PROJECT EDITORS: Emily Bestler, James Uebbing
ASSOCIATE EDITOR: Julia Myer
EDITORIAL COORDINATOR: Karyn Gullen Browne
EDITORIAL STAFF: Linda Grossman, Peter Childers
DESIGN: Susan Lusk

Cover illustration by Kye Carbone

Printed and bound in the United States of America

Library of Congress Cataloging in Publication Data

Walter Pater.
    (Modern critical views)
    Bibliography: p.
    Includes index.
    1. Pater, Walter, 1839–1894—Criticism and interpreta-
tion—Addresses, essays, lectures. I. Bloom, Harold.
II. Series.
PR5137.W28   1985   824'.8   84-28580
ISBN 0–87754–612–6

Chelsea House Publishers
Harold Steinberg, Chairman and Publisher
Susan Lusk, Vice President
A Division of Chelsea House Educational Communications, Inc.
133 Christopher Street, New York, NY 10014

Contents

Editor's Note

This volume is a selection of the best and most representative criticism that is now available on the great critic Walter Pater. It is arranged in the chronological order of these essays' publication.

I have begun this book with my own "Introduction" to a volume of Pater's selected writings, which emphasizes his enormous if sometimes hidden influence upon modern literature. This is followed by Graham Hough's defense of Pater's critical temperament, written at the height of T. S. Eliot's anti-Paterian sway over Anglo-American letters.

The editor's own essay on *Marius the Epicurean* introduces certain strains in Pater's achievement which are more fully examined in Ian Fletcher's remarkable pamphlet, reprinted here in full because Fletcher seems to me to have understood Pater better than anyone else, from Pater's own day until now. J. Hillis Miller's brilliant "partial portrait" of Pater uncovers the uncanny affinity between the author of *Appreciations* and the Deconstructive moment in contemporary criticism.

Gerald Monsman's searching account of *Gaston de Latour* is followed by Perry Meisel's sensitive analysis of Pater's characteristic thematic imagery. Billie Inman's enormous knowledge of Pater's reading informs her sketch of the intellectual context of the celebrated "Conclusion" to the *Renaissance.* The book ends with an advanced account of Paterian textuality and its labyrinths by Jay Fellows, who brings to Pater a vision derived from Pater's central and inescapable precursor, John Ruskin.

Introduction

. . . What is this song or picture, this engaging personality presented in life or in a book, to me? What effect does it really produce on me? Does it give me pleasure? and if so, what sort of degree of pleasure? How is my nature modified by its presence, and under its influence?

— PATER, Preface to *The Renaissance*

. . . Why should a poem not change in sense when there is a fluctuation of the whole of appearance? Or why should it not change when we realize that the indifferent experience of life is the unique experience, the item of ecstasy which we have been isolating and reserving for another time and place, loftier and more secluded.

— STEVENS, "Two or Three Ideas"

"AESTHETIC" CRITICISM

Pater is a great critic of a kind common enough in the nineteenth century—Coleridge, Lamb, Hazlitt, De Quincey, above all Ruskin—but scarcely to be found in the twentieth. Difficult to define, this sort of critic possesses one salient characteristic. His value inheres neither in his accuracy at the direct interpretation of meaning in texts nor in his judgments of relative eminence of works and authors. Rather, he gives us a vision of art through his own unique sensibility, and so his own writings obscure the supposed distinction between criticism and creation. "Supposed," because who can convince us of that distinction? To adapt Shelley's idea of the relation between poetry and the universe, let us say that criticism creates the poem anew, after the poem has been annihilated in our minds by the recurrence of impressions blunted by reiteration. Ruskin's or Pater's criticism tends to create anew not so much a particular work of art but rather the precisely appropriate consciousness of the perceptive reader or viewer. This does not mean that these great critics are monuments to the Affective Fallacy, or that literary historians with Formalist tendencies are justified in naming Ruskin and Pater as critical Impressionists. Oscar Wilde, who brilliantly vulgarized both his prime precursors, insisted that their work treated "the work of art simply as a starting-point for a new creation." Matthew Arnold had asserted that the "aim of criticism is to see the object as in itself it really is." A few years later, implicitly invoking Ruskin against Arnold, Pater slyly added that "the first step towards seeing one's object as it really is, is to know one's impression as it really is, to discriminate it, to realise it distinctly." Wilde, attempting to complete his master, charmingly amended this to the grand statement that "the primary aim of the critic is to see the object as in itself it really is not." Between Arnold's self-deception and Wilde's wit comes Pater's hesitant and skeptical emphasis upon a peculiar kind of vision, with which he identifies all aesthetic experience.

We owe to Pater our characteristic modern use of "aesthetic," for he emancipated the word from its bondage to philosophy, both when he spoke of the "aesthetic critic" in his "Preface" to *The Renaissance*, and when he named the work of Morris and Rossetti as the "aesthetic poetry" in *Appreciations*. Vulgarized again by his ebullient disciple Wilde, and by the parodies of Wilde as Bunthorne in Gilbert and Sullivan's *Patience*, and of Pater himself as Mr. Rose in W. H. Mallock's *The New Republic*, Pater had to endure the debasement of "aesthete" as a term, and we endure it still. Pater meant us always to remember what mostly we have forgotten, that "aesthete" is from the Greek *aisthetes*, "one who perceives." So the "aesthetic critic" is simply the perceptive critic, or literary critic proper, and "aesthetic poetry" is precisely the contemporary poetry that is most perceptive, that is, in one's judgment most truly poetry.

Pater's key terms as a critic are "perception" and "sensation," which is response to perception. "Vision" for Pater, as for Blake, is a synonym for Coleridge's or Wordsworth's "Imagination," and Pater further emulated Blake by questing after the "spiritual form" of phenomena as against "corporeal form." This is the "form" that: "Every moment . . . grows perfect in hand or face," according to the almost preternaturally eloquent "Conclusion" to *The Renaissance*. In the marvelous "Postscript" (on "Romanticism") to *Appreciations*, Pater traces the genesis of form:

> . . . there are the born romanticists, who start with an original, untried *matter*, still in fusion; who conceive this vividly, and hold by it as the essence of their work; who, by the very vividness and heat of their conception, purge away, sooner or later, all that is not organically appropriate to it, till the whole effect adjusts itself in clear, orderly, proportionate form; which form, after a very little time, becomes classical in its turn.

Vividness and *heat* purge away from the Romantic idea all that is not form, and form is the reward of the aesthete or perceptive man, if he has the strength to persist in his purgation. "In the end, the aesthetic is completely crushed and destroyed by the inability of the observer who has himself been crushed to have any feeling for it left." That dark observation is by Wallace Stevens, an heir (unwilling) of Pater's aestheticism. A more accurate observation of the aesthete's defeat comes from as great an heir, more conscious and willing, who attributed to Pater's influence his poetic generation's doomed attempt "to walk upon a rope, tightly stretched through serene air." Yeats nevertheless got across to the other side of the Nineties, and carried Pater alive into our century in *Per Amica Silentia Lunae* (1917) and *A Vision* (1925, 1937). Pater's vision of form culminates in Yeats's Phase 15: "Now contemplation and desire, united into one, inhabit a world where every beloved image has bodily form, and every bodily form is loved." Pater, for whom the attained form demanded purgation, an *askesis* (to which I shall return), hesitantly held back from this Yeatsian version of a High Romantic Absolute.

To know Pater, and to apprehend his influence not only on Stevens and Yeats, but on Joyce, Eliot, Pound, and many other writers of our century, we need to place Pater in his Oedipal context in the cultural situation of his own time. The pleasures of reading Pater are intense, to me, but the importance of Pater transcends those pleasures, and finally is quite out of proportion to Pater's literary achievement, fairly large as that was. Pater is the heir of a tradition already too wealthy to have required much extension or variation when it reached him. He revised that tradition, turning the Victorian continuation of High Romanticism into the Late Romanticism or "Decadence" that prolonged itself as what variously might be called Modernism, Post-Romanticism or, self-deceivingly, Anti-Romanticism, the art of Pound's Vortex. Though Pater compares oddly, perhaps not wholly adequately, with the great Victorian prose prophets, he did what Carlyle, Ruskin, Newman, Arnold could not do: he fathered the future. Himself wistful and elaborately reserved, renouncing even his own strength, he became the most widely diffused (though more and more hidden) literary influence of the later nineteenth upon the twentieth century. In its diffusion, particularly in America, the Paterian influence was assimilated to strikingly similar elements in Nietzsche and Emerson, a process as indubitable as it is still largely unstudied. When Yeats proclaimed the "profane perfection of mankind" or Pound or Stevens their images of the poet as a crystal man, they combined Pater with Nietzsche and Emerson (both of whom he seems to have neglected). "Just take one step farther," Nietzsche urged, and "love yourself through Grace; then you are no longer in need of your God, and the whole drama of fall and redemption is acted out in yourself." "In the highest moments, we are a vision," is the antinomian counsel of Emerson. Pater's first essay, "Diaphaneitè," read to an Oxford literary group in 1864, presented the artist as a transparent or crystal image of more-than-human perfection, an

Apollonian hero. How often, in Modern poetry, we have heard these strains mingled, until by now our latest poets alternately intoxicate and eradicate themselves in the inhuman effort that might sustain a vision so exalted. Pater, though a theorist of the Dionysian, evaded the heroic vitalism of a Nietzsche or the quasi-divine self-reliance of an Emerson, declining to present himself either as prophet or as orator. Yet his baroque meditations upon art, hieratic and subdued, touch as firmly upon the ruinous strength of our major Modern poets as any other precursor of our sensibility does.

PRIVILEGED MOMENTS

Pater's context begins with his only begetter, Ruskin, whose effect can be read, frequently through negation, throughout Pater's work. Believing, as he says in "Style," that imaginative prose largely took the place of poetry in the modern world, Pater necessarily assumed, consciously I think, the characteristic malady of Post-Enlightenment poetry, the new creator's anxiety-of-influence in regard to his precursor's priority, which becomes a menacing spiritual authority, in a direct transference from the natural to the imaginative world. Ruskin, despite his irrelevant mania for ferocious moralizing, is the major "aesthetic critic," in Pater's sense, of the nineteenth century. Stylistically, Pater owed more to Swinburne, but stance rather than style is the crucial indebtedness of a poet or imaginative prose writer. This is Swinburne; *sounds* like Pater, yet menaces him not at all:

> All mysteries of good and evil, all wonders of life and death, lie in their hands or at their feet. They have known the causes of things, and are not too happy. The fatal labour of the world, the clamour and hunger of the open-mouthed all-summoning grave, all fears and hopes of ephemeral men, are indeed made subject to them, and trodden by them underfoot; but the sorrow and strangeness of things are not lessened because to one or two their secret springs have been laid bare and the courses of their tides made known; refluent evil and good, alternate grief and joy, life inextricable from death, change inevitable and insuperable fate.

Swinburne is speaking of Michelangelo, Aeschylus, Shakespeare; masters of the Sublime, whose mastery does not lessen "sorrow and strangeness." The accent here becomes Pater's (Cecil Lang surmises that Gautier's prose is behind Swinburne's, and Gautier also affected the early Pater), but the attitude, superficially akin to Pater's, is profoundly alien to the Epicurean visionary. Swinburne broods on knowledge and powerlessness, but Pater cared only about perception, about seeing again what Michelangelo, Aeschylus, Shakespeare *saw*. Ruskin's Biblical style was no burden to the Hellenizing Pater, but Ruskin's critical stance was at once initial release yet ultimate burden to his disciple. For this is Pater's Gospel, but it is Ruskin's manifesto: ". . . the greatest thing a human soul ever does in this world is to see something, and tell what it saw in a plain way. Hundreds of people can talk for one who can think, but thousands can think for one who can see. To see clearly is poetry, prophecy and religion all in one." Pater was not concerned to tell what he saw in a plain way, but he was kindled by this exaltation of seeing.

Ruskin himself, though uniquely intense as a prophet of the eye, belonged to the Spirit of the Age in his emphasis, as Pater well knew. The primal source of later Romantic seeing in England was Wordsworth, who feared the tyranny of the eye, yet who handed on to his disciples not his fear of the visual, nor (until much later) his Sublime visionary sense, but his program for renovation through renewed encounters with visible nature. Carlyle, a necessary link between Wordsworth and Ruskin, equated the heroism of the poet with "the seeing eye." But a trouble, already always present in Wordsworth and Coleridge, developed fully in Ruskin's broodings upon vision. *Modern Painters III* (1856) distinguishes "the difference between the ordinary, proper, and true appearances of things to us; and the extraordinary, or false appearances, when we are under the influence of emotion, or contemplative fancy; false appearances, I say, as being entirely unconnected with any real power or character in the object, and only imputed to it by us." This imputation of life to the object-world Ruskin called the "pathetic fallacy" and judged as "a falseness in all our impressions of external things." The greatest order of poets, the "Creative" (Shakespeare, Homer, Dante), Ruskin declared free of the pathetic fallacy, finding it endemic in the second order of poets, the "Reflective or Perceptive" (Wordsworth, Keats, Tennyson). Himself a thorough Wordsworthian, Ruskin did not mean to deprecate his Reflective (or Romantic) grouping, but rather to indicate its necessary limitation. Like Pater after him, Ruskin was haunted throughout his life and writings by Wordsworth's "Intimations" Ode, which objectified for both critics their terrible sense of bereavement, of estrangement from the imaginative powers they possessed (or believed themselves to have possessed) as children. Both Ruskin and Pater began as Wordsworthian poets, and turned to imaginative prose partly because of the anxiety-of-influence induced in them by Wordsworth.

Ruskin's formulation of the pathetic fallacy protests the human loss involved in Wordsworth's compensatory imagination. As such, Ruskin's critique prophesies the winter vision of Wallace Stevens, from "The Snow

Man" through to "The Course of a Particular." When Stevens reduces to what he calls the First Idea, he returns to "the ordinary, proper, and true appearances of things to us," but then finds it dehumanizing to live only with these appearances. So the later Ruskin found also, in his own elaborate mythicizings in *Sesame and Lilies* and related books, and in the Wordsworthian autobiography, *Praeterita*, that closed his work. What Wordsworth called "spots of time," periods of particular splendor or privileged moments testifying to the mind's power over the eye, Ruskin had turned from earlier, as being dubious triumphs of the pathetic fallacy. Pater, who subverted Ruskin by going back to their common ancestor Wordsworth, may be said to have founded his criticism upon privileged moments of vision, or "epiphanies" as Joyce's Stephen, another Paterian disciple, was to term them.

The "epiphany," for us, has been much reduced, yet still prevails as our poets' starting-point for moving from sensation to mastery, or at least to self-acceptance:

> Perhaps there are times of inherent excellence,
>
> Perhaps there are moments of awakening,
> Extreme, fortuitous, personal, in which
>
> We more than awaken. . . .

But Stevens's good moments, as here in *Notes Toward a Supreme Fiction*, have receded even from the modified Wordsworthianism that Pater offered as privileged moments, or pathetic fallacies raised to triumphs of perception. For Ruskin's "Perceptive" poets are Pater's "Aesthetic" poets, not a second order but the only poets possible in the universe of death, the Romantic world we have come to inhabit. Joyce's Stephen, recording epiphanies as "the most delicate and evanescent of moments," is recollecting Pater's difficult ecstasy that flares forth "for that moment only." The neo-orthodox, from Hopkins through Eliot to Auden, vainly attempted to restore Pater's "moments" to the religious sphere, yet gave us only what Eliot insisted his poetry would not give, instances of "the intense moment / Isolated, with no before and after," the actual art (such as it is) of *Four Quartets* even as it was of *The Waste Land*. Pater remains the most honest recorder of epiphanies, by asking so little of them, as here in the essay on the poet Joachim Du Bellay in *The Renaissance*:

> A sudden light transfigures a trivial thing, a weathervane, a windmill, a winnowing flail, the dust in the barn door; a moment—and the thing has vanished, because it was pure effect; but it leaves a relish behind it, a longing that the accident may happen again.

"He had studied the nostalgias," like his descendant in Stevens's more qualified vision, and he did not pretend we could be renovated by happy accidents. Yet he offered a program more genuinely purgative than High Romanticism had ventured:

> . . . painting and poetry . . . can accomplish their function in the choice and development of some special situation, which lifts or glorifies a character, in itself not poetical. To realise this situation, to define, in a chill and empty atmosphere, the focus where rays, in themselves pale and impotent, unite and begin to burn . . .

This, from the early essay on "Winckelmann," presents the embryo of a Paterian epiphany. Here is such an epiphany at its most central, in the crucial chapter "The Will as Vision" of *Marius the Epicurean:*

> Through some accident to the trappings of his horse at the inn where he rested, Marius had an unexpected delay. He sat down in an olive garden, and, all around him and within still turning to reverie. . . . A bird came and sang among the wattled hedgeroses: an animal feeding crept nearer: the child who kept it was gazing quietly: and the scene and the hours still conspiring, he passed from that mere fantasy of a self not himself, beside him in his coming and going, to those divinations of a living and companionable spirit at work in all things. . . .
>
> In this peculiar and privileged hour, his bodily frame, as he could recognize, although just then, in the whole sum of its capacities, so entirely possessed by him—Nay! actually his very self—was yet determined by a far-reaching system of material forces external to it. . . . And might not the intellectual frame also, still more intimately himself as in truth it was, after the analogy of the bodily life, be a moment only, an impulse or series of impulses, a single process . . . ? How often had the thought of their brevity spoiled for him the most natural pleasures of life . . . . —To-day at least, in the peculiar clearness of one privileged hour, he seemed to have apprehended . . . an abiding place. . . .
>
> Himself—his sensations and ideas—never fell again precisely into focus as on that day, yet he was the richer by its experience. . . . It gave him a definitely ascertained measure of his moral or intellectual need, of the demand his soul must make upon the powers, whatsoever they might be, which had brought him, as he was, into the world at all. . . .

All of Pater is in this passage. Wordsworth lamented the loss of an earlier glory, ultimately because such glory was equal to an actual sense of immortality. He celebrated "spots of time," not because they restored that saving sense, but in the hope they testified to his spirit's strength over a phenomenal world of decay, and so modestly hinted at some mode of survival. Ruskin, until he weakened (on his own terms), insisted on the Homeric strength of gazing upon ocean, and seeing no emblem of continuity but only pure physical nature: "Black or clear, monstrous or violet-coloured, cold salt water it is always, and nothing but that." Pater's Marius has been found by a skeptical but comforting compromise between the natural visions of Wordsworth and Ruskin. "Peculiar and privileged," or "extreme, fortuitous, personal" as Stevens was to call it, the time of reverie abides in Ruskin's "pure physical nature," yet holds together in continuity not only past and present but what was only potential in the past to a sublimity still possible in the future. The self still knows that it reduces to "sensations and ideas" (the subtitle of *Marius the Epicurean*), still knows the brevity of its expectation, knows even more strongly it is joined to no immortal soul, yet now believes also that its own integrity can be at one with the system of forces outside it. Pater's strange achievement is to have assimilated Wordsworth to Lucretius, to have compounded an idealistic naturalism with a corrective materialism. By de-idealizing the epiphany, he makes it available to the coming age, when the mind will know neither itself nor the object but only the dumbfoundering abyss that comes between.

HISTORICISMS:
RENAISSANCE AND ROMANTICISM

Pater began to read Ruskin in 1858, when he was just nineteen, eight years before he wrote his first important essay, "Winckelmann." From then until the posthumously published writings, Pater suffered under Ruskin's influence, though from the start he maintained a revisionary stance in regard to his precursor. In place of Ruskin's full, prophetic, even overwhelming rhetoric, Pater evolved a partial, hesitant, insinuating rhetoric, yet the result is a style quite as elaborate as his master's. The overt influence, Pater buried deep. He mentioned Ruskin just once in his letters, and then to claim priority over Ruskin by two years as the English discoverer of Botticelli (as late as 1883, Ruskin still insisted otherwise, but wrongly). Ruskin is ignored, by name, in the books and essays, yet he hovers everywhere in them, and nowhere more strongly than in *The Renaissance* (1873), for Pater's first book is primarily an answer to *The Stones of Venice* (1851, 1853) and to the five volumes of *Modern Painters* (1843–1860). Where Ruskin had deplored the Renaissance (and located it in Italy between the fourteenth and sixteenth centuries), elevating instead the High Middle Ages, Pater emulated the main movement of English Romanticism by exalting the Renaissance (and then anticipated later studies by locating its origins in twelfth-century France). Yet the polemic against Ruskin, here as elsewhere, remains implicit. One of Pater's friends reported that once, when talking of Ruskin's strength of perception, Pater burst out: "I cannot believe that Ruskin saw more in the church of St. Mark than I do." Pater's ultimate bitterness, in this area, came in 1885, when Ruskin resigned as Slade Professor of Fine Art at Oxford. Pater offered himself for the professorship, but it went to one Hubert Von Herkomer, and not to the author of the notorious book on the Renaissance, whose largest departure from Ruskin was in opposing a darker and hedonistic humanism to the overtly moral humanism of his aesthetic precursor.

The vision of Pater's *Renaissance* centers upon the hope of what Yeats was to call Unity of Being. Drawing his epigraph from the Book of Psalms, Pater hints at the aesthetic man's salvation from the potsherds of English Christianity in the 1860's: "Though ye have lain among the pots, yet shall ye be as the wings of a dove covered with silver, and her feathers with yellow gold" (Psalms 68:13). The aesthetic man, surrounded by the decaying absolutes inherited from Coleridge-as-theologian, accepts the truths of solipsism and isolation, of mortality and the flux of sensations, and glories in the singularity of his own peculiar kind of contemplative temperament. Pater would teach this man self-reconcilement and self-acceptance, and so Unity of Being. In the great figures of the Renaissance— particularly Botticelli, Michelangelo, Leonardo—Pater presents images of this Unity of aesthetic contemplation. Ruskin, a greater critic than Pater, did not over-idealize the possibilities of aesthetic contemplation, not even in books as phantasmagoric as *The Queen of the Air*. Pater's desperation, both to go beyond Ruskin and to receive more from art, is at once his defining weakness in comparison to Ruskin, and his greater importance for what was to come, not just in the 1880's and 1890's, but throughout our century.

In his vision of the Renaissance, Pater inherits the particular historicism of English Romanticism, which had found its own origins in the English Renaissance, and believed itself a renaissance of that Renaissance. Between the High Romantics and Pater many losses were felt, and of these Darwin compelled the largest. *The Renaissance* is already a Darwinian book, rather in the same way that *The Stones of Venice* was still a Coleridgean book. Pater's moral tentativeness necessarily reflected his own profound repressions, including his aversion to heterosexuality, and the very clear strain of sadomasochism in his psyche. But the intellectual sanction of Pater's skeptical Epicureanism was provided by the prevalent skepticism even of religious apologias in the age of Newman and the Oxford Movement. Evolution, whether as presented by Christian historicisms or by Darwin himself, gave the self-divided Pater a justification for projecting his temperament into a general vision of his age's dilemmas. His later work, considered further on in this Introduction, found a governing dialectic for his skepticism in the Pre-Socratics and Plato, but in *The Renaissance* the personal projection is more direct, and proved more immediately influential.

The "Preface" to *The Renaissance* outlines a cycle in the concept of renaissance, which goes from an early freshness with "the charm of *ascêsis*, of the austere and serious girding of the loins in youth" to "that subtle and delicate sweetness which belongs to a refined and comely decadence." The Greek word *ascêsis* (or *askesis*) originally referred to athleticism, but easily transferred itself, even in ancient time, to an exercise in spiritualizing purgation. Paterian *askesis* is less a sublimation (as it seems when first used in the "Preface") than it is an aesthetic self-curtailment, a giving-up of certain powers so as to help achieve more originality in one's self-mastery. An Epicurean or hedonistic *askesis* is only superficially a paradox, since it is central in the Lucretian vision that Pater labored to attain. For Lucretius, truth is always in appearances, the mind is a flow of sensory patterns, and moral good is always related directly to pleasurable sensations. But intense pleasure, as Epicurus taught, is grossly inferior to possessing a tranquil temperament. Pater's Epicureanism in *The Renaissance* was more radical, and hesitates subtly at exalting a quasi-homosexual and hedonistic humanism, particularly in the essays on Leonardo and on Winckelmann.

In the essay on "Two Early French Stories," Pater identifies his "medieval Renaissance" with "its antinomianism, its spirit of rebellion and revolt against the moral and religious ideas of the time." Pater's own antinomianism is the unifying element in his great first book, as he elaborately intimates "a strange idolatry, a strange rival religion" in opposition to the Evangelical faith of Ruskin and the revived orthodoxies of the Oxford Movement. The extraordinary essay on Botticelli, a triumphant prose poem, sees in his Madonna "one of those who are neither for Jehovah nor for His enemies," and hints at a sadomasochistic sadness with which Botticelli conceives the universe of pleasure he has chosen. In the essay on Leonardo, which may be Pater's finest poem, the visionary center is reached in the notorious (and wholly magnificent) passage on *La Gioconda*, which Yeats brilliantly judged to be the first Modern poem, but which he proceeded to butcher by printing in verse form as the first poem in *The Oxford Book of Modern Verse* (1936). Yeats, in his "Introduction," asked an insightful and largely rhetorical question: "Did Pater foreshadow a poetry, a philosophy, where the individual is nothing, the flux of *The Cantos* of Ezra Pound, objects without contour . . . , human experience no longer shut into brief lines, . . . the flux . . . that within our minds enriches itself, re-dreams itself . . . ?"

Freud, in his study of Leonardo, found in the Mona Lisa the child's defense against excessive love for his mother, by means of identifying with her and so proceeding to love boys in his own image, even as he had been loved. In one of his most troubling insights, Freud went on to a theory of the sexual origins of all thought, a theory offering only two ways out for the gifted; a compulsive, endless brooding in which all intellectual curiosity remains sexual, or a successful sublimation, in which thought, to some extent, is liberated from its sexual past. Is Pater, throughout *The Renaissance*, and particuarly in the "Leonardo" and the "Conclusion," merely a fascinating, compulsive brooder, or has he freed his thought from his own over-determined sexual nature? Some recent studies reduce Pater only to the former possibility, but this is to underestimate an immensely subtle mind. Here is the crucial passage, not a purple patch but a paean to the mind's mastery over its own compulsiveness:

> The presence that rose thus so strangely beside the waters, is expressive of what in the ways of a thousand years men had come to desire. Hers is the head upon which all "the ends of the world are come," and the eyelids are a little weary. It is a beauty wrought out from within upon the flesh, the deposit, little cell by cell, of strange thoughts and fantastic reveries and exquisite passions. Set it for a moment beside one of those white Greek goddesses or beautiful women of antiquity, and how would they be troubled by this beauty, into which the soul with all its maladies has passed! All the thoughts and experience of the world have etched and moulded there, in that which they have of power to refine and make expressive the outward form, the animalism of Greece, the lust of Rome, the mysticism of the middle age with its spiritual ambition and imaginative loves, the return of the Pagan world, the sins of the Borgias. She is older than the rocks among which she sits; like the vampire, she has been dead many times, and learned the secrets of the grave; and has been a diver in deep seas, and keeps their fallen day about her; and trafficked for strange webs with Eastern merchants, and, as Leda, was the mother of Helen of Troy, and, as Saint Anne, the mother of Mary; and all this has been to her but as the sound of lyres and flutes, and lives only in the delicacy with which it has moulded the changing lineaments, and tinged the eyelids and the hands. The fancy of a perpetual life, sweeping together ten thousand experiences, is an old one; and modern philosophy has conceived the idea of humanity as wrought upon by, and summing up in itself, all modes of thought and life. Certainly Lady Lisa might stand as the embodiment of the old fancy, the symbol of the modern idea.

Most broadly, this is Pater's comprehensive vision of an equivocal goddess whom Blake called "the Female Will" and the ancient Orphics named *Ananke*, meaning "Necessity." Pater dreads and desires her, or perhaps desires her precisely through his dread. Desire dominates here, for the sight of her is a privileged moment, an epiphany of the only divinity Pater truly worshipped. In the essay following, on "The School of Giorgione," Pater speaks of "profoundly significant and animated instants, a mere gesture, a look, a smile, perhaps—some brief and wholly concrete moment—into which, however, all the motives, all the interests and effects of a long history, have condensed themselves, and which seem to absorb past and future in an intense consciousness of the present." The Lady Lisa, as an inevitable object of the quest for all which we have lost, is herself a process moving toward a final entropy, summing up all the estrangements we have suffered from the object-world we once held close, whether as children, or in history. She incarnates too much, both for her own good and for ours. The cycles of civilization, the burden our consciousness bears, render us latecomers but the Lady Lisa perpetually carries the seal of a terrible priority. Unity of Being she certainly possesses, yet she seems to mock the rewards Pater hoped for in such Unity. A powerful juxtaposition, of the ancient dream of a literal immortality, of living all lives, and of Darwinism ("modern philosophy"), ends the passage with an astonishing conceptual image. The Lady Lisa, as no human could hope to do, stands forth as a body risen from death, and also as symbol of modern acceptance of Necessity, the non-divine evolution of our species. She exposes, as Pater is well aware, the hopelessness of the vision sought by *The Renaissance*, and by all Romantic and Post-Romantic art.

Yet, with that hopelessness comes the curious reward of the supreme Paterian epiphany. Rilke remarked of the landscape behind the Madonna Lisa that "it is Nature which came into existence . . . something distant and foreign, something remote and without allure, something entirely self-contained. . . ." Following Rilke, the psychologist J. H. Van den Berg associates this estrangement of an outer landscape with the growth of a more inward, alienated self than mankind had known before:

> The inner life was like a haunted house. But what else could it be? It contained everything. Everything extraneous had been put into it. The entire history of the individual. Everything that had previously belonged to everybody, everything that had been collective property and had existed in the world in which everyone lived, had to be contained by the individual. It could not be expected that things would be quiet in the inner self.

In his way, Van den Berg, like Rilke, sides with Ruskin and not with Pater, for the implicit argument here is that the Romantic inner self cost too much in solipsistic estrangement. But Pater was a divided man, humanly wiser than he could let himself show as a Late Romantic moralist-critic. His vision of the Mona Lisa is as much a warning as it is an ideal. This, he says, is our Muse, mistress of Unity-of-Being. The poets of the Nineties, including the young Yeats, chose to see the ideal and not to heed the warning. The further work of Pater, after *The Renaissance*, shows the Aesthetic Critic accepting his own hint, and turning away from self-destruction.

One cannot leave the "Conclusion" to *The Renaissance* without acknowledging the power which that handful of pages seems to possess even today, a hundred years after their composition. In their own generation, their pungency was overwhelming; not only did Pater withdraw them in the second edition, because he too was alarmed at their effect, but he toned them down when they were restored in the third edition. The skeptical eloquence of the "Conclusion" cost Pater considerable preferment at Oxford. There is a splendidly instructive letter from John Wordsworth (clerical grandnephew of the poet) to Pater, written in 1873, indignantly summing up the "Conclusion" as asserting: "that no fixed principles either of religion or morality can be regarded as certain, that the only thing worth living for is momentary enjoyment and that probably or certainly the soul dissolves at death into elements which are destined never to reunite." One can oppose to this very minor Wordsworth a reported murmur of Pater's: "I wish they would not call me a hedonist. It gives such a wrong impression to those who do not know Greek."

Early Pater, in all high seriousness, attains a climax in those wonderful pages on the flux-of-sensations, and the necessity of dying with a faith in art, that conclude *The Renaissance*. Written in 1868, they came initially out of a review of William Morris's poetry that became the suppressed essay on "Aesthetic Poetry." They gave Pater himself the problem of how he was to write up to so fierce a demand-of-self: "To burn always with this hard, gemlike flame, to maintain this ecstasy, is success in life."

FICTIVE SELVES

Pater's own life, by his early standards, was only ambiguously a success. His work after *The Renaissance* is of three kinds, all of them already present in his first book. One is "imaginary portraits," a curious mixed genre, of which the novel *Marius the Epicurean* is the most important, and of which four excellent shorter examples are given [elsewhere]: the semi-autobiographical "The Child in the House," two stories from the book called *Imaginary Portraits*, and a classical example from *Greek Studies*. Another grouping of Pater's work, critical essays, was mostly gathered in *Appreciations*, from which I have selected liberally. The last group, classical studies proper, stand a little apart from the rest of his work, are more lightly represented in this book, and will be considered at the close of this Introduction.

"Imaginary portraits," in Pater's sense, are an almost indescribable genre. Behind them stand the monologues of Browning and of Rossetti, the *Imaginary Conversations* of Landor, perhaps Sainte-Beuve's *Portraits contemporains*. Like *The Renaissance* and *Appreciations* they are essays or quasi-essays; like "The Child in the House" they are semi-autobiographical; yet it hardly helps to see "Sebastian Van Storck," or "Denys l'Auxerrois" or "Hippolytus Veiled" as being essays or veiled confessions. Nor are they romance-fragments, though closer to that than to short stories. It may be best to call them what Yeats called his Paterian stories, "Mythologies," or "Romantic Mythologies." Or, more commonly, they could be called simply "reveries," for even at their most marmoreal and baroque they are highly disciplined reveries, and even the lengthy *Marius the Epicurean* is more a historicizing reverie than it is a historical novel. "Reverie" comes from the French *rêver*, "to dream," and is already used in music to describe an instrumental composition of a dreamlike character. The power and precariousness alike of Pater's reveries are related to their hovering near the thresholds of wish-fulfillment. I suspect that Pater's nearest ancestor here is Browning, even as Ruskin looms always behind Pater's aesthetic criticism. Just as Browning made fictive selves, to escape his earlier strain of Shelleyan subjectivity in the verse-romances *Pauline*, *Paracelsus*, and *Sordello*, so Pater turned to "imaginary portraits" to escape the subjective confession that wells up in his "Leonardo da Vinci" and "Conclusion" to *The Renaissance*. On this view, *The Renaissance* is Pater's version of Shelley's *Alastor* or Keats's *Endymion*; it is a prose-poem of highly personal Romantic quest after the image of desire, visualized by Pater in the Mona Lisa. Turning from so deep a self-exposure, Pater arrives at his kind of less personal reverie, a consciously fictive kind.

Pater had no gifts for narrative, or drama, or psychological portrayal, and he knew this well enough. Unlike Browning, he could not make a half-world, let alone the full world of a mythopoeic master like Blake. Pater, who intensely admired both poets, oriented his portraits with more specific reference to the most inescapable of Romantic poets, Wordsworth, concerning whom he wrote the best of his essays in strictly literary criticism. In the nearly-as-distinguished essay on "Coleridge," Pater justly praises Wordsworth as a more instinctual poet than Coleridge. Wordsworth is praised for "that flawless temperament . . . which keeps his conviction of a latent intelligence in nature within the limits of sentiment or instinct, and confines it to those delicate and subdued shades of expression which perfect art allows." Pater, too consciously, seeks in his portraits to be instinctual rather than intellectual, hoping that thus he can avoid drama and self-consciousness. Unfortunately, he cannot sustain the Wordsworthian comparison, as again he knew, for though he shared Wordsworth's early naturalism, he lacked the primordial, Tolstoyan power that sustains poems like "The Ruined Cottage," "Michael," "The Old Cumberland Beggar." Yet he yearned for such power, and would have been a Wordsworthian novelist, like George Eliot and Hardy, if he had found the requisite strength. But this yearning, poignantly felt all through the beautiful Wordsworth essay, was a desperate desire for his opposite. Wordsworth lived in nature, Pater in a dream. Longing for the sanctities of earth, Pater found his true brothers in Rossetti and Morris, poets of phantasmagoria, and his true children in Yeats and the Tragic Generation. The "imaginary portraits" are crucial to our understanding of Pater, but as art they are equivocal achievements, noble but divided against themselves.

SORROWS OF INFLUENCE

Pater is not the greatest critic English Romanticism produced—Coleridge and Ruskin vie for that eminence—but he is certainly the most underrated major nineteenth-century critic, in our own time. He is superior to his older rival, Arnold, and to his disciple, Wilde, both of whom receive more approval at this moment. Yet even as a literary critic he is evasive, and remains more a master of reverie than of description, let alone analysis, which is alien to him. This becomes a curious critical strength in him, which requires both description and analysis to be apprehended.

   Appreciations begins with the extraordinary essay on "Style," which is Pater's *credo* as a literary critic. As the essay urges awareness of the root-meanings of words, we need to remember that "style" originally meant an ancient instrument for writing on a waxed tablet, and having one pointed end for incising words, and one blunt end for rubbing out writing, and smoothing the tablet down. We might also remember that "appreciations" originally meant "appraisals." Before appraising Wordsworth, Coleridge, Rossetti, Morris, Lamb, and others, Pater offers us a vision of his stylistic attitude, incisive but also ascetic. Ian Fletcher, Pater's best scholar, reminds us that Pater's idea of style is "as a mode of perception, a total responsive gesture of the whole personality." Since Pater's own style is the most highly colored and self-conscious of all critics who have written in English, there is a puzzle here. Pater attempted to write criticism as though he were style's martyr, another Flaubert, and his insistence upon *askesis*, the exercise of self-curtailment, hardly seems compatible with a whole personality's total response. We do not believe that the style is the man when we read Pater, and a glance at his letters, which are incredibly dull and nonrevelatory, confirms our disbelief. Pater's style, as befits the master of Wilde and Yeats, is a mask, and so Pater's idea of style and his actual style are irreconcilable. As always, Pater anticipates us in knowing this, and the essay "Style" centers upon this division.

Prose, according to Pater, is both music's opposite and capable of transformation into the condition of music, where form and matter seem to dissolve into one another. Pater's subject is always the mystery of utter individuality in the artistic personality; his style strives extravagantly to award himself such individuality. Whether in matter or style, Pater has therefore a necessary horror of literary influence, for to so desperate a quester after individuality *all* influence is over-influence. Pater's subject-matter is also Ruskin's and Arnold's; his style is also Swinburne's, or rather one of Swinburne's styles. Unlike Emerson and Nietzsche, who refused to see themselves as latecomers, Pater's entire vision is that of a latecomer longing for a renaissance, a rebirth into imaginative earliness. The hidden subject of *Appreciations* is the anxiety of influence, for which Pater's remedy is primarily his idea of *askesis*. "Style" urges self-restraint and renunciation, which it calls an economy of means but which in Pater's actual style seems more an economy of ends. Ruskin, threatening precursor, was profuse in means and ends, master of emphasis and of a daemonic, Sublime style, which in his case *was* the man. Swerving from Ruskin, Pater turns to Flaubert in "Style," seeking to invent a father to replace a dominant and dangerous aesthetic parent. But guilt prevails, and Pater's anxiety emerges in the essay's long concluding paragraph, which astonishingly seems to repeal the special emphasis of everything that has come before. "Good art, but not necessarily great art," Pater sadly murmurs, suddenly assuring us that greatness depends not upon style but on the matter, and then listing Dante, Milton, the King James Bible, and Hugo's *Les Misérables*, which seems rather exposed in this sublime company, and hardly rivals Flaubert in its concern with form. By the test of finding a place in the structure of human life, Hugo will receive the palm before Flaubert, Ruskin before Pater, Tennyson (secretly despised by Pater) before Rossetti and Morris. The final *askesis* of the champion of style is to abnegate himself before the burden of the common life he himself cannot bear.

In the essay "Wordsworth," Pater has the happiness of being able to touch the commonal through the greatest mediating presence of nineteenth-century poetry. The essays on Wordsworth of Arnold and, *contra* Arnold, of A. C. Bradley, have been profoundly influential on rival schools of modern Wordsworthian interpretation, and Pater has not, but a reading of the three essays side by side will show Pater's superiority. His Wordsworth is neither Arnold's poet of Nature nor Bradley's poet of the Sublime, but rather a poet of instinctual pagan religion. Wordsworth would have been outraged by Pater's essay, and most modern scholars agree that Pater's Wordsworth is too much Pater's Marius and too little Wordsworth. Against which, here is Pater's account of Wordsworth's ac-tual religion, *as a poet*:

> Religious sentiment, consecrating the affections and natural regrets of the human heart, above all, that pitiful awe and care for the perishing human clay, of which relic-worship is but the corruption, has always had much to do with localities, with the thoughts which attach themselves to actual scenes and places. Now what is true of it everywhere, is truest of it in those secluded valleys where one generation after another maintains the same abiding place; and it was on this side, that Wordsworth appre-hended religion most strongly. Consisting, as it did so much, in the recognition of local sanctities, in the habit of connecting the stones and trees of a particular spot of earth with the great events of life, till the low walls, the green mounds, the half-obliterated epitaphs seemed full of voices, and a sort of natural oracle, the very religion of those people of the dales, appeared but as another link between them and the earth, and was literally a religion of nature.

What is most meaningful for Pater are those voices coming from low walls, green mounds, tombstones. These things remain *things* in Wordsworth, wholly other than ourselves, yet we are deeply affected by what emanates from them. Pater was converted by them to the only religion he ever sincerely held, "literally a religion of nature." Just as the spots of time gave Wordsworth not a sense of the Divine, but precise knowledge to what point and how his own mind displayed a mastery over outward sense, so for Pater the spots of time he located in works of art gave a precise knowledge of the limited efficacy of the great Romantic program for renovation. The Romantics, as Pater understood and Arnold did not, were not nature-poets, but rather exemplars of the power of the mind, a power exerted against the object-world, or mere universe of death. Like Ruskin, and like Yeats and Stevens, Pater is a Romantic critic of Romanticism. Whether Pater writes on Giorgione or Winckelmann, the myth of Dionysus or Plato and the Doctrine of Change, Rossetti or Wilde, he writes as a conscious post-Wordsworthian, and his true subject is the partial and therefore tragic (because momentary) victory that art wins over the flux of sensations. The step beyond Pater is the one taken by his disciple, Yeats, who insists on the tragic joy of art's defeat, and who in his savage last phase celebrates the flux, exulting in his own doctrine of change.

Pater, withdrawing in *Appreciations* as in *Marius* from hailing the Heraclitean flux, is most moved by Wordsworth's quiet and primordial strength, the instinctual power of "impassioned contemplation." The eloquent and compassionate essay on "Coleridge" begins from Pater's recognition that Coleridge lacked this strength, and goes on to reject Coleridge's theological reliance upon outworn Absolutes. More strikingly, Pater pioneers in rejecting the Organic Analogue that Coleridge popularized. The motto of Pater's essay on Coleridge might well come from Nietzsche: "But do I bid thee be either plant or phantom?" Coleridge, Pater suggests, bid us be both, and so "obscured the true interest of art," which is to celebrate and lament our intolerably glorious condition of being mortal gods.

Beyond his steady defense of art's dignity against metaphysical and religious absolutes, Pater's nobility and uniqueness as a nineteenth-century literary critic stem from his insistence that the later nineteenth-century poet "make it new," even as that poet (like Pater himself) remains fully conscious of the inescapable sorrows of influence. Such a poet wanders in the half-lights of being a latecomer, trailing after the massive, fresh legacy of Goethe, Wordsworth, Blake, Hugo, Keats, Shelley, Baudelaire, Browning, even as Pater trailed after De Quincey, Lamb, Hazlitt, Coleridge, Arnold and the inescapable Ruskin, quite aside from Swinburne and the unmentioned Emerson and Nietzsche. Pater is still the best critic Pre-Raphaelite poetry has had, largely because he understood so well the anxiety of influence consciously present in Rossetti and unconsciously at work in Morris. The great essay on Morris, "Aesthetic Poetry," properly close to the "Conclusion" to *The Renaissance* which was quarried from it, presents Pater's most unguarded vision of poetic experience, so that Pater inevitably suppressed it:

> . . . exotic flowers of sentiment expand, among people of a remote and
> unaccustomed beauty, somnambulistic, frail, androgynous, the light al-
> most shining through them. . . . The colouring is intricate and delirious,
> as of "scarlet lilies." The influence of summer is like a poison in one's
> blood, with a sudden bewildered sickening of life and all things. . . . A
> passion of which the outlets are sealed, begets a tension of nerve, in
> which the sensible world comes to one with a reinforced brilliancy and
> relief—all redness is turned into blood, all water into tears. . . . One
> characteristic of the pagan spirit the aesthetic poetry has . . . —the sense
> of death and the desire of beauty: the desire of beauty quickened by the
> sense of death. . . .

Remarkably hinting that sadomasochistic yearnings and the anxiety of being a late representative of a tradition are closely related, Pater
implies also that the heightened intensity of Morris and Rossetti (and of
Pater) compensates for a destructively excessive sexual self-consciousness.
The sensible world becomes phantasmagoria because one's own nature is
baffled. A critic who understands the dialetic of style, as Pater magnifi-
cently did, is in no need of psychoanalytic reduction, as these essays on
Morris and Rossetti show. *Appreciations*, which influenced Wilde and Yeats,
Joyce and Pound, and more covertly Santayana and Stevens, has had little
influence upon modern academic criticism, but one can prophesy that
such influence will yet come. In a letter (January 8, 1888) to the young
poet Arthur Symons, Pater recalled the marvelous dictum of Rossetti:
"Conception, my boy, FUNDAMENTAL BRAINWORK, that is what makes the
difference in all art." Pater's apt purpose in this recall was to urge Symons,
and the other poets of his generation—Yeats, Dowson, Lionel Johnson—to
make it new again through the fundamental brainwork necessary to overcome anxieties-of-influence. Here is the prophecy, addressed to the Paterian
poets of the Tragic Generation, which Pound and his Modernists attempted to fulfill:

> I think the present age an unfavourable one to poets, at least in England.
> The young poet comes into a generation which has produced a large
> amount of first-rate poetry, and an enormous amount of good secondary
> poetry. You know I give a high place to the literature of prose as a fine
> art, and therefore hope you won't think me brutal in saying that the
> admirable qualities of your verse are those also of imaginative prose; as I
> think is the case also with much of Browning's finest verse. . . .

The Poundian dictum, that verse was to be as well written as
prose, initially meant Browningesque verse and Paterian prose, as Pound's
early verse and prose show. That literary Modernism ever journeyed too
far from its Paterian origins we may doubt increasingly, and we may
wonder also whether modern criticism as yet has caught up with Pater.

CENTRIFUGAL AND CENTRIPETAL

In the important essay on Romanticism that he made the "Postscript" to *Appreciations*, Pater insisted that: "Material for the artist, motives of inspiration, are not yet exhausted . . . ," yet he wondered how "to induce order upon the contorted, proportionless accumulation of our knowledge and experience, our science and history, our hopes and disillusion . . ." To help induce such an order seems to be the motive for *Plato and Platonism* (1893) and the posthumously published *Greek Studies* (1895). The Plato of Walter Pater is Montaigne's Plato (and probably Shelley's), a skeptical evader of systems, including his supposed own, whose idea of order is the dialectic: "Just there, lies the validity of the method—in a dialogue, an endless dialogue, with one's self." Clearly this is Pater more than Plato, and we need not wonder why Pater favored this above his other books. In the chapter "The Genius of Plato," Pater gives us another reverie, an idealized imaginary portrait of what he would have liked the mind of Pater to be. A comparison with Emerson's Plato (also influenced by Montaigne) is instructive, for the Plato of *Representative Men* is criticized for lacking "contact," an Emersonian quality not far removed from "freedom" or wildness. Unlike Plato, the author of the *Dialogues*, Walter Pater's visionary indeed lacks "contact," even as Pater severely made certain he himself lacked it.

Pater gives us the author of *The Republic* as "a seer who has a sort of sensuous love of the unseen," and whose mythological power brings the unseen closer to the seen. This Plato is possible and possibly even more than marginal, yet he does seem more Ficino or Pico della Mirandola than he was Plato, for he is more a poet of ideas than a metaphysician, and more of a solipsistic Realist than an Idealist. Above all, he is Pater's "crystal man," a model for Yeats's vision of an *antithetical* savior, a greater-than-Oedipus who would replace Christ, and herald a greater Renaissance than European man had known.

From reading both Hegel and Darwin, Pater had evolved a curious dialectic of history, expounded more thoroughly in *Greek Studies*, using the terms "centripetal" and "centrifugal" as the thesis and antithesis of a process always stopping short of synthesis:

> All through Greek history we may trace, in every sphere of the activity of the Greek mind, the action of these two opposing tendencies,—the centrifugal and centripetal. . . . There is the centrifugal, the Ionian, the Asiatic tendency, flying from the centre . . . throwing itself forth in endless play of undirected imagination; delighting in brightness and colour, in beautiful material, in changeful form everywhere, in poetry, in

philosophy . . . its restless versatility drives it towards . . . the development of the individual in that which is most peculiar and individual in him. . . . It is this centrifugal tendency which Plato is desirous to cure, by maintaining, over against it, the Dorian influence of a severe simplification everywhere, in society, in culture. . . .

The centrifugal is the vision of Heraclitus, the centripetal of Parmenides, or in Pater's more traditional terms from the "Postscript" to *Appreciations*, the centrifugal is the Romantic, and the centripetal the Classic. Pater rather nervously praises his Plato for Classic correctiveness, for a conservative centripetal impulse against his own Heraclitean Romanticism. Reductively, this is still Pater reacting against the excesses of *The Renaissance*, and we do not believe him when he presents himself as a centripetal man, though Yeats was partially persuaded, and relied upon Pater's dialectic when he created his own version of an aesthetic historicism in *A Vision*.

Pater, in his last phase, continued to rationalize his semi-withdrawal from his own earlier vision, but we can doubt that even he trusted his own hesitant rationalizations. We remember him, and read him, as the maker of critical reveries who yielded up the great societal and religious hopes of the major Victorian prose-prophets, and urged us to abide in the mortal truths of perception and sensation. His great achievement, in conjunction with Swinburne and the Pre-Raphaelites, was to empty Ruskin's aestheticism of its moral bias, and so to purify a critical stance appropriate for the apprehension of Romantic art. More than Swinburne, Morris, Rossetti, he became the father of Anglo-American Aestheticism, and subsequently the direct precursor of a Modernism that vainly attempted to be Post-Romantic. I venture the prophecy that he will prove also to be the valued precursor of a Post-Modernism still fated to be another Last Romanticism. We can judge, finally, this ancestor of our own sensibility as he himself judged Plato:

His aptitude for things visible, with the gift of words, empowers him to express, as if for the eyes, what except to the eye of the mind is strictly invisible, what an acquired asceticism induces him to rank above, and sometimes, in terms of harshest dualism, oppose to, the sensible world. Plato is to be interpreted not merely by his antecedents, by the influence upon him of those who preceded him, but by his successors, by the temper, the intellectual alliances, of those who directly or indirectly have been sympathetic with him.

GRAHAM HOUGH

The Paterian Temperament

As it happens, he makes precisely this attempt himself, in *The Child in the House*, which has as its intention "the noting, namely, of some things in the story of his spirit, in that process of brain-building, by which we are, each one of us, what we are". There is no clearer guide to the elements that go to compose Pater's temperament. The note which is first struck is one which we do not usually associate with Pater—the note of domesticity and homeliness. He was later very uncommunicative about the circumstances of his own life, but what the first few pages of *The Child in the House*, with an almost Jamesian circumlocution, contrive to say, is that he was brought up in a suburb and loved it; and that ever after, this delightful, English and typically bourgeois sense of home remained quite fundamental to him.

> With Florian then the sense of home became singularly intense, his good fortune being that the special character of his home was in itself so essentially home-like. As after many wanderings I have come to fancy that some parts of Surrey and Kent are, for Englishmen, the true land-scape, true home-counties, by right, partly, of a certain earthy warmth in the yellow of the sand below their gorse-bushes, and of a certain grey-blue mist after rain, in the hollows of the hills there, welcome to fatigued eyes, and never seen farther south; so I think that the sort of house I have described, with precisely those proportions of red-brick and green, and with a just perceptible monotony in the subdued order of it, for its distinguishing note, is for Englishmen at least typically home-life.

This is true enough, and delicately observed; but not, one would have said, the appropriate *ambiente* for burning with a hard gemlike flame.

On further reflection one realises that the passages in Pater which are done with most affection are often descriptions of homely and unexotic scenes; and that a tension between the familiar pieties and later ways of feeling that appear to contradict them plays a considerable part in the Paterian ethics.

> The wistful yearning towards home, in absence from it, as the shadows of evening deepened, and he followed in thought what was doing there from hour to hour, interpreted to him much of a yearning and regret he experienced afterwards, towards he knew not what, out of strange ways of feeling and thought in which, from time to time, his spirit found itself alone.

His longing for emotional security characteristically finds its satisfaction in the physical image of a familiar childhood spot, "a place 'inclosed' and 'sealed' ", as he calls it with pre-Freudian simplicity, from which it is yet possible to look out upon other fields and other ranges of experience: "a womb with a view", in the crisper idiom of Palinurus.

From the outside world two streams of impressions flow in upon him, impressions of beauty and impressions of pain.

> From this point he could trace two predominant processes of mental change in him—the growth of an almost diseased sensibility to the spectacle of suffering, and, parallel with this, the rapid growth of a certain capacity of fascination by bright colour and choice form— . . . marking early the activity in him of a more than customary sensuousness, "the lust of the eye", as the Preacher says, which might lead him, one day, how far! Could he have foreseen the weariness of the way! In some music sometimes the two sorts of impressions came together, and he would weep, to the surprise of older people.

The lust of the eye brings with it a sort of weariness: later he speaks of "the tyranny of the senses", "a passionateness in his relation to fair outward objects, an inexplicable excitement in their presence, which disturbed him, and from which he half-longed to be free". In music (all art aspires to the condition of music) impressions of pain and impressions of beauty are both present; "a touch of regret or desire" mingles with his memory of beautiful objects, and "the longing for some undivided, entire possession of them". To the reader of Pater these sentiments are all familiar enough; what is important here is the effort at introspective research, the attempt to trace attitudes which, when they appear in his writing, are often put down to pose or fashion, to their real origins in childhood. One need not regret the absence of a later psychological sophistication, which if it might have taught him to push the investigation further, would also probably have made the confession impossible.

He likes to find some sanction for his sensuous preoccupations, "the necessity he was under of associating all thoughts to touch and sight", in Christianity, which, almost as much as ancient Greek religion, contrives to translate a great part of its spiritual truth into visible forms: and this absorption of Christianity into his private myth, or of his private myth into Christianity, is made easier by the dominance in him of the sense of pity (is there not some proverb about pity being akin to love?), the fusion of the sense of beauty and the sense of pain. For in Pater pity takes a sensuously appreciable form, "fastening those who suffered in anywise to his affections by a kind of sensible attachment".

We see the development of this in *Marius*, where it is in part the sense of pity, or to put it more noncommittally, some consequence of the feeling for suffering—the sight of the girl and her crippled brother, of the workman's boy injured by a fall of brickwork—that takes him beyond his earlier Epicureanism. And a similar complex of feeling seems to lie behind Pater's favourite cultural myth—the outcrop of pagan culture in the Christian world. Pater refers often to Heine's notion of the gods in exile taking modest employment under the new dispensation, and the two fantasies *Denys l'Auxerrois* and *Apollo in Picardy* deal with this theme. If they are not particularly successful this is probably because Pater is not altogether clear about what he is trying to do. Denys-Dionysus has "a fondness for oddly-grown or even misshapen but potentially happy children; for odd animals also: he sympathised with them all, was skilful in healing their maladies, saved the hare in the chase, and sold his mantle to redeem a lamb from the butcher". Yet he is later suspected of a brutal murder committed with a great vine-axe. Apollyon-Apollo "seemed able to draw the wild animals too, to share their sport, yet not altogether kindly. Tired, surfeited, he destroys them when his game with them is at an end: breaks the toy; deftly snaps asunder the fragile back. . . . The small furry thing he pierced with his arrow fled to him nevertheless caressingly, with broken limb, to die palpitating in his hand." Denys and Brother Apollyon both apparently symbolise the same thing, "the power of untutored natural impulse, of natural inspiration". Is not Pater trying to suggest some obscure alliance in the natural world between love and pain, something beyond the pleasure principle which moves "the springs and handles of that great machine in things, constructed so ingeniously to play pain-fugues on the delicate nerve-work of living creatures"; a something which even Christian feeling finds it hard to assimilate?

The child in the house goes on to experience the fear of death—"the fear of death intensified by the desire of beauty"; and this fear is not, as often happens, suggested to his mind by religious books, but arises spontaneously; and religious sentiment first occurs to him as something that might light up and dignify these sombre imaginings. Hence comes a preoccupation with at least the externals of the religious life.

> He began to love, for their own sakes, church lights, holy days, all that belonged to the comely order of the sanctuary, the secrets of its white linen, and holy vessels, and fonts of pure water; and its hieratic purity and simplicity became the type of something he desired always to have about him in actual life.

But it is not wholly a matter of externals; the hieratic solemnities, originally appreciated as a means of tempering his own glooms and terrors, became symbolical of daily life at the most ideally perfect level.

> Thus a constant substitution of the typical for the actual took place in his thoughts. Angels might be met by the way, under English elm or beech-tree; mere messengers seemed like angels, bound on celestial errands; a deep mysticity brooded over real meetings and partings; . . . All the acts and accidents of daily life borrowed a sacred colour and significance.
>
> Sensibility—the desire of physical beauty—a strange biblical awe, which made any reference to the unseen act on him like solemn music, these qualities the child took away with him, when, at about the age of twelve years, he left the old house, and was taken to live in another place.

The essay ends with a recurrence to the note of its beginning, the sentiment of home. The child has been looking forward to the change from the old house, but at the end, a clinging back to the old surroundings comes over him, "so intense that he knew it would last long, and spoiling all his pleasure in a thing so eagerly anticipated."

It would not be hard to relate most of the later developments of Pater's nature to this piece of *recherche du temps perdu*. (It is not unlike Proust, with more primness and reticence, and none of the self-critical wit.) Through all the careful delicacy of the writing the flavour of what has often been called Pater's morbidity is still apparent. Morbid is often a question-begging term; but what is really meant by it here is I suppose the suggestion in Pater's writing of some half-developed sexual deviation, of which we catch hints in the alliance between love and pain, the half-fear of sensuous impressions, the resultant languor. And this raises the question of a prevalent sexual unbalance in much of the work of the aesthetic school: the dominance of erotic reverie in Rossetti; the incapacity or refusal of normal sexual experience in Ruskin and Pater; the more obvious manifestations of both in the nineties; all so generally felt that in popular speech the word "aesthetic" not uncommonly carries with it something of this connotation. Remembering too the continual evidences of homosexual feeling in Pater's life and writing, one almost inevitably begins to form a composite picture of a kind of temperament in which more or less suppressed erotic fantasy, combined perhaps with the frustration or diversion of normal sexuality; a preoccupation with the periphery of religious experience; a tremulous sensitiveness to aesthetic impressions; a conscious pursuit of beauty; and the conscious cultivation of a precious or elaborate style, all play a major part; and the more usual kinds of adjustment and efficiency become unimportant. The type reached its climax of development in the *poètes maudits*, mostly of a slightly later generation, in England and in France; for they translated their sensibilities into terms of actual life; in Pater's more sheltered and more cautious career the characteristics are less obvious. It is I suppose sufficiently plain that the origins of this kind of attitude, if not congenital, at any rate go very far back in Pater's life, and owe very little to the social circumstances in which he found himself; though it is no doubt true that the influence of the Paterian ethos on a later literary generation is in part time's revenge on Victorian convention—the convention that the only possible type of sexual behaviour is tender romantic love consummated by perpetual monogamy. There is little danger now of that particular convention exercising a stifling effect on letters; but there is a new kind of Puritanism, a sort of self-conscious post-analytical rectitude, a knowing superiority over non-Freudian self-deceivers, which results in a tacit disapproval of the Paterian temperament, without much effort to do what is alone critically relevant, to find the effect of this temperament on the quality of his writing. This task is not made any easier by the fact that so many of what profess to be judgments on his work are really judgments on his psycho-physical constitution.

Yeats began the *Oxford Book of Modern Verse* with the Gioconda passage from *The Renaissance*. To a later generation for whom modern verse meant something that began to happen in the twenties, the point of this was not immediately obvious. Yeats's compilation, as well as a great deal of his own prose writing, served to remind them of the considerable influence of Pater's manner on the early part of this century. Its real character has perhaps not been wholly understood. For all that Pater says about the tyranny of the senses, his writing is not really marked by any particular acuteness of sense-perception. It is in fact mainly concerned with the moral and emotional overtones of sensuous experience, the feelings that arise posthumously from experiences of sound, form and colour, and the thoughts that are the products of those feelings. Much of Pater's work, in the *Imaginary Portraits*, for instance, consists of attempts to relate a philosophical attitude, such as that of Sebastian van Storck, to a temperament, to a culture, and beyond that, to a landscape and a physical environment. A thing which is worth doing; for the most rigorously logical system is after all the residual deposit of a thousand impressions that have gone perhaps unheeded, the ghosts of people, of places, of forgotten childhood impressions; which ultimately, however, fall into an ordered scheme under the power of a formalising intellect. He does indeed describe physical things, but tends at once to translate them from sensations into sentiments. Often his own ruling sentiments take charge, and he justifies this by choosing for his most elaborate set-pieces subjects which have some coincidence with his own dominant moods—Mona Lisa, and Botticelli's Venus. But even the marbles of Aegina, which might seem to offer little room for Pater's obsessions, become the occasion of a passage on the combination of tenderness and cruelty: and the red hawthorn, the first experience of beauty in *The Child in the House*, instigates a reflection on regret and longing, and its connection with the tyranny of the senses. This perpetual dominance of a certain emotional mood leads to some monotony in the writing, and to a languor in its rhythms. It is not only Mona Lisa's eyelids that are a little weary; Pater's generally seem to be so too. As a purely literary quality this languor was to be deliberately sought after by Pater's disciples, as we can see in Yeats's early essays; but in Pater himself it is the consequence of emotional obsession; and of conflict also, conflict going on quietly, and far underground, but still perpetual. There is a sense of constraint, too, in the more highly wrought passages, as of a man determined on sincerity, yet afraid of saying too much. And this constraint is closely connected with one of Pater's major virtues, a scrupulousness, a resolve, if not to say everything, at least not to under- or overstate what is said. This gives Pater's virtuosity a quite different accent from that of other practitioners of decorative prose, Ruskin, for instance, or de Quincey. Decorative prose of any kind, however, arouses little enthusiasm in our day; and perhaps no one but Yeats could in 1936 have boldly transcribed the Gioconda passage as poetry. Yet that is probably what it was—the only kind of poetry possible to a man like Pater, without the energy of self-dramatisation necessary for full creative work. Pater's practice of the genre is distinguished by a sense of order and control that is rare in prose poetry.

He is open to the charge of preciosity and affectation, and his deliberate obliviousness of most of the interests of mankind will always be viewed with impatience by those who demand a more obvious kind of effectiveness. We have shown, I suppose, that it was psychologically inevitable, a part of Pater's basic longing for home as a place enclosed and sealed against the turbulence of the outside world. Historically, the important thing to say is that this withdrawal was necessary. There were more than enough influences at work in late Victorian life to drag the arts into the commonplace of day-to-day existence. In an age that was boiling up for the Boer War and the windy degradation of the daily press it was necessary that a small group of hierophants should keep the sacred flame burning in some still retreat. It was not perhaps particularly good for their own health; the atmosphere of shrines is notoriously insalubrious. But it is not a very profitable exercise to estimate the value of an attitude like Pater's apart from its effect; its justification is that in a world not inclined to be sympathetic to such delicate plants, it has continued to exist; and continues to represent a certain phase of our culture. And it would be a mistake to suppose that Pater's preoccupations were altogether apart from the main stream of cultural development. One might reply to objections against Pater's achievement in the words he himself uses about criticism:

> In truth the legitimate contention is, not of one age or school of literary art against another, but of all successive schools alike, against the stupidity which is dead to the substance, and the vulgarity which is dead to form.

It is in this after all quite fundamental conflict that retired and highly specialised natures like Pater's are capable of producing lasting effects: and it has been the purpose of this chapter to suggest that Pater's part in the struggle was a not dishonourable one.

HAROLD BLOOM

The Place of Pater:
"Marius the Epicurean"

T he Aesthetic Movement in England
(*circa* 1870–1900) is usually tracked to its sources in the literary Paris of
the 1850s. The poets Théophile Gautier and Charles Baudelaire are thus
viewed as being the inventors of the new sensibility exemplified in the life
and work of Algernon Swinburne, James Whistler, Walter Pater, and their
immediate followers—George Moore, Oscar Wilde, Aubrey Beardsley,
Simeon Solomon, Ernest Dowson, Lionel Johnson, Arthur Symons, and
the young William Butler Yeats. Whistler, an American and a painter,
rightly felt that he owed everything to Paris and himself and nothing to
English tradition. But behind Swinburne and Pater were three generations
of English Romanticism, from the poetry of Blake and Wordsworth on
through to the Victorian Romanticism of the Pre-Raphaelite poets and
painters. In the midst of this tradition one finds a more direct source of
English Aestheticism: the literary theories of Arthur Henry Hallam, as set
forth in a review of his friend Alfred Tennyson's poetry some twenty years
before Gautier and Baudelaire created their sensibility out of Delacroix,
Poe, and their own complex natures.

Yeats remarked that he had found his literary aesthetics in Hallam
before coming under Pater's influence. Hallam contrasted Shelley and
Keats as "poets of sensation" with Wordsworth as a "poet of reflection":

Susceptible of the slightest impulse from external nature, their fine
organs trembled into emotion at colors, and sounds, and movements,

From *The Ringers in the Tower*. Copyright © 1971 by The University of Chicago Press.

unperceived or unregarded by duller temperaments . . . So vivid was the
delight attending the simple exertions of eye and ear, that it became
mingled more and more with their trains of active thought, and tended
to absorb their whole being into the energy of sense.

Marshall McLuhan observed that the theme of Hallam's essay is
usually the theme of Pater and of T. S. Eliot: the Copernican revolution in
poetry that saw a change in the direction of poetic art, from "the shaping
of the poetic object . . . to the shaping of psychological effects in the
reader," as McLuhan phrases it. Eliot disliked Pater's work, as he disliked
most of the Romantic tradition, but critics tend now to agree that he has
a place in that tradition despite himself.

Walter Pater's place in Romantic tradition was a consciously chosen one, and only recently have readers begun to see again what that
place was. In his lifetime Pater was a shadowy but famous figure, vaguely
blamed by the public as being the half-sinister and withdrawn theorist
whom extravagant disciples—Wilde, Beardsley, Moore—would cite as the
authority for their more extreme stances in art and in life. This Pater of
popular tradition is so vivid a part of literary folklore that any critic ought
to be wary of clearing away the myth. We would lose the "tremendous
Ritualist" who had lost all faith, and who burned his poems because they
had been too pious, but who felt frustrated nonetheless when he was
prevented (by his friends) from being ordained. A still greater loss would
be the Pater who is reputed to have walked the Oxford meadows in the
cool of the evening, murmuring that the odor of the meadow-sweet gave
him pain: "It is the fault of nature in England that she runs too much to
excess."

Aside from his assured place in the great line of English eccentrics,
Pater is one of the central figures in the continuity between Romanticism,
Modernism, and the emergent sensibility still in the process of replacing
Modernism today. Pater's most ambitious and extensive work, the historical novel *Marius the Epicurean*, is in itself one of the more remarkable
fictional experiments of the later nineteenth century, but it has the added
value now of teaching us something about our own continuity with the
past that otherwise we could not wholly know.

Currently fashionable sensibility, two-thirds of the way through
the century, is perhaps another ironic disordering of Paterian sensibility.
Pater is halfway between Wordsworth and ourselves. But he is more than a
link between, say, the sensibility of Keats and that of the late Yeats or late
Stevens; he is a kind of hinge upon which turns the single gate, one side
of which is Romantic and the other modern poetry. Marius himself may
be little more than an idealized version of Pater's own self-consciousness,

and yet Marius, more than any fictional character of our age, is the representative modern poet as well as the representative man of literary culture who remains the only audience for that poet. If one holds in mind a handful of our age's lyrical poems at their most poignant, say Yeats's *Vacillation* and *The Man and the Echo*, with Stevens's *The Course of a Particular* and *Of Mere Being*, and imagines a possible poet who might make those poems into a story, one gets the sensibility and even the dimmed, half-willing, self-defeated fate of Pater's Roman quester.

"His Sensations and Ideas" is the subtitle of *Marius the Epicurean*. At the center of the novel is the flux of sensations; at its circumference whirl a succession of ideas of the good life, all of them inadequate beside the authenticity of the central flux. This inadequacy is highly deliberate:

> . . . with this sense of the splendour of our experience and of its awful brevity, gathering all we are into one desperate effort to see and touch, we shall hardly have time to make theories about the things we see and touch. What we have to do is to be for ever curiously testing new opinions and courting new impressions, never acquiescing in a facile orthodoxy. . . .

That is Pater at his most central, in the famous "Conclusion" to *The Renaissance*, written in 1868. Thinking of this "Conclusion," and of its effect on the "Tragic Generation" of Wilde, Aubrey Beardsley, Ernest Dowson, Lionel Johnson, and their companions, Yeats eloquently complained that Pater "taught us to walk upon a rope, tightly stretched through serene air, and we were left to keep our feet upon a swaying rope in a storm." Pater's reply is more eloquent still:

> While all melts under our feet, we may well catch at any exquisite passion, or any contribution to knowledge that seems by a lifted horizon to set the spirit free for a moment, or any stirring of the senses, strange dyes, strange colours, and curious odours, or work of the artist's hands, or the face of one's friend. Not to discriminate every moment some passionate attitude in those about us, and in the brilliancy of their gifts some tragic dividing of forces on their ways, is, on this short day of frost and sun, to sleep before evening.

Eliot complained that Pater was neither a critic nor a creator but a moralist, whether in *Marius*, *The Renaissance*, or elsewhere. Clearly Pater, whenever he wrote, was all three, like Eliot himself. The confusion of purposes, in both men, was well served by a late version of Romantic art, the usual mode for each being a flash of radiance against an incongruous or bewildering background. In this "privileged" or "timeless" moment of illumination, the orthodox religious quest of the later writer found its equivocal conclusion, but the skeptical, more openly solipsistic Pater tended to remain within a narrower vision, confined to what he himself naturalistically could see.

Because of this restraint, *Marius* is a surprisingly unified narrative for all its surface diversity. At first reading one can feel that its motto might well be the tag from Nennius affixed by David Jones to his *Anathemata*: "I have made a heap of all that I could find," or perhaps Eliot's line in *The Waste Land*: "These fragments I have shored against my ruins." Pater gives us the tale of Cupid and Psyche from Apuleius, an impressionistic account of the *Pervigilium Veneris*, a supposed oration of Cornelius Fronto, a version of a dialogue of Lucian, and a paraphrase of selected meditations of Marcus Aurelius. Critics have suspected his motives: they argue that Pater resorted to imitation because he could not invent a story, create a character, dramatize a conflict, or even present a conversation. This is true enough. We hardly *hear* anything said in Pater's novel, and few events occur that are not historical. Critics less prejudiced than Eliot have also questioned the accuracy of Pater's summations of philosophical creeds, and others have indicated the absence of all theological content from the presentation of Christianity in the closing pages of the book. All true, and all irrelevant to the achievement of *Marius*, which remains a unified reverie or aesthetic meditation upon history, though a history as idealized and foreshortened as in Yeats's *A Vision*, a thoroughly Paterian work.

Pater and Yeats made magical associations between aspects of the Renaissance and their own times. Yeats extended the parallel to different phases of Byzantine culture, with an arbitrariness justified by his needs as a lyrical poet not content with the limitations of lyric. Pater's *Marius* is founded on a more convincing and troubling resemblance, between Victorian England in the 1880s and Rome in the Age of the Antonines, two summits of power and civilization sloping downward in decadence. The aesthetic humanism of Marius, poised just outside of a Christianity Pater felt to be purer than anything available to himself, is precisely the desperately noble and hopeless doctrine set forth in the "Conclusion" to *The Renaissance*. Like Pater, Marius is committed to the universe of death, loving it the better for every evidence of decay. "Death is the mother of beauty" in Pater as in his immediate ancestor, the poet of the *Ode to Psyche* and the *Ode on Melancholy*, and in his immediate descendant, the poet of *Sunday Morning* and *Esthétique du Mal*. There is a morbidity in Pater, not present in Keats or in Stevens, the spirit of sadomasochism and inversion, the infantile regressiveness of his *The Child in the House*, and the repressed destructiveness that emerges in some of his *Imaginary Portraits*. Something of this drifts into *Marius The Epicurean*, through the subtly evaded homosexuality of the love of Marius first for Flavian and then for Cornelius, and in the reveries on human and animal victims of pain and martyrdom. But what morbidity there is distracts only a little from the central theme of the book, which is Pater's own version of Romanticism, his individual addition of strangeness to beauty. For Wordsworth the privileged moments, "spots of time," gave precise knowledge of how and to what extent his power of mind reigned over outward sense. "I see by glimpses now," Wordsworth lamented, but the glimpses revealed the glory of human imagination, and recalled a time when the poet stood alone, in his conscious strength, unaided by religious orthodoxies. For Pater the spots of time belonged to the ascendancy of what Wordsworth called "outward sense," and the dying Marius is still an "unclouded and receptive soul," sustained by "the vision of men and things, actually revealed to him on his way through the world." The faith, to the end, is in the evidence of things seen, and in the substance of things experienced. Certainly the closest analogue is in the death poem of Stevens, *Of Mere Being*, where the palm that rises at the end of the mind, the tree of mere being, has on it the life-enhancing aureole of an actual bird:

> The bird sings. Its feathers shine . . .
> The bird's fire-fangled feathers dangle down.

The burden of *Marius the Epicurean* is the burden of modern lyric, from Wordsworth to Stevens, the near solipsism of the isolated sensibility, of the naked aesthetic consciousness deprived of everything save its wavering self and the flickering of an evanescent beauty in the world of natural objects, which is part of the universe of death. As a critic, Pater derived from Ruskin, and went further in alienation. This stance of experiential loss and aesthetic gain is familiar enough to contemporary analysts in several disciplines. It was while Pater labored at the composition of *Marius* that the unconscious was formally "discovered" (about 1882), and thus the Romantic inner self received its definitive formulation. Societies (Victorian and Antonine) disintegrate, and individuals (Pater and Marius) lose all outward connections. Pater would have understood immediately the later description of the unconscious proposed by the phenomenologists: an index of the remoteness in the self's relationships with others. The famous description of the Mona Lisa in Pater's *Renaissance*, anthologized by Yeats as the first modern poem, is just such a vision of the unconscious: what J. H. Van den Berg, the phenomenological psychiatrist, defines as "the secret inner self, the innerworld in which everything the world has to offer is shut away." Van den Berg, as it happens, is referring to Rilke's account of Leonardo's lady and her landscape, but Rilke writes of the painting much in Pater's spirit. The landscape, Rilke observes, is as estranged as the lady, "far and completely unlike us." Both represent what Van den Berg calls "things-in-their-farewell," a beauty purchased by estrangement.

This, I think, is the most relevant context in which to read *Marius the Epicurean*. *Marius* is the masterpiece of things-in-their-farewell, the great document in English of the historical moment when the unconscious came painfully to its birth. Where Wordsworth and Keats, followed by Mill and Arnold, fought imaginatively against excessive self-consciousness, Pater welcomes it, and by this welcome inaugurates, for writers and readers in English, the decadent phase of Romanticism, in which, when honest, we still find ourselves. What Pater, and modernist masters following him, lack is not energy of apprehension, but rather the active force of a synthesizing imagination, so titanic in Blake and Wordsworth. Yet this loss—in Yeats, Joyce, Stevens—is only an honest recognition of necessity. Except for the phenomenon of a last desperate High Romantic, Hart Crane, the faith in the saving, creative power of the imagination subsides in our time. Here too Pater is the hinge, for the epiphanies of Marius only help him to live what life he has; they do not save him, nor in the context of his world, or Pater's, or ours, can anyone be saved.

As an artist, Pater was essentially a baroque essayist, in the line of Sir Thomas Browne and De Quincey, and the aesthetic achievement of Marius is of a kind with the confessions of those stylists. Yeats, at least, thought *Marius* to be written in the only great modern prose style in English. One can add Yeats, in his still undervalued prose, to the line of Browne, De Quincey, and Pater, and indeed the influence of Pater remains to be traced throughout all of Yeats's prose, early or late, particularly in the marvelous *Autobiographies*. Criticism has said little to the purpose about this late tradition of highly mannered prose, whose elaborate and conscious harmonies have an affinity with the relatively more ascetic art of James, and reach their parodistic climax in Joyce. Our expectations of this prose are mistaken when we find it to be an intrusion, of any kind, between ourselves and its maker; it is as much of his vision as he can give to us, and its self-awareness is an overwhelming attempt to exorcize the demon of discursiveness. The marmoreal reverie, whether in *Marius* or in Yeats's *Per Amica Silentia Lunae* and *A Vision*, is allied to other modernist efforts to subvert the inexorable dualism of form and content.

Pater has the distinction of being one of the first major theorists in the modern phase of this effort. He rejected the organic analogue of Coleridge, by which any work of art is, as it were, naturalized, because he feared that it devalued the intense and solitary effort of the artist to overcome natural limitation. In his essay on *The School of Giorgione* he could speak of art as "always striving to be independent of the mere intelligence, to become a matter of pure perception, to get rid of its responsibilities to its subject or material." This ideal is impossible, and prompts the famous and misleading formula: "All art constantly aspires towards the condition of music." What stimulated Pater to this extravagance was his obsessive concern with what Stevens states so simply in one of his *Adagia*: "One has a sensibility range beyond which nothing really exists for one. And in each this is different." The peculiar structure of *Marius The Epicurean* emanates from the primacy Pater gives to sensibility, in his own special sense of that complex faculty.

Paterian "sensibility" is nothing less than the way one sees, and so apprehends, everything of value in human experience, or in the art that is the best of that experience. Poetry and *materia poetica*, Stevens says, are the same thing. *Marius* is a gathering of *materia poetica*, taken out of one moment of European history, on the chance of illuminating a later moment. The late Victorian skeptic and Epicurean, of whom Pater and Wilde are definitive, is emancipated from his immortality, and suffers the discontent of his own passion for ritual. Pater, as was notorious, studied the nostalgias of religion only in terms of form and ceremony. The passionate desire for ritual, in Pater and in his Marius, as in the Yeats of *A Prayer For My Daughter*, is not a trivial matter, because the quest involved is for the kind of innocence and beauty that can only come from custom and from ceremony. The social aspect of such innocence may be pernicious, but fortunately Pater, unlike Yeats, offered only visionary politics.

Marius the Epicurean is constructed as a series of rituals, each of which is absorbed into its successor without being destroyed, or even transcended. As art was ritual for Pater, so life is ritual for Marius, the ordering principle always being that no form or possibility of life (or of art) is to be renounced in favor of any other. This could be described, unkindly and unfairly, as a kind of polymorphous perversity of the spirit, a refusal to pay the cost of choosing a single aim for culture, or of meeting the necessity of dying by a gracious yielding to the reality principle. What can be urged against Pater, fairly, is that he evaded the novel's ultimate problem by killing off Marius before the young man grasps the theological and moral exclusiveness of Christianity. Marius could not remain Marius and renounce; forced to make the Yeatsian choice between perfection of the life and perfection of the work he would have suffered from a conflict that would have destroyed the fine balance of his nature. Whether Pater earns the structural irony of the novel's concluding pages, as a still-pagan Marius dies a sanctified Christian death, is quite legitimately questionable.

But, this aside, Pater's novel is unflawed in its odd but precise structure. The four parts are four stages on the life's way of Marius, but the continuities of ritual pattern between them are strong enough to set up a dialectic by which no apparent spiritual advancement becomes an aesthetic retreat. The consequence is that the spiritual quest is not from error to truth, but only from alienation to near-sympathy. Thus the first part opens with the most humanly appealing presentation of a belief in the book, as we are given the ancestral faith of Marius, "the Religion of Numa." Here there is no skepticism, but a vision of home and boyhood, the calm of a natural religion that need not strain beyond the outward observances. The world of sense is at home in the child and his inherited faith, which climaxes by his initiation into the world of literature, beautifully symbolized by the story of Cupid and Psyche. The tentative love of Marius for Flavian is precisely the awakening of the literary sense under the awareness of death that Pater traces in the "Conclusion" to *The Renaissance*, and the premature death of Flavian, his one masterpiece left imperfect, inaugurates the first crisis Marius must suffer.

Resolving this crisis is the "conversion," by himself, of Marius to Epicureanism, the doctrine of Aristippus. Though Epicureanism (and its Stoic rival, as represented by Aurelius and Fronto) is supposedly the dominant element of only the second part of the novel, its presence in the book's title is no accident, as in the broad sense Marius, like Pater, lives and dies an Epicurean. For the Epicureanism involved is simply the inevitable religion of the Paterian version of sensibility, or the "aesthetic philosophy" proper. "Not pleasure, but fullness of life, and 'insight' as conducing to that fullness—energy, variety, and choice of experience . . . ," is Pater's best summary of the doctrine, with his added warning that "its mistaken tendency would lie in the direction of a kind of idolatry of mere life, or natural gift. . . ."

The first crisis of this Epicureanism comes at the close of Part II, with Marius's recoil from the sadistic games of the arena, a recoil fascinating for everything that it suggests of the repressed masochism of both Marius and his creator. Like Flaubert, that other high priest of the religion of art, Pater has a way of wandering near the abyss, but *Marius* is no *Salammbô*, and finds no place in the litany of the Romantic agony. But the cruelty of the world, the pain and evil that border so near to Marius's exquisite realm of sensation and reverie, awaken in him a first movement of skepticism toward his own Epicureanism.

Part III develops this sense of limitation with regard to the fruits of sensibility, but by exploiting a more fundamental flaw in the Paterian vision. The self-criticism here is illuminating, not just for this book but for the whole of Pater, and explains indeed the justification for the elaborately hesitant style that Pater perfected. Isolation has expanded the self, but now threatens it with the repletion of solipsism. The Stoic position of Aurelius and Fronto is invoked to contrast its vision of human brotherhood with the more selfish and inward cultivation of Aristippus. But the limits of Stoicism are rapidly indicated also, even as exemplified in its noblest exponent, the philosophic emperor. The climax of Part III comes with marvelous appropriateness, in the quasi-Wordsworthian epiphany experienced by Marius, alone in the Sabine Hills. Moved by the unnamed Presence encountered in this privileged hour, Marius is prepared for the supernatural revelation that never quite appropriates him in the fourth and final part of the novel.

Here, in the closing portion, Pater's skill in construction is most evident. Part IV builds through a series of contrasts to its melancholy but inevitable conclusion. We pass from the literary neo-Platonism of Apuleius with its fanciful daemons aiding men to reach God, on to the aesthetically more powerful vision of the Eucharist, as Marius is drawn gradually into the Christian world of Cornelius and Cecilia. This approach to grace through moral sympathy is punctuated beautifully by a triad of interventions. The first is the dialogue in which the great satirist Lucian discomfits a young philosophic enthusiast, teaching the Paterian lesson that temperament alone determines our supposed choice of belief. Next comes a review of a diary of observed sufferings by Marius, coupled with an account of recent Christian martyrdoms. Finally there is the deeply moving last return home by Marius. Reverently, he rearranges the resting-places of his ancestors, in full consciousness that he is to be the last of his house. He goes out to his fate with the Christian knight, Cornelius, offering up his life in sacrifice for his friend, and dies anonymously among unknown Christians, his own quest still unfulfilled. "He must still hold by what his eyes really saw," and at the last Marius still longs to see, and suffers from a deep sense of wasted power. He is a poet who dies before his poems are written, and even the great poem that is his life is scarcely begun. The attentive reader, confronted by Marius's death, is saddened by the loss, not of a person, but of a major sensibility. And for such losses, such yieldings of a fine sensibility to the abyss, there are no recompenses.

We return always, in reading Pater, to the "Conclusion" of *The Renaissance*, where he spoke his word most freely. The lasting power of *Marius the Epicurean* stays with us not as an image, or series of images, but as a memory of receptivity, the vivid sense of a doomed consciousness universal enough to encompass all men who live and die by a faith in art:

> . . . we have an interval, and then our place knows us no more. Some spend this interval in listlessness, some in high passions, the wisest, at least among "the children of this world," in art and song. For our one chance lies in expanding that interval, in getting as many pulsations as possible into the given time. Great passions may give us this quickened sense of life, ecstasy and sorrow of love, the various forms of enthusiastic activity, disinterested or otherwise, which come naturally to many of us. Only be sure it is passion—that it does yield you this fruit of a quick-ened, multiplied consciousness. Of this wisdom, the poetic passion, the desire of beauty, the love of art for art's sake, has most; for art comes to you professing frankly to give nothing but the highest quality to your moments as they pass, and simply for those moments' sake.

IAN FLETCHER

Walter Pater

P ater's reputation was at its height in
the twenty years after his death. Lately, there has been an intensified
interest in his work; although with reservations. Prejudice and fashion are
to blame. The very word 'Pater' has come to be associated with an
undisciplined impressionistic criticism, and one or two rather uncharacteristic
passages, such as the prose-poem on the Mona Lisa, are assumed to be
broadly representative. The modern critic is often suspicious of any work
which falls outside fairly strict categories: how can he compare such works
with others and 'place' them with a suitable conviction? This difficulty
applies to Pater with peculiar force. His work seems to lie in a twilight of
categories between criticism and creation; between art and literary criticism, *belles-lettres*, classical scholarship, the *journal intime* and the philosophic novel. Few readers are sufficiently catholic to judge him, not
simply as a critic of art or of literature, but as something at once more or
less than these things. Pater's work represents above all the triumphs and
failures of a temperament. It records in his own words 'a prolonged quarrel
with himself.' As in most domestic arguments there is a good deal of
repetition: personal isolation, the means of transcending it, the good life
as tension between moral rigour and culture, and the final defeat of
isolation through ritual, sympathy and the sacrifice of personality—topics
like these are worried over, established, developed, qualified, re-interpreted.
Under many disguises, Pater is a self-explorer, honest and severe, who
touches, in the process, on interests central to his own time. His style,
though mannered, is one of the most individual and hypnotically satisfy-

ing in English: the faithful counterpart of that exhausting backward and forward struggle with himself. For Pater was incapable of renunciation: he lived in a world where 'we must needs make the most of things', even of things incompatible or dangerous. What unites these interests and evasions?

II

Much of Pater's work is transposed and distanced autobiography. In a short 'imaginary portrait', *The Child in the House*, Pater attempts to re-shape the past as it might have been relived by his adult self. Here he examines scrupulously his own sensuous education; and strives to account for the richness and oddity of his temperament. Like Pater, the child is precociously aware of isolation, and the close association of pain and beauty:

> An almost diseased sensibility to the spectacle of suffering, . . . and the rapid growth of a certain capacity of fascination by bright colour and choice form . . . marking early the activity in him of a more than customary sensuousness, 'the lust of the eye', . . . which might lead him, one day, how far! Could he have foreseen the weariness of the way!

The weariness belongs to the priest of art, who did not so much make, as have imposed upon him, 'the sacrifice of a thousand possible sympathies'. For sharply though he responded to the beauty of colours and forms, Pater was himself singularly plain and timid.

In *The Child in the House* Pater regards home, an experience for the child, a symbol for the adult, as a sanctuary from spiritual wandering. Adult life is equated with exile, and in several of Pater's experiments in ruminative fiction, men come back to die at home with a sense of fulfilment. The child is seen as a conventional animal, prizing even the restraints laid upon him as reassurance: childhood routine provides the source of Pater's lifelong concern with ritual as the most efficacious of man's instruments for spiritual communication: ritual provides life with a set of ideal symbols, and at the level of ritual the otherwise frightening and destructive experiences of beauty and terror can be related, however frailly, to daily habit.

Pater's personal history, whatever the raw excitements of the inner life, had none of the squalor and excitement of some of his contemporaries. His father died while he was still an infant; his mother while he was at boarding school, and his two sisters were sent to complete their education abroad: these events must have pointed his sense of isolation. In 1858, he went up to Oxford. After taking a second class in schools, and tutoring privately for a year or two, he was elected in 1864 a Fellow of Brasenose. The remainder of his life, with the exception of some years spent partially in London, was passed quietly in Oxford, where his sisters kept house for him. In his youth, Pater had been attracted towards at least the outer shows of Christianity. By the time of his election, however, he had become strongly influenced by the popular and plausible notions of Comte. Both in conversation and writing he was now known as a lover of irony and smoothly destructive paradox. In the most important of his early essays, that on Coleridge as philosopher (1866), there are overt anti-Christian implications and confident asperities of tone: implications and asperities carefully toned down in the revised version published in *Appreciations* (1889). In spite of such scepticism, Pater persisted for some time in attempting to take orders, an attempt which seems to have crystallized under Keble's influence, and may have determined Pater's view that beliefs are transmitted by temperament.

The 1860s in England were a period of crisis in opinion. In periodicals such as *The Fortnightly Review*, the troubled English mind struggled with competing loyalties to science and religion, to authority and 'the free play of mind', reaching a remarkably articulate stage of self-consciousness. Pater was an avid reader of the more intellectual magazines of the time, and for him, as for others, they provided something essential, an insight not only into his own personal doubts, but into the spirit of the age. This uneasy movement of the English mind underlies all Pater's earlier writing, and as the uneasiness was never wholly resolved he cannot be said to have arrived at a 'settled position'. It was in such magazines as *The Fortnightly* that Pater published most of the essays contained in his first, and one of his central books, *Studies in the History of the Renaissance* (1873), itself a glancing contribution to the problem of evolving a new ethic to replace partially discredited traditional beliefs.

By the middle of the 1870s, though he had now a distinct place in the world of letters, Pater's mild academic ambitions remained unsatisfied. He seems to have been a conscientious but not conspicuously successful tutor, though his pupils, Gerard Manley Hopkins among them, remembered him with affection. 'Don't suppose', Field Marshal Haig, visiting Oxford after the First World War, is reputed to have remarked in his blunt, laconic fashion, 'there's a man called Pater still here? Taught me something about the writing of English.' Pater's administrative powers were slender; he was not a good committee man, and there are many amusing stories about his vagueness at College meetings. But more decisive reasons accounted for Pater's failure to exercise an influence on Oxford life commensurate with his abilities. *The Renaissance* had alarmed the Master of Balliol, the most powerful single personality in the university, Benjamin Jowett. And Oxford's ingratitude to Pater, both during his lifetime and after his death, is, on wider grounds, not surprising. Neither in his gifts, nor in his eccentricities, was Pater a typical Oxford man. He was not an exact scholar; he was not in large companies a ready or amusing talker. He owed his Fellowship partly to his gifts as a stylist, but even his style was not in the main Victorian tradition of Oxford prose. It was not the innocently luminous style of Newman, of Dean Mansel, or, with a little more of professional mannerism, Matthew Arnold; the style that is like the perfection of Common Room conversation. Pater's style with its elaborate and refined cadences appeals to the inner rather than the outer ear. The reader must construe as he reads. Yet that prose of Pater's, many felt, with all its artifice, could be profoundly subversive. He could be seen as 'a corruptor of youth'.

Already in the early 1870s Pater had begun to modify some of the more extreme positions adopted in *The Renaissance*. His mood was shifting with the shifting tides of the time. The forces of tradition (some would have said of reaction) were being rallied by the new Oxford Idealism. But there were deeper sources of change within Pater himself. Over the years he had begun to feel the limitations of a self-regarding ethic that sought the meaning of life in the intensity of highly-charged moments of experience. He had proclaimed that creed in the 'Conclusion' to *The Renaissance*, with a confidence which, as so often in Pater, already marked disquiet; in the second edition he suppressed the 'Conclusion' altogether, restoring it with careful modifications in the third. This timidity sprang from the very popularity of the book, especially with the younger generation, whose general misunderstanding of *The Renaissance* was to Pater as painful as it was surprising.

Such innocence and isolation point to Pater's uncertainty about an audience, about his own private self and his public role as writer, further emphasized by the fact that in some moods he saw his art as essentially 'private'. In his disciples, Pater's uncertainties were disconcertingly resolved: 'is this then what I am?' Wilde, the most systematic (and most dangerous) vulgarizer of his ideas, might well have been writing a parable of the master's relationship with his younger admirers in *Dorian Gray*, where the hero's double, the portrait, changes while his own face remains a beautiful *tabula rasa*.

In 1881, Pater resigned his position as a tutor at Brasenose, though not his Fellowship, and devoted the next three years to the arduous composition of *Marius the Epicurean*. This was a work on a much larger scale than anything he had previously attempted; designed to expand and rectify the deliberately elliptical statements of the 'Conclusion', and to place them in a concrete historical setting and in the context of an imagined life story. For Marius, Pater's hero, the wistful quest with which the book is concerned does arrive at some sort of goal. Marius, at the end of the tale, is on the threshold of Christian belief, having transcended isolation through the sympathy that leads to action and self-sacrifice. But Marius also transcends isolation through the sense of at last belonging, again wistfully and on the outer fringes, to a society of like-minded souls, the society of the primitive Christian Church, for which Pater's miniature emblem, in *Marius the Epicurean*, is the decorous beauty of the household of Cecilia.

Most of Pater's later writing in some sense supplements *Marius*. In 1887, he collected together four essays in ruminative fiction, *Imaginary Portraits*, and in 1889 published a rather miscellaneous collection of critical studies, *Appreciations*. This includes the famous essay on 'Style', the outcome of a crisis personal no less than æsthetic. *Plato and Platonism* (1893) was the last book published in his lifetime. Pater presents Plato as an impressionist philosopher, as tentative in judgement as the author of *Marius* himself. The book is also interesting as one of the earliest clear statements in English of the position of historical relativism. Pater feels it is not the business of a lecturer on Plato to abstract certain doctrines as typically Platonic, and to decide whether they are true, false or meaningless; it is rather to grasp Plato as a man, and to grasp the world in which Plato moved, and to try to show how natural it is that such a man, in such a world, should have such ideas. *Plato and Platonism* was Pater's own favourite among his books; perhaps because it was based on lectures it is written in an unusually relaxed style.

When he wrote *The Renaissance*, the young Pater thought of religion as merely one of several high passions: but there seems to be evidence that his later response was not merely to the beauty of outward Christian observance but to the moral beauty of the Christian life. And his last, unfinished, essay deals sympathetically with Pascal as an example of 'the inversion of . . . the æsthetic life'. He was a devout attendant at the services in Brasenose Chapel, and in the 'friary' of Saint Austin's, a small Anglo-Catholic chapel lost in the slums of South East London, he may have found a living and contemporary image of the primitive Christian community. His interest in it, together with eight years of spending his vacations in London, reflect the effort made in his last years to subdue the sense of isolation by identifying himself with some dedicated group, however marginal. Pater may have thought that the literary world of

London would offer him a more lively and admiring social ambiance than Oxford. Writers, mostly much younger men, such as George Moore, Arthur Symons, William Sharp and Lionel Johnson, looked up to Pater as a master; but he seems to have mixed little with them socially, nor does he figure as a person in classic works of literary reminiscence of the 1880s and 1890s, such as Yeats's *Autobiographies*. London, in the end, proved perhaps as much a desert for Pater as Oxford: like the Desert Fathers he remained (however unwillingly) a hermit to the end.

Pater's own kindness to, and interest in, other people was plain and effortless. But, prizing as he did his own personality above everything else—it was, for him, the only certain element in experience—Pater lacked that final requisite of all personal relationships, the ability to surrender personality. Much of Pater's writing consists in a deliberate mythologizing of his friends, as though, in Eliot's words, he was constantly seeking through personal relationships something beyond them. In his *Imaginary Portraits*, he created ideal types such as Emerald Uthwart, based in some of their traits on friends, but so acutely idealized that they become in effect incarnations of everything, so unlike what he was, that Pater wished to be himself. Pater's isolation was also an inevitable function of his vocation. Like Flaubert, he was the martyr of an ideal of style. Like Flaubert, his life was unified, not by the sequence of the ordinary human passions, romantic love, family responsibility, worldly ambition, but by the single purpose of creating high literature. For Pater, art no less than life was ritual; a total discipline which involved, in that poignant phrase of his already quoted: 'the sacrifice of a thousand possible sympathies'. Even though a collection of his letters has recently been published, Pater's 'mystery' remains as opaque as ever. His natural costiveness, unlike the exuberance of James, made him a grudging letter writer, while his life was given some stability by the continued presence of his two sisters, one of them a woman of considerable intelligence. He had no need to search desperately for friends. The materials for an adequate biography are perhaps no longer available. The outer man so largely eluding us, we must seek the inner man in the books; books which both reveal and hide those secrets of personality, where, in considering this strangely reserved and yet almost indiscreetly candid writer, the critic must begin and end.

III

Pater's earlier essays are dominated by a group of related ideas: human isolation within the 'flux' (a flux of which human personality is itself part), the relativist spirit of the modern world and the importance of temperament, which Pater opposes to the rigidity of 'character'. Such a picture of an unstable, ungraspable world is coloured by Pater's sense of personal isolation, but reflects also the troubled intellectual climate of the 1850s and 1860s.

Newman's conversion to Catholicism in 1845 had robbed the Anglican Church of its moral and intellectual centre. The shift among some of the more intellectual Oxford divines towards Latitudinarianism is reflected in the famous *Essays and Reviews* (1860). These 'modernists' subordinated religion to the 'verifying faculty' of scientific law, and suggested that the Church should exist in a fluid state, without fixed principles. Even a man of the Right, like Dean Mansel, whom Pater much admired, tended to undercut scepticism with scepticism. Newman was to prolong this line of argument in his *Grammar of Assent* (1870), appealing to the limits of positive knowledge, the unbearableness of uncertainty, and to the impracticability of basing fundamental assents on merely syllogistic arguments. His appeal, on behalf of faith, was to the sense of awe and the convergences of probability. In *The Development of Christian Doctrine* (1846), which he wrote, standing up, on the verge of conversion, in agony and tears, Newman had hit upon the notion of evolution which was beginning to transform science and historical theory. It was the dissolvent, rather than the defensive element in such daring Christian thinkers which most profoundly attracted the young Pater. What the prevailing scepticism implied for him was not a weapon against crude free thought; it was rather a personal liberation from the constraints of dogma; it offered the possibility of dallying unashamedly with a self-pleasing ethic, without sacrificing the sensuous aspects of religion.

This dissolvent element pervades Pater's essay on Coleridge—the main theme is not Coleridge's poetry or his criticism but his metaphysics. Pater attacks Coleridge for his aspiration towards the Absolute, which he sees as an expression of mental sickliness in revolt against the patient tentativeness of scientific method (in a lecture to his students, Pater was once to create a mild furore by describing monastic religion as resembling 'a beautiful disease'). Knowledge, for Pater, is essentially a matter of the specific, and Coleridge is to be blamed for tamely accepting the conclusions of traditional Christianity, and seeking to justify them in a new and abstruse manner, instead of applying his fine critical spirit to the sources through which it is claimed that Revelation has been made. Moreover, 'urbanity' for Pater, as for Arnold, is one of the requisites of culture. One should be able to survey the dilapidation of a cherished theory into picturesque ruin with a condoning smile. This urbanity Coleridge, according to Pater, lacks: and the consequent roughness of form of most of his prose works and his excess of seriousness—'a seriousness arising not from any moral principle, but from a misconception of the perfect manner' —are his typical defects. Pater than proceeds to show how irrelevant metaphysics are to the spirit of the nineteenth century:

> Modern thought is distinguished from ancient by its cultivation of the 'relative' spirit in place of the 'absolute'. . . . To the modern spirit nothing is, or can be rightly known, except relatively and under conditions. The philosophical conception of the relative has been developed in modern times through the influence of the sciences of observation. Those sciences reveal types of life evanescing into each other by inexpressible refinements of change. Things pass into their opposites by accumulation of undefinable quantities. . . . The faculty for truth is recognized as a power of distinguishing and fixing delicate and fugitive detail. The moral world is ever in contact with the physical, and the relative spirit has invaded philosophy from the ground of the inductive sciences. There it has started a new analysis of the relations of body and mind, good and evil, freedom and necessity. Hard and abstract moralities are yielding to a more exact estimate of the subtlety and complexity of our life. Always, as an organism increases in perfection, the conditions of its life become more complex. Man is the most complex of the products of nature. Character merges into temperament: the nervous system refines itself into intellect. Man's physical organism is played upon not only by the physical conditions about it, but by remote laws of inheritance, the vibrations of long-past acts reaching him in the midst of the new order of things in which he lives. When we have estimated these conditions he is still not yet simple and isolated; for the mind of the race, the character of the age, sway him this way or that through the medium of language and current ideas.

Thus, for Pater, the morality of his own age was necessarily more complex and flexible than that of a writer like Coleridge, who, for all his speculative, roving genius, still believed wholeheartedly in 'hard and abstract moralities' (in, say, the Ten Commandments): whereas for Pater all moral problems tended to become special cases. (This, indeed, is what led him, as early as 1874, to write an admirable essay on *Measure for Measure*.) The *Studies in the History of the Renaissance* is his earliest attempt to organize the tentative method over a fairly wide range of instances, though within a definable context; to organize a search for fixed points within the bewildering flux of the modern world.

IV

The Renaissance was intended as a prolegomenon to a new age: an age whose choicer spirits might achieve oneness with themselves through æsthetic contemplation. The topics dealt with range from the thirteenth to the eighteenth centuries. For Pater, the Renaissance was not a phenomenon confined narrowly to one place or period, but a widespread, discontinuous and prolonged movement of the European spirit; its essence, the vivid and disruptive impact of the values of Greek life, thought and art on the jaded or one-sided local traditions of European culture. Pater thought of these jaded and one-sided traditions as mainly those of the Christian Middle Ages, but not wholly so; for he saw Winckelmann, the eighteenth-century German Hellenist, who is the subject of one of his best essays, as reacting not against Christianity, but against the decadence of early Humanism itself, against a sterile neo-Classical eighteenth-century orthodoxy, and as seeking out the reality, rather than the conventional picture, of ancient Greece. Yet Winckelmann is a little set apart from Pater's other Renaissance types. They all, painters and poets, had the sense of discovering in the classical world something *new*, and the possibility of renewed creation. Winckelmann, their belated descendant, had the sense, rather, of recovering something *lost*. The Hellenistic past, for Winckelmann, becomes the starting point of a mode of contemplation, rather than of creation. He anticipates the critical attitude which, for Pater, was the attitude of the nineteenth-century mind at its best.

To the historians of the eighteenth century, the Renaissance suggested mainly the re-acquisition of classical learning, the new taste for Roman (rather than Greek) antiquities that marks the fifteenth and sixteenth centuries, first in Italy, and then through the other civilized parts of Europe. It meant the rise of the Humanists and the fall of the Schoolmen. But Pater's own century had acquired a more subtle, vivid and objectively defined historical sense. The Renaissance was now seen as the re-birth of Man, a re-birth of individuality, the beginning, in fact, of the Modern World. In Pater's own age, this wistfulness about a past, now for the first time so sharply conceived by historians that it could be explored, in imagination, as the present can be conceived, combined with a typical Victorian unease. This led many to project an 'ideal moment' into the past. But the views of writers who romantically idealized selected portions of the past were often quite unrelated to historical actualities; Pater wrote as a scholar, if a somewhat vagrant one.

Pater's method, in *The Renaissance*, of exploring not so much a period as a movement of history through selected individuals, places him in line with Michelet, with the German romantic historians, and in a sense even with Carlyle. History for him has both a dramatic interest and a practical bearing. In Burckhardt's famous *Civilization of the Renaissance in Italy* (1860) Pater saw a way of concentrating on sudden luminous moments of a period, of a movement, rather than attempting to draw a flat systematic map of it. This approach had an obvious attraction for a writer who believed passionately both in the fruitfulness of the tentative approach, and in the isolation of all individuals within the 'flux'. There is, however, one important difference between Burckhardt and Pater. Burckhardt tended to insist over-sharply on distinctions between 'historical periods', periods which, we are more and more realizing, are less realities than conveniences of the historian. Pater emphasized the essential continuity of the Renaissance with the Middle Ages on the one hand, and with modern times on the other, and in this he is in line with present historical research. He also differed from the leading historians of his time in the special nature of his interest in the individual. For Pater, as for Sainte Beuve, it is rather the man behind a work of art or literature (rather than, for instance, the 'style of an age') that gives a work unity. Art, for him, existed for personality's sake; and he saw the shaping of personality, through the creation and appreciation of art, as, in a sense, the highest kind of art. It is here that he is fundamentally a moralist, not a mere (or pure) critic of literature or art.

The 'Preface' summarizes Pater's critical method. Pater begins with Arnold's definition of the critic's first duty as being 'to see the object as in itself it really is', but significantly adds 'in æsthetic criticism the first step towards seeing one's object as it really is, is to know one's own impression as it really is'. For Pater, the impression is our sole contact with anything external to ourselves. Pater parts company from Arnold in stressing Hellenism and muting Hebraism. Whereas both Pater and Arnold use literature as the basis for a theory of life, Pater follows much more consistently the corollary of culture as an inward process. Arnold is too glib when he relates the instinct for the good life to literature as represented by the submission to 'the best that has been thought and said' and to the problem of the good life in relation to others. For Pater this is not possible: believing as he does that man is fundamentally isolated, and that the senses are all that men have in common. Culture at this stage appears only as a harmony of sensations in the individual life, and for this reason he extends (Arnold was indifferent to the other arts) Arnold's concern with literature to painting and sculpture.

Pater's method of great receptivity and intensification of personality through contemplation of the work of art is an ideal for the few, not the many, in his own age; and in its insistence on the appreciative approach offers a consumer's rather than a producer's view of art. Here is a typical passage:

The æsthetic critic, then, regards all the objects with which he has to do, all works of art, and the fairer forms of nature and human life, as powers or forces producing pleasurable sensations, each of a more or less peculiar . . . kind. This influence he feels and wishes to explain, analysing it and reducing it to its elements. To him, the picture, the landscape, the engaging personality in life or in a book, *La Gioconda*, the hills of Carrara, Pico of Mirandola, are valuable for their virtues, as we say, in speaking of a herb, a wine, a gem; for the property each has of affecting one with a special, unique impression of pleasure. Our education becomes complete in proportion as our susceptibility to these impressions increases in depth and variety.

A certain looseness in the texture of his argument is typical of Pater. He tends to use abstract concepts decoratively; to isolate ideas rather than to relate them, and when he ascribes so much to the 'fineness of truth' of the single word, he often treats it, or other fragments or details of larger wholes (a piece of decorative or symbolic detail in a painting, say) as if it were an æsthetic sufficiency. Yet the apparent want of discrimination between the different levels of pleasure therein gives a misleading impression of Pater's total attitude. The mention of *persons* as well as *things* must involve the moral dimension, since the æsthetic critic is contemplating what is *responsive*. The impressions, also, received from even the simplest objects of contemplation which Pater lists here—a herb, a wine, a gem—are, in fact, complex. The 'unique' impression is the uniqueness of a complex whole; whose elements, or some of them, may be broadly or closely similar to elements of other complex wholes. By not adverting to this point, Pater seems to leave out from the critic's function the task of comparison, and grading, of broadly or partly similar wholes, and the notion of a hierarchy or different kinds of wholes.

The chief qualifications of the æsthetic critic are, for Pater, alertness, openness, a clear notion of what he is trying to isolate. But Pater was not primarily concerned with pure æsthetic theory, he is a practical critic: he feels that the man who 'experiences impressions strongly, and drives directly at the analysis and discrimination of them, has no need to trouble himself with the abstract question of what beauty is in itself or what is its exact relation to truth or experience'. Yet, though he appears to isolate Beauty in an uncompromising Art for Art's sake fashion, Pater had to admit that the perfection of oneself in relation to beautiful objects must at least indirectly involve the moral perfection of oneself in relation to others, for among 'the objects with which criticism deals' are 'artistic and accomplished forms of human life'.

The single essay in *The Renaissance* which deals most directly with 'artistic and accomplished forms of human life' is that on Winckelmann, with whom Pater felt a profound personal sympathy. Winckelmann grew up in eighteenth-century Germany without any advantages, was largely self-taught, and dedicated himself passionately to the study of Greek antiquity. His example was the foundation of Goethe's struggle to acquire a classical balance between breadth of culture and intensity of feeling: 'One *learns* nothing from him, but one *becomes* something.' And in this sense Winckelmann is the supreme example of the transmission of culture through temperament. Pater saw in Winckelmann's story the example of a life full of 'distinguishing intensity', a life of rich being, not of mere doing. As an art critic, also, Pater admired Winckelmann for his feeling for the concrete, his lack of shame in handling the sensuous side of Greek art. For the spectator, Pater noted approvingly, the intellectual and the spiritual are properly merged in the sensuous. Yet from the example of Winckelmann, Pater realized the sacrifice involved in the æsthetic life.

From this stringent ideal of the cultivated man as receptive specta-tor rather than violent originator, Pater arrives at the theory of the conduct of life he inculcates in the 'Conclusion' to *The Renaissance*. This is a highly compressed, evocative document. Pater gives, first, his own version of Hume's and Mill's phenomenalism. The sole unit of experience is 'the impression'. All that is actual is a single sharp moment, gone before it can be said to be. Yet there lingers inexplicably within that moment the relic, more or less fugitive, of other such moments gone by. These moments are in perpetual flight, but their onset can be 'multiplied', and their impact made more vivid by 'the high passions'. As the moment is isolated by analysis from its context, so the observer is abstracted from his social frame: he is cut off alike from the solidity of the world and from social solidarity:

> Experience, already reduced to a swarm of impressions, is ringed round for each one of us by that thick wall of personality through which no real voice has ever pierced on its way to us, or from us to that which we can only conjecture to be without. Every one of those impressions is the impression of the individual in his isolation, each mind keeping as a solitary prisoner its own dream of a world.

The price to be paid for the freedom of the human sensibility to seek first and foremost the heightening of its sensations is a high one. The solid world, the social world, even the vague assurance of something beyond the veil, all go. The purpose of such language with its melancholy emphasis on dissolution and isolation is to set the stage for the real message of the 'Conclusion'. This is that we should multiply and intensify our sensations at all cost: that not the wisdom of experience, but the excitement of experiencing, is the one thing necessary:

> Not to discriminate every moment some passionate attitude in those about us, and in the very brilliancy of their gifts some tragic dividing of forces on their ways, is, on this short day of frost and sun, to sleep before evening. . . . We have an interval, and then our place knows us no more. . . . Our one chance lies in expanding that interval, in getting as many pulsations as possible into the given time. High passions may give us this quickened sense of life, ecstasy and sorrow of love, the various forms of enthusiastic activity. . . . Of this wisdom, the poetic passion, the desire of beauty, the love of art for its own sake has most. For art comes to you, professing frankly to give nothing but the highest quality to your moments as they pass, and simply for those moments' sake.

This is not, however, the mere creed of Art for Art's sake: it is Art for the sake of a specially conceived morality. For Pater, as Professor Kermode has pointed out, 'art is what is significant in life, and so sensibility or insight, corruptible as it is, is the organ of moral knowledge, and art, for all its refusal to worship the idols of vulgar morality, is the only true morality; indeed it is nothing less than life itself'. Intensities, for Pater, were not all in one narrowly monotonous key, the key, for instance, of sublimated or tantalized sexuality: making love was an intense experience, so was a mystic's vision, so were the overtones of 'a chorus-ending in Euripides'. (For all his talk about intensifying and multiplying sensations, he does not quite cultivate them for their own sake: he seeks through them rather the unification of personality.) Yet, after Pater wrote, it was impossible for critics and artists to continue in the naïvely moralistic view of art that had marked even a great critic like Ruskin or a painter of genuine integrity like Holman Hunt.

V

The Renaissance possesses distinct unity of tone; but its total effect remains somewhat baffling. This partly derives from its being a federation of periodical essays, published over a period when Pater's thought was in rapid evolution. Pater was himself probably aware of the resulting inconsistencies, but he may have accepted these as records of his mental history and the 'Preface' and the 'Conclusion' clearly represented attempts at a final blend. The culminating essay, that on Winckelmann, was the earliest composed and recalls the scepticisms of the Coleridge essay. The essay on the French proto-Renaissance, 'Two Early French Stories' and the 'Joachim du Bellay' had appeared in 1872, five years after the 'Winckelmann' and a

year before *The Renaissance* was published. These two essays gesture towards a shadowy theme: a cyclic movement in the Renaissance itself from
twelfth- and thirteenth-century France to the France of the Pléiade. Other
themes may be distinguished. We are made aware, for example, of prepara-
tions for the emergence by the end of the book of that culture hero of the
nineteenth century, Goethe; in the first essay phrases limit the vivid
rebelliousness of the French middle ages; its openness to the return of the
Pagan Venus, its intellectual curiosity, the free play of its human affections: 'the perfection of culture', Pater tells us, 'is not rebellion but peace';
its end a 'deep moral stillness'. And such perfection finds its most complete embodiment in Goethe. In the 'Preface' Pater associates beauty in
landscape, painting and the fair forms of human life, while that becomes
transposed in the 'Conclusion' into 'the face of one's friend'. At times he
lingers over what is virtually some Platonic belief in the body's beauty as
vehicle of the soul, index of an inward harmony and completeness. Pico
della Mirandola, for example, retains a medieval chivalry of intellect, a
readiness to encounter the most mysterious and uncouth ideas in the belief
that 'nothing which has ever interested living men and women can wholly
lose its vitality'. Pico, like Pater himself, evades renunciations: the old
Gods survive the flame of his conversion and Pico furnishes too an
example of that transmission of culture by beauty of form and personality.
       'The fair face of one's friend': Pater discreetly alludes to 'the vague
and wayward loves' of Michelangelo and Leonardo, to the passionate male
friendships of Winckelmann. But such are later corrected by the intense
but chaste relationship of Marius with Flavian and with Cornelius. Even
·in the earlier book, the ideal is less the homosexual, than the Platonic, the
androgynous; that point where the beauty of male and of female dissolve
in a higher accordance, though the Androgyne, as so often in the later
nineteenth century, can be other than healing; in one of Michelangelo's
works we meet that 'face of doubtful sex, set in the shadow of its own
hair'. The image of the androgyne, of an untroubled centrality one might
argue, is related itself to an idea that persists through *The Renaissance*: the
tendency of the individual arts to transcend their formal limits and aspire
to the condition of music, most non-discursive of all arts. Personality
itself, at its fairest, most developed, has precisely such an aspiration,
associated with the ideal of transpicuousness we encounter in Pater's first
surviving prose work, 'Diaphaneitè', and later found by Pater in the moral
sexlessness of Greek sculpture. But that triumph of form over matter
remains associated in a manner almost mystical with death, like the swoon
of Leda in Yeats's sonnet 'Leda and the Swan', 'only the abstract lines
remain, in a great indifference'. The Pléiade, Pater tells us, were insatia-

ble of music and in Du Bellay's most famous poem, the 'Hymn to the Winds', 'matter itself becomes almost nothing; the form almost everything'. The theme is resumed in the Giorgione essay, where Pater describes Giorgione's school as refining on that 'feverish, tumultuously coloured world of the old citizens of Venice—exquisite pauses in time, in which arrested thus, we seem to be spectators of all the fullness of existence and which are like some consummate extract or quintessence of life'. Here, Pater involves us in a Keatsian dying-into-life. We have the profile of a *symboliste* theory of art, the essay on Giorgione has been seen, too, as anticipating Clive Bell's notion of 'significant form'.

Art critics have indeed been milder to Pater than have the literary critics, though his descriptions of paintings share the expressive qualities of his discussion of literary texts. The method is to mime the emotional effect of a work of art through the tone and cadence of his prose and (like Ruskin, in this field his master) he extends the spatial effects of an art work into the temporal. Pater was contemporary with the first scientific historians of art in Germany and occasionally embodies their findings (not always fortunately; he limits Giorgione's canon to one painting); but he remains distinctly light on technical as opposed to dramatic or meditative description and was no haunter of archives. Yet art historians of severe method, such as Berenson and Herbert Horne, have put on record their debt to Pater.

At his best, Pater allows the reader sufficient plain visual data to share in, or to resist, his interpretation of the work of art. In describing Botticelli's *Birth of Venus*, for example, he intuitively remarks the slender, unripe, Gothic idiom of the Goddess's body. And this insight is followed by a sensitive record of the painting's faintly menacing detail:

> An emblematical figure of the wind blows hard across the gray water, moving forward the dainty-lipped shell on which she sails, the sea 'showing his teeth', as it moves in thin lines of foam, and sucking in, one by one, the falling roses, each severe in outline, plucked off short at the stalk, but embrowned a little, as Botticelli's flowers always are. Botticelli meant all this imagery to be altogether pleasurable; and it was partly an incompleteness of resources, inseparable from the art of that time, that subdued and chilled it; but his predilection for minor tones counts also; and what is unmistakable is the sadness with which he has conceived the goddess of pleasure, as the depositary of a great power over the lives of men.

This 'quotation' from Botticelli can indeed be applied to much of the master's work, even if Pater consistently underestimates the achievements of the Florentine Renaissance, describing it as 'in many things, great rather by what it designed than by what it achieved'.

VI

If the Botticelli passage is a triumph, there may be reservations about the second most famous passage in Pater: his evocation of Leonardo's famous portrait of a lady, the Gioconda, or the Mona Lisa. This lady has a smiling mouth and is set, not in a domestic background, but as Pater puts it 'in that cirque of fantastic rocks, as in some faint light under sea'.

> The presence that rose thus so strangely beside the waters, is expressive of what in the ways of a thousand years man had come to desire. Hers is the head upon which all 'the ends of the world are come' and the eyelids are a little weary. It is a beauty wrought out from within upon the flesh, the deposit, little cell by cell, of strange thoughts and fantastic reveries and exquisite passions. Set it for a moment beside one of those white Greek goddesses or beautiful women of antiquity, and how would they be troubled by this beauty, into which the soul with all its maladies has passed? All the thought and experience of the world have etched and moulded there, in that which they have of power to refine and make expressive the outward form, the animalism of Greece, the lust of Rome, the reverie of the Middle Ages with its spiritual ambition and imaginative loves, the return of the pagan world, the sins of the Borgias.

There follows the passage which Yeats printed as free verse in his *Oxford Book of Modern Verse*, followed by two sentences of summary:

> She is older than the rocks among which she sits; like the vampire, she has been dead many times, and learned the secrets of the grave; and has been a diver in deep seas, and keeps their fallen day about her; and trafficked for strange webs with Eastern merchants; and, as Leda, was the mother of Helen of Troy, and, as Saint Anne, the mother of Mary; and all this has been to her but as the sound of lyres and flutes, and lives only in the delicacy with which it has moulded the changing lineaments, and tinged the eyelids and the hands. The fancy of a perpetual life, sweeping together ten thousand experiences, is an old one; and modern thought has conceived the idea of humanity as wrought upon by, and summing up in itself, all modes of thought and life. Certainly Lady Lisa might stand as the embodiment of the old fancy, the symbol of the modern idea.

The Mona Lisa as the embodiment of the old fancy. Even there Pater attributes more to the painting than is readily legible. There are clear embarrassments in attempting to discover verbal equivalents for visual experience and Pater is not writing scientific art criticism. The passage represents a reverie on the painting as on Leonardo's work in general; but it remains more than self-indulgent fantasy. First, we may note that the passage occurs in the middle of the Leonardo essay, at the centre of *The Renaissance*, and its significance radiates backward and forward, back to what is embodied in history, forward to what is as yet only symbolized, or prescribed. The description collects phrases which Pater uses of the master's other works, for the Mona Lisa's face is the final embodiment of an image that obsessed Leonardo; that same face impressing itself on the icons of Saint John, Saint Anne and the Madonna and, as may be gathered from a copy of the now lost painting, of Leda and the Swan. To take one example of phrases recollected, as in some trance, from other parts of the essay we can cite that 'diver in deep seas' reflecting the earlier 'faint light under sea' which on the literal level could be the varnish that both preserves and distorts the painting. Laid over paint first as preservative, later to lend some mellow, speciously antique patina, it chills the spring of colour, but adds mystery. The painting has also ripened through time in the sense of being interpreted and re-interpreted, each analysis thickening the varnish that lies over Leonardo's original paintwork.

Pater's account assumes into itself much of the history of that interpretation. For Vasari, in the sixteenth century, Lisa's smile is pleasing; the painting pre-eminently life-like; Leonardo is seen as one who controls nature by making a perfect model of it, as in primitive magic. The Romantic critics shift to the notion of portraiture as bodying forth the subjectivity of the sitter, so that smile and landscape which the sixteenth century may have seen as unfinished or formalized become willed and significantly related.

Pater associates landscape and face more firmly than his predecessors and Sir Kenneth Clark concludes that he is right: the rocky backgrounds of Leonardo's portraits show a real understanding of the forces that led to their structure; but there are also landscapes of fantasy, projections not of Lisa's but Leonardo's inner world. With Lanzi in the eighteenth and through to Hazlitt and Stendhal in the early nineteenth century, interpretation of the haunting smile proceeds from gaiety to equivocation: the smile belongs equally to mistress and to saint. Michelet, who sees Leonardo as prophet and type, interprets the smile as delight at scientific 'forbidden knowledge' mingled with irony at the expense of an old world that is passing: Leonardo as the first modern man, though the smile is nervous, troubled. Pater takes Michelet into the regions of myth, and French critics writing immediately before Pater provide him with vocabulary; the smile is now satanic, sibylline, voluptuous, caught in the mystery of half-light, and Gautier, touching on Leonardo's obsessive faces, provides the final touches: 'We have seen their faces, but not upon this earth; in some previous existence perhaps; through the subtle modelling we divine the beginnings of fatigue . . . a spirit entirely modern . . .

beneath the form expressed, one feels a thought which is vague, infinite, inexpressible, like a musical idea . . . images already seen. . . .' Vasari's 'jesters and singers' whom rumour suggested Leonardo had employed to 'protract the subtle expression', Pater finally modulates into the 'flutes and lyres' of Swinburne's *Laus Veneris*. (Swinburne's description of some heads of Michelangelo, written in 1868, had a considerable effect on Pater's style of this period.)

Pater's Mona Lisa has assumed by now the lineaments of the Romantic Fatal Woman, who enters men's lives from beyond history and is an indication of the autonomy of images that live their life independently of the minds to which they give themselves. She resolves the painful antimonies of pleasure-pain; knowledge-mystery; orgasm-death. Leonardo is oracle; no victim, but victor over his Image. That image sums up all the forces that lay behind the Renaissance of which Leonardo made a model, but the image now needs re-mastering.

Anthony Ward has persuasively argued that Pater's own image of the Lady Lisa is intended as a model for the future, a model which will enable him in the determinist nightmare of the Darwinian world to 'go on writing'. Mr Ward reminds us of Pater's distinction in the essay 'Style' between the 'masculine', the 'controlling, rational, forming, power' of the artist, exerted on the 'feminine', the brute amorphous mass of the artist's experience, which constitutes 'soul' as opposed to 'mind', a related distinction. Organization achieved by mind is the design made on the web of the artist's experience; in Pater's case what he knew of reality as he had been taught to see it by Darwin. Man was merely 'the most complex of the products of nature'. The tissues of his brain were indeed 'modified by every ray of light and sound'; he was under the influence of 'natural law' or in Pater's own despairing term 'necessity'. And to continue paraphrasing Mr Ward, Darwin also taught Pater that though man's consciousness, his being, was fragmented into moments which changed even as they were being formed, these fragments bore in them 'the central forces of the world'. In Pater's view, an organic development involved the notion that though the organism was in constant change, at each moment in its development it vestigially contained legible upon it a sort of synoptic history of development. This 'web' is reflected by submitting it to the controlling power of design. In so far as an artist can reduce the incoherent flux of experience to design he will be able to emancipate himself from that incoherence. To the extent that the power of design affects the artist's own response to the incoherence and determinism of the nightmare, it will establish his freedom from it and the type of such a design is the Mona Lisa. As Anthony Ward puts it: 'The modern, Schelling said, must create his own mythology out of the material given to the intelligence of his age.' In the Mona Lisa, we may see Pater struggling to evolve the myth, or artistic model, which would locate and give expression to that material. 'He was intent on . . . making the ideas he wished to express saturate and become identical with the vessel made to contain them.' He wished to define the image on the female 'fabric of his dreams'. And he wishes the fabric of dreams to be legible upon the image. In *The Daughter of Herodias*, Leonardo's picture, the characters, Pater says, are: 'clairvoyants, through whom, as through delicate instruments, one becomes aware of the subtler forces of nature, and the modes of their action, all that is magnetic in it'. They are significant examples in which we actually see those forces at work on human flesh. Pater was trying to create an image or model, a design, into which he could pour all the female fluid matter of his understanding of the world so as to locate it there and make it legible. . . . Mona Lisa contains each of the three particulars Mr Ward has defined and she satisfies at the same time the masculine demands Pater was making in that she reduces the three particulars to a design. 'Men in the ways of a thousand years' can be translated into Walter Pater himself. The Lady Lisa is expressive of what he himself desires and 'the ways of a thousand years' does not only function legitimately as a liturgical gesture: it is also an attempt to give universality and authority to the image. The Mona Lisa is a 'head', a single entity upon which 'all the ends of the world are come', concentrating in a single finite image all man's relation to the objects about him, his sense of their 'tyranny'. 'Wrought out from within upon the flesh, the deposit, little cell by cell.' The image, that is to say, is a changing one. It develops as it is conceived. The flux enters into it but is controlled, and the phrase 'deposited little cell by cell' clearly shows knowledge of the doctrine of organic development. We are also told of the accumulative nature of the image, since from Leonardo's childhood, we have seen it 'defining itself on the fabric of his dreams'. In the moment of our apprehension of her face we may see all history vestigially legible, 'all the thought and experience of the world . . .' She contains a synoptic history of the development of civilization, 'the animalism of Greece', etc.

Evolution introduced a new conception of time into English consciousness. In a moment there were concentrated 'a thousand experiences'. In the notion of carbon Pater says there was both the notion of coal and of the diamond. The artist's role was thus to collapse the growth of a thing into one of his moments of vision, and to contradict temporal development. He was to make the moment 'wholly concrete'.

The image of the Mona Lisa represents in the words of the

Giorgone essay 'an exquisite pause in time . . . in which we seem to be spectators of the fullness of all existence'. And in such moments, man was free from the world's deliquescence. And the Mona Lisa is also free, spectator of all existence, yet although detached from her experience she has still organized it into her design and so is able to free herself from it, yet though freed from the experience, that experience cannot be denied and must be expressed. She at once resists and so gives expression to the 'magnetic nightmare'. She shows the action of mind on soul, shows man dealing with his experience so as to control it, thus, giving him back his sense of freedom. She is at once the realization and the suggestion of an artistic idea. And to Mr Ward's invocation of Darwin, we can add contemporary biological theory, particularly that of Virchow, who posits in his *Cellular Pathologie* of 1858 'an eternal law of continuous development' in terms of cells, which recalls not merely the Mona Lisa but the phraseology of the early essay on Coleridge.

The more we examine this so called 'purple panel' the more we find that it is dense with meaning.

VII

In *The Renaissance* Pater had been trying to fix the secret individual experiences of a few personalities who in his scheme of values mattered supremely, by attempting to define in them some central quality, some fixed point in the flux. That fixed point was best illustrated in Michelangelo by the Biblical phrase 'Out of the strong came forth sweetness'. In Leonardo, the fixed point was the conflict between the scientist's curiosity and the artist's love of beauty; and so on. But there was one great objection to making ideal types out of actual historical personages. Anybody who has actually existed remains, even after his death, subject to the flux. New scholarly discoveries have altered, for instance, since Pater's time, our view of Giorgione, of whom Pater accepted only one picture as provenly authentic; and even where there has not been this type of development, we cannot help seeing Pater's Leonardo or his Botticelli as doubly distant in time from us; as presented to us through the subtly distorting medium of Pater's own late nineteenth-century sensibility (and our view of that sensibility is itself a subtly distorted mid-twentieth-century view). It was Pater's awareness of this fundamental flaw in the notion of making art out of history that turned him from writing about historical figures, idealized into types, and towards writing, as in *Imaginary Portraits* and *Marius the Epicurean*, about imaginary figures who could be,

without possibility of reduction, ideal types. He decided to create characters who had no historical existence, who could still, like the characters in
The Renaissance, be incarnations of the unending development of culture,
but who could be fixed, like works of art. There are likely to be no such
shifts in our evaluations of Pater's purely imaginary characters. What they
have in common is that they are all gifted or dedicated natures, born out of
due time. Duke Karl is the herald of a serene neo-classicism in a Germany
desolated by religious wars; Sebastian van Storck is torn between the life
of feeling and the passion for metaphysics, and chilled by the abstractions
of Spinozan philosophy. In other such stories (some of them were published posthumously) we find buried Hellenism irrupting into the Gothic
twilight. Brother Apollyon is really Apollo in exile, while Denys of
Auxerre re-enacts the ritual death of Dionysus as Lord of Misrule, so
playing out Pater's notion that ritual remains, while beliefs falter. All the
subjects of Pater's *Imaginary Portraits* are destroyed by the age in which
they live, but remain unchanged at the centre; portents of change, they
are themselves unchanging; all of them die unreasonably and almost
casually, drastically, yet in a way that seems irrelevant to their life-patterns.
The effect of these 'imaginary portraits' is curiously cold, though impressive. We do not feel our way into these stories; rather we reflect on them
from a distance. Perhaps we are supposed to have heard them before (as in
the case of Dionysus and Apollo, with their harsh cycles, we certainly are)
but told in another tone of voice. They reflect Pater's own predicament;
images of himself projected into history, full of the sense of exile, never
communicating.

VIII

Marius the Epicurean, Pater's central work, an extended 'imaginary portrait', makes sense on two levels: first, as a scholarly imaginative re-
creation of second-century Antonine Rome; secondly as a subtle, trenchant
and indirect analysis of High Victorian England. Pater was quite open in a
letter to a friend about the contemporary bearing of the book:

> I regard this matter as a sort of duty. For you know I think that there is a
> . . . sort of religious phase possible for the modern mind, the conditions
> of which phase it is the main object of my design to convey.

Certain obvious affinities existed between Pater's England and
Marcus Aurelius's Rome. Both were centres of vast empires, both govern-
ments were internally stable; both intermittently at war with other races
on the frontier. More profoundly, both provided an intellectual climate in

which a bewildering number of competing faiths and philosophies were able to flourish. The Antonine period represented for Pater the ripe autumn of the Graeco-Roman world, and one of the implications of *Marius* is that in Victorian England the almost over-ripe fruit of civilization is also hanging heavy on the bough.

From the Broad Church historians, like Thomas Arnold or Dean Stanley, Pater may well have derived the notion that societies passed through the same life-cycles as individuals and that God's providence was constantly active, so disrupting the determined patterns of history. For the Broad Church historians, Rome provided the model of a finished civilization while our own was, on a higher level, still pursuing its course. God's providence intervened largely through the process of religion *accommodating* itself to progress, and it is this principle of accommodation that Pater seems to have in mind, when he refers to 'a religious phase possible to the modern mind', one which will take into account the 'flux' and by so doing will transcend it. Another indication of the manner in which Providence asserted itself through history was furnished by ritual. When Pater attended Mass at a High Anglican Church such as St Alban's, Holborn, he could not fail to notice that the celebrant was wearing the formal evening dress of a Roman gentleman of the second century. Myth, on the other hand, to Pater, as to Arnold, expressed something fluid, though some myths no longer religiously responded to seemed to possess a permanent poetic value. It is, therefore, in ritual, rather than in the abstract moral and metaphysical appeal of religion or in naked mysticism that Pater is interested:

> Players and painted stage took all my love
> And not those things that they were emblems of.

But the deeper significance of *Marius* is that it explores Pater's inner life more coherently than the scattered brilliances of *The Renaissance* were able to do. Marius is essentially Pater himself with a personal beauty that he never had, seeking and finding a life of communion and sacrifice for which Pater only wistfully longed.

The structure of *Marius* resembles that of Pater's other 'imaginary portraits'. Character is genuinely evoked, but at a distance. The people in *Marius* never make a brutal impact on one another; they never converse. Their ideas reach us through diaries, lectures and Platonic fable. This is partly tact on Pater's part, for he knew he had none of the ordinary novelists's gifts. It is partly also a deliberate method of indicating the essential isolation of the central figure and of embodying character, as Pater's own character in life was essentially embodied, through the artistic presentation of the emotional impact of ideas.

The book opens with a sensitive account of the old, simple Roman religion of the household gods, of hearth and field; a rustic religion of 'usages and sentiments' rather than dogma, of 'natural piety'. Perhaps this is comparable to the old high-and-dry Anglicanism of Pater's childhood. Marius, the child-priest, is soon orphaned, leaves the security of his childhood home, and loses his attachment to the old Pagan religion. In Pisa, he meets the young aesthete Flavian whose physical beauty and moral corruption are epitomes of the decaying Pagan world. Flavian has literary ambitions and his 'euphuism'—here seen as art without morality— has, for Pater, obvious topical relevance to the creed of Art for Art's sake. The First Part of *Marius* ends with the death of Flavian, still struggling to finish his masterpiece, the *Pervigilium Veneris*.

Marius, though not infected by Flavian's corrupt sophistication, is deeply moved by his death. He realizes that for the Pagan there is no consolation in the face of death. It is the first of several emotional crises, which also become moral and intellectual crises, and which are all concerned with the gulf between the living and the dead and man's bafflement, awe or horror in the face of death. Rejecting the philosophy of 'flux', from Aristippus of Cyrene, Marius learns to concern himself less with troubling thoughts than with the happy ordering of the feelings, 'life as the end of life'. This is not a crude hedonism, but a method of tactful discrimination. Marius then proceeds to Rome to become Marcus Aurelius's secretary, and the pointed contrast between the refined egoism of his own Epicureanism and the stern disinterestedness of the Emperor's Stoicism has its effect. He now begins to think of Epicureanism as an essentially adolescent philosophy. From a discourse of Cornelius Fronto, a teacher of rhetoric at Rome, Marius conceives the notion that morality may indeed be a kind of artistic ordering of life, but comparable to the ordering Fronto finds in the universe itself, that of a single great polity.

But, to Marius, Fronto's metaphysics also seem painfully abstract. He admires much more the practical discipline which Aurelius has made of the Stoic philosophy, but his admiration cools when he realizes that the Emperor's love of humanity is rather abstract, too. And this disillusionment is reinforced by the spectacle of Aurelius's helpless grief at the death of his child. Stoicism cannot meet the test of death. At this time Marius has a spiritual experience of supreme importance. Riding among the Sabine Hills, he senses, behind the veil of matter, an unseen friend or guide, and so arrives at the notion of a personal creator, utterly different from the vague principle of cosmic order of the Stoics. Even through his early Cyrenaicism, Marius had preserved a certain austerity of temperament, and at the time when, through a knightly young figure,

Cornelius, he meets a community of Christians, he is already preparing himself, though unconsciously, for his own sacrificial death.

In Christianity Marius is to find all that he found good in Paganism: the sense of communion; humble acceptance of the good things of the earth (unlike Aurelius's proud rejection of them); the heightened response to life of a refined Cyrenaicism; the moral dignity of Stoicism itself—but all transcended, not rejected. The inclusion of Paganism in its noblest forms in Christianity is symbolized for Marius by 'the fragments of older architecture, the mosaics, the spiral columns' which compose the architecture of the Christian catacomb in Cecilia's house. And Marius's development towards Christianity is by way of culture not self-denial: not by the sacrifice of any one of the aspects of the self but by the 'harmonious development of all the parts of human nature, in just proportion to one another'. (All this is very plausible, but not particularly Christian.) For the Church under the Antonines radiates the full beauty of holiness through its poetry and music, establishing a tradition that was to last to Pater's own day.

Marius's first contact with Christianity is, typically, through death, through the catacomb. At the graves of the Christian martyrs, he learns that death can be joy; but he is also initiated into life, into natural love, when the family of the gracious Cecilia becomes for him an emblem of the heavenly family of the Church itself. And witnessing the eucharistic celebration, he feels that he has at last found something to hold by, dimly sensing there a redemptive cyclic movement: 'There was here a veritable consecration, hopeful and animating, of the earth's gifts, of old dead and dark matter itself, now in some way redeemed at last, of all that we can touch and see . . . and in strong contrast to the wise emperor's renunciant and impassive attitude towards them.'

For Marius, this is a new 'spirit' investing old rites, not a new 'matter': ritual as ever remains the fixed element in religion, though myth changes. Marius's own hope for the future now rests mainly on his friendship with Cornelius. In this friendship, he seems to reach out in imagination to a happier and holier future, and it is in this spirit that Marius sacrifices himself for Cornelius's safety, dying, consoled by Christian rites, in a Christian household. 'His death, according to their generous view in this matter (being) of the nature of a martyrdom; and martyrdom, as the Church has always said, a kind of sacrament with plenary grace.' Christian by Nature, not Grace, poor Marius, and it is pleasant to think that his relics, in later years, may have been venerated as those of an early martyr: but the conclusion of the book has its subdued ironies. Marius's end seems weariness rather than exaltation: Marius the spectator has become Marius the actor, having overcome the 'endless dialogue of the mind with itself' and commitment leads only to self-destruction.

As a work of art, *Marius* has a dense and logical structure, based on a series of contrasts, dialectical or ironic. Flavian placed over against the rather unreal figure of Cornelius; the severe beauty of Cecilia juxtaposed with the 'malign' beauty of the Empress Faustina; the Roman games with the martyrs, 'athletes of God'. But minor incidents are easily overlooked. Marius's visit to his own family catacomb, as the last of his race, lends an added poignancy to the feeling that he can identify himself with 'the coming world', through his friendship with Cornelius, who is to marry Cecilia. Even the much criticized insertion of a translation of Apuleius's *Cupid and Psyche* has complete relevance to Marius's developing philosophy: it serves 'to combine many lines of meditation, already familiar into the ideal of a perfect imaginative love, centred upon a type of beauty entirely flawless and clean . . . in contrast with that ideal . . . men's actual loves . . . might appear to him . . . somewhat mean and sordid'. And Pater would have known the tradition of allegorizing the fable as the soul's desire for union with God.

IX

Surprisingly little of Pater's criticism is directed towards English literature as distinct from subjects derived from painting, sculpture or antiquity. The essay on *Measure for Measure* retains some interest; but apart from one or two reviews, this aspect of his work is not rewarding.

The essay on Wordsworth in *Appreciations*, originally published in 1874, strongly counterpoints the 'Conclusion' to *The Renaissance* and remains a cardinal example both of his *finesse* and his failings as a literary critic. It appeared some years before Arnold's fine essay on Wordsworth, at a time when, for various reasons, Wordsworth was beginning to lose the hold he had once had, especially on younger readers. Pater was, therefore, drawing attention to a poet recognized as great but beginning, partly because of the bulk and unevenness of his performance, to be a little neglected. He had already in *The Renaissance* strikingly isolated what was for him Wordsworth's greatest virtue, meditative pathos. Perhaps the gravest defect of this essay (it is inherent in the 'appreciative' method as such, which will always pay more attention to texture than to structure, to moments of intensity than to the background they arise from) is the failure to see that the 'alien element . . . something tedious and prosaic . . .'

in Wordsworth is not only inseparable from, but often serves to heighten Wordsworth's moments of grand concentration. Pater's essay conjures up a spectral Wordsworth, purged of all that is 'alien' and 'prosaic', but purged also of his large craggy individuality. He scales the great poet down to something smaller, sweeter, smoother than life-size:

> His life of eighty years is divided by no very profoundly felt incidents: its changes are almost wholly inward, and it falls into broad, untroubled, perhaps somewhat monotonous spaces. What it most resembles is the life of one of those early Italian or Flemish painters, who, just because their minds were full of heavenly visions, passed, some of them, the better part of sixty years in quiet, systematic industry. This placid life matured a quite unusual sensibility, really innate in him, to the sights and sounds of the natural world . . . The poem of *Resolution and Independence* is a storehouse of such records: for its fulness of imagery it may be compared to Keats's *Saint Agnes' Eve*.

Pater would not have known about Annette Vallon, but he ought to have noticed that the French Revolution, for Wordsworth, was 'a profoundly felt incident'; and he ought to have noticed that a line in the poem he is mentioning, *Resolution and Independence*: 'And mighty poets in their misery dead', does not reflect anything at all like this Flemish placidity. But it is acute of him to isolate 'Resolution and Independence' for its 'fulness of imagery', though at the same time when he compares it with *The Eve of St Agnes*, he again shows the limitations of his method. 'Resolution and Independence' is a poem with a tough underlying moral structure, of self-discovery and self-rebuke, an underlying almost didactic structure that would have appealed to, say, Pope or Dr Johnson; where *The Eve of St Agnes* is self-indulgent erotic fantasy distanced miraculously into art. But Pater is extremely effective when he deals more generally with Wordsworth's qualities:

> Clear and delicate at once, as he is in the outlining of visible imagery, he is more clear and delicate still, and finely scrupulous, in the noting of sounds; so that he conceives of noble sound as even moulding the human countenance to nobler types, and as something actually 'profaned' by colour, by visible form, or image. . . .

And in the following passage he rises to the full height of his subject though even here, as we follow the mannered cadences, we may have a slight uneasy sense that Pater's Wordsworth is a little too much like the young Marius, a little too self-consciously appreciating the simple ritual dignities of the Roman religion of the boundaries and the soil:

Religious sentiment, consecrating the affections and natural regrets of the human heart, above all, that pitiful awe and care for the perishing human clay, of which relic-worship is but the corruption, has always had much to do with localities, with the thoughts which attach themselves to actual scenes and places. Now what is true of it everywhere, is truest of it in those secluded valleys where one generation after another maintains the same abiding-place; and it was on this side, that Wordsworth apprehended religion most strongly. Consisting, as it did so much, in the recognition of local sanctities, in the habit of connecting the stones and trees of a particular spot of earth with the great events of life, till the low walls, the green mounds, the half-obliterated epitaphs seemed full of voices, and a sort of natural oracles, the very religion of those people of the dales appeared but as another link between them and the earth, and was literally a religion of nature. It tranquillized them by bringing them under the placid rule of traditional and narrowly localized observances. 'Grave livers', they seemed to him, under this aspect, with stately speech, and something of that natural dignity of manners, which underlies the highest courtesy.

It is perhaps easiest to 'place' Pater as a critic by comparing him with his rather older contemporary, Arnold. He has neither Arnold's flair—sometimes also a weakness—for the ambitious generalization nor Arnold's uncanny gift, sometimes as in his treatment of Pope and Dryden, unscrupulously used, for picking on the very quotation that will appear to prove his point. He tries to focus on what might be called the sensuous aspects of literature, aspects which seem to him to have an almost physical resonance, rather than, like Arnold, on literature as 'a criticism of life'. Partly because of this, he is a humbler critic than Arnold. Arnold is always arrogantly sure that he is right, even in the quite numerous instances where his successors have almost unanimously decided that he is crashingly wrong. Pater shows a sounder general taste in what for him is more or less contemporary literature, than Arnold. Arnold makes a great fuss about a very minor pair, the de Guérins, and about one of the world's great bores, Sénancour. Pater mentions with praise, in passing, Stendhal, Blake, Flaubert, none of them 'safe' or fashionable authors in his time. Again, Pater is always a scholar as Arnold quite strikingly is not one. Furthermore, Pater is perhaps the first English critic of importance to have the historical sense very profoundly developed. It is that sense which makes him, on the whole, avoid too arrogant 'placing', or absolute judgements. He wishes to *see* a work of literature or art as vividly as possible in its historical setting, rather than to rap its knuckles in a schoolmasterly way, for not conforming to the moral and social standards of Dr Arnold's Rugby. He is less superficial than Arnold about, for instance, the Greeks; Arnold saw them as bathed perpetually in a white Apollonian light; Pater knew about the dark, earthy side of Greek religion. But against all this there has to be set the fact that Arnold, unlike Pater, could occasionally speak of poetry with the authority which only a good practising poet possesses; and that Arnold, as a critic, even when he is most wrong-headed, speaks always with moral urgency, a concern about the social function of the arts, which was not Pater's *métier*. Perhaps those who know both writers find in Pater more that is gently suggestive and stimulating; in Arnold, more to excite, more to admire, and more to dislike.

X

One comes back, again and again, in discussing Pater, to the idea of style; style as a mode of perception, a total responsive gesture of the whole personality rather than—for all Pater's own very notable stylistic mannerism—a mere way of arranging words. Pater's essay 'Style', an expansion of a review of Flaubert's *Correspondence*, was published towards the end of his life and from its unusual firmness of statement may constitute something of an æsthetic *credo*. Pater begins by remarking that the distinction between poetry and prose has been pushed too far and, following Hazlitt and anticipating Eliot, stresses that poetry should possess the virtues of good prose. Following Arnold, Pater believes that prose is 'the special and opportune art of the modern world', its flexibility enabling it to deal, far better than Victorian verse, with modern life's complexities. He makes De Quincey's distinction between the literature of power and that of knowledge: the literature of knowledge has as its criterion truth of fact only; but imaginative prose is to be judged for its fineness of truth, the writer's personal sense of fact, exactness of transposition of the inner vision.

It is natural for a writer to shape the pattern of his attention to fact to his ingrained flair for fitness. But human beings are infinitely various, and the quality of a given piece of literature will depend not on mere transposition of fact, but on fact in its infinite variety as experienced by a specific personality. The writer must have a scholar's tact, for his material, language, is as much a 'given' thing as the raw material of the sculptor. The liberties he takes will show his recognition of the expanding potentialities of language as well as its agreed civilized limits; just the degree to which he oversteps these limits will be an index to the balance of his imagination and his taste. The notion of the flux applies also, with an especially moving pungency, to language. Words slip, slide, flatten out under excessive pressures. The artist-scholar will be acutely aware both of the root-meanings of words and of the constant shifts of their actual meanings in changing contexts; he will aspire to a purged and yet ranging vocabulary, including elements of both the racy and the recondite. He must be aware of developments in philosophy and science—how to tame, for example, ferocious words like 'transcend', 'ideal', 'phenomenon', breaking into the language about this time, so that literature will not be shut out of the expanding vocabulary of the modern scientific intellectual.

But all such requisites of style are subdued to the architectonic quality that reveals the shaping presence of 'mind', guaranteeing the tact of the writer's omissions. All the laws of good writing aim, thus, at an identity almost of word with object, so that word, phrase, sentence, sequence of cadences seems almost to *become* what it presents. (Compare the remark, in the Giorgione essay which I earlier quoted, about all the arts aspiring to the condition of music, since in music the distinction between matter and form is as far as possible annihilated.)

This doctrine of confluence of matter and form leads Pater on to Flaubert's notion of the *mot juste*. But he is forced to reject Flaubert's insistence on the artist's impersonality, since, for Pater, style essentially mirrors the uniqueness of temperament, 'is the man'.

> One seems to detect the influence of a philosophic idea . . . of a natural economy, of some pre-existent adaptation, between a relative, somewhere in the world of thought, and its correlative, somewhere in the world of language,—both alike, rather, somewhere in the mind of the artist. . . .

Flaubert seems to believe that we know what we are thinking in a purely non-verbal way. For Pater, the process is not so much that of an existent idea in search of expression as of the clarification of the thought itself. In the moment of difficulty for a good writer, it is not the 'exact' word that is wanting, what is wrong is some tangle in the actual thinking itself. The problem of style is, fundamentally, one of self-transparency, of supple self-reflection.

Even if the architectonic ideal of 'mind' in style is satisfied, this does not imply that *great* as opposed to *good* literature will result. For Pater concludes his essay by telling us that greatness in literature depends not on form but matter, not on handling, but substance; on the range and depth of the human interest of its theme.

> Given the conditions I have tried to explain as constituting good art;— then, if it be devoted further to the increase of men's happiness, to the

redemption of the oppressed, or the enlargement of our sympathies with each other, or to such presentment of new or old truth about ourselves and our relation to the world as may ennoble and fortify us in our sojourn here, or immediately, as with Dante, to the glory of God, it will be also great art . . . it (will have) something of the soul of humanity . . . and find its logical, its architectural place, in the great structure of human life.

This argument undercuts not merely the ideal of unified matter and form, but the whole of Pater's earlier insights into the nature of literary art. Pater had, indeed, already recognized the limitations of his intellectualist ideal, by admitting the presence of a further element in style, that of 'soul', exhibited mainly in devotional literature of a highly personal type. If the quotation above is to be taken as his final position, then Pater has renounced Æstheticism and submitted to a simple Christian humanitarianism. However, the issue is not so plain. In his writings after 'Style' we find little practical outcome, and in 'Style' itself, the architectonic ideal itself is not observed. The æsthetic unit, for Pater, remains fixed at the sentence, if necessary, a sentence extended by parenthesis, distinction and qualification to paragraph length. That style is a matter of *perception*, not of cadence or euphony, is the principle laid down in the essay; but one finds so often in Pater the isolated cadence or sentence making its impact by itself; one must pause after every sentence to adjust oneself to a new rhythm (not a new turn of argument). In 'Style' itself, the plea for a flexible prose and the rejection of Flaubert are only loosely connected. We must read 'Style', with its jagged transitions, as a set of related perceptions, or set, even, of ultimately isolated perceptions, held together only by their occurrence within a common periphery. A typical passage of argument may make this clearer:

> Music and prose literature are, *in one sense*, the opposite terms of art. . . . *If* music be the ideal of all art whatever, precisely because in music it is impossible to distinguish the form from the substance . . . then, literature, by finding its specific excellence in the absolute correspondence of the term to its import, will be but fulfilling the condition of all artistic quality in things everywhere, of all good art.

It is rather like a proportion sum: let a be b. Pater attempts first to disarm us by that qualifying phrase 'in one sense', and once we are off guard the innocent word 'if' is used to establish as an axiom what has been proposed entirely without empirical justification. In such a passage Pater is modulating logic æsthetically, subjecting our pleasure in seeing an argument properly worked out to our pleasure in what I. A. Richards has called 'a music of ideas'. Pater's ideal vocabulary is purged and ranging, scholarly but adventurous; but his actual vocabulary, even at its most mature and discriminating in the finally revised *Marius* (1892) (the relation of this to 'Style' has been acutely analysed by Mr Edmund Chandler), consists of many words that are either precious, intensive or cloudy. His vocabulary is purged and scholarly, but very narrow; that of a special, even an intensely private, personality. And though Pater asserts that literature is great through the dignity of its broad human interests, what, as Mr Chandler asks, are we to make of this passage:

> . . . not only scholars, but all disinterested lovers of books, will always
> look to (literature), as to all other fine art, for . . . a sort of cloistral
> refuge, from a certain vulgarity in the actual world. A perfect handling of
> a theory like Newman's *Idea of a University*, has for them something of
> the uses of a religious 'retreat'.

The assumption here still seems to be that art is closed, finished, perfect, while life has an indefinitely open texture. Art is the moral object, intrinsically superior to everyday reality, not a means of encountering experience with greater openness and alertness. So Pater's actual criticism remains fixed always upon the work of art as a thing in itself, and does not move beyond the work of art to its wider or deeper human relevance. He comes back always to his private sensibility, and the immediate modifications a work of art has produced in that; all wider ranges of interest are left out of consideration. 'Style' perhaps represents an honest awareness of the limitations of his own attitudes to art and life, and his own inability at a late stage of development to transcend these. For the scholar-artist, as opposed to the creative artist, art is not liberation, the escape from involvement or emotion through an apparently self-dependent world; but a kind of short-circuiting of emotion, from the work of art back to the work of art.

XI

Pater's reputation falls into four broad phases; the first lasting till 1885, the year of the publication of *Marius*. Early critics were baffled both by the method and the manner of *Studies in the History of The Renaissance* despite the frame of 'Preface' and 'Conclusion'. The challenge of a new type of criticism proved too much; it raised the unanswered question as to whether Pater was scholar or dilettante; irresponsible apologist for an amoral aestheticism or serious moralist. Until the publication of *Marius* then it proved difficult to control an image of so controversial, yet so obscure, a figure as the quiet tutor of Brasenose. The almost uniformly suspicious, sometimes patronizing, almost always crass, reviews of *The Renaissance* gave way to a more respectful response to *Marius*, yet even then reviewers tended to regard *Marius* as a clarification, rather than as a radical re-ordering of the insights contained in the 'Conclusion'. Still, from 1885 on Pater was increasingly treated as a writer of extreme originality, and sometimes, indeed, as a literary saint. *Appreciations* and *Plato and Platonism*, in particular, led critics to evolve an antithesis between the difficult 'brilliances' of *The Renaissance* and the 'friendliness' of the later prose. By the end of the century, Pater's reputation had been established as stylist, as creative critic, as the propagandist of æstheticism (associated with Rossetti, Swinburne and Burne-Jones) and even by some as a genius. Edward Thomas's study of 1913 sets out and partially succeeds in diminishing the stylist. The loss of innocence of so many in the first World War, the grey rather than red thirties, were hardly periods in which Pater could comfortably survive. His *alma mater* found him an embarrassing shade, so near a parody of an actual Oxford, that he had to be dismissed through gossip or with an elegant sneer. More astringent sneers proceeded from Cambridge: Dr Leavis observing that Rossetti no more burned with 'a hard gem-like flame' than did Pater. And there the matter rested until the work of Professors Graham Hough and Kermode.

Pater's one indisputably great disciple, W. B. Yeats, began to lead scholars back to the master. In particular, the close relation of Pater to the twentieth century began to be explored. In the 1960s, Pater attracted much criticism, both precise and imaginative, chiefly from the United States. *Marius* and the *Imaginary Portraits* became the focus of attention. The old naturalist and realist criteria for fiction had now been abandoned and the boundaries between prose and poetry could be defined far less rigidly than before. A new image of Pater as a myth-maker of considerable power began to emerge, while other scholars began to relate Pater more and more to the central concerns of his age. This approach, however, tended to mute somewhat the sharply individualized nature of Pater's work.

What can the general reader profitably gather from Pater's work? He will probably find *The Renaissance, Marius* and the *Imaginary Portraits* (including *Apollo in Picardy*) more rewarding than other volumes. But the sustaining interest of reading him will be less the impetus, the sense of design, than the sudden recurring felicity of image or cadence; a cadence as evocative it may be as 'the legend of Leda, the delight of the world breaking from the egg of a bird'; an epiphany such as this from the essay on Du Bellay:

A sudden light transfigures a trivial thing, a weathervane, a windmill, a winnowing flail, the dust in the barn door; a moment—and the thing has vanished, because it was pure effect; but it leaves a relish behind it, a longing that the accident may happen again.

Or an image, complete, precise yet mysterious as this of the effeminate, menacing Dionysus:

He will become, as always in later art and poetry, of dazzling whiteness; no longer dark with the air and sun, but like one . . . brought up under the shade of Eastern porticoes or pavilions, or in the light that has only reached him softened through the texture of green leaves; honey-pale, like the delicate people of the city, like the flesh of women, as those old-vase painters conceive of it, who leave their hands and faces untouched with the pencil on the white clay.

Or this description of the paintings of Watteau: the sense of an ending indeed:

The storm is always brooding through the massy splendour of the trees, above those sun-dried glades, or lawns, where delicate children may be trusted, thinly clad; and the secular trees themselves will hardly outlast another generation.

We read Pater not because we expect to be dominated by him, but because we enjoy being surprised by him. And like many unmethodical writers, who depend on disconnected intuition, he has a gift of chiming in through his intuitions with the more organized perceptions of some writers who have succeeded him: much of the highly methodized æsthetics of Yeats exist in a kind of evasive or tangential state in Pater. Pater's place as an influential writer in a diffused sense has yet to be explored: historical relativism; the symbolical energies of English poetry from Yeats onward; the spirit of tactful accommodation of cultural scepticism to spiritual inwardness; the sense of the inner life's sanctities, all these directions have some of their roots in Pater. He remains the classic example of a type of temperament in whom we can recognize certain subdued and almost inexpressible moments of the self, its moments of wistfulness and hesitation and its partial triumphs of perception; and more than Marius, or any of those shadowy half-created characters in the *Imaginary Portraits*, he has created himself for us in his *œuvre* as a permanently significant symbolical figure: the most complete example, the least trivial, of the æsthetic man.

J. HILLIS MILLER

Walter Pater: A Partial Portrait

Walter Pater is, along with Coleridge, Arnold, and Ruskin, one of the four greatest English literary critics of the nineteenth century. He is also, of the four, the most influential in the twentieth century and the most alive today, although often his influence can be found on writers who deny or are ignorant of what they owe to him. Pater is effective today as a precursor of what is most vital in contemporary criticism.

Pater may be placed in various lines or triangulated on various topographical surfaces. A slightly different perspective on him is gained through each of these various mappings, genealogies, or filiations. He is the nearest thing to Nietzsche England has, as Emerson is Nietzsche's nearest match in America. This could be put less invidiously by saying that Nietzsche is the Pater of the German-speaking world, Emerson the Pater of America. The three together form a constellation, with many consonances and dissonances among the three stars. Toward the past, Pater belongs to the line of English Romanticism, moving from the great Romantics—particularly Wordsworth and Coleridge, in this case—through Tennyson to the Pre-Raphaelites, among whom, along with Ruskin and Swinburne, Pater is a major critical voice. Another affiliation would link Pater to the English Protestant and empirical tradition going back to Locke and to the Puritan autobiographers of the seventeenth century, with their emphasis on private witnessing as the only genuine test of truth. The "aesthetic critic," in Pater's definition of him, must ask first and last, "What is this song or picture, this engaging personality presented

From *Daedalus* 105, no. 1 (Winter 1976). Copyright © 1976 by J. Hillis Miller.

in life or in a book, to *me*? What effect does it really produce on me?" Pater is also, however, one of the most important "translators" into Victorian England of Hegelian thought and of German idealism generally. He won his fellowship at Brasenose College, Oxford, as much for his first-hand knowledge of German as for his ability as a classicist. More important than all these associations, perhaps, is the filament that connects Pater with that strand of Western tradition which has been most antithetical to Plato: Heraclitus, the atomists, Epicurus, Lucretius, Joachim of Flora, Bruno, Spinoza, and Goethe.

In the other direction, toward the future, Pater's progeny also form more than one genetic line. Pater's influence on Yeats and, less obviously, on Wallace Stevens was decisive. This influence spread to other poets and novelists of the twentieth century: Joyce, Pound, Eliot, and many others. By way of Proust and the critics of the *Nouvelle Revue Française*, Pater is one of the progenitors of modern subjectivistic, "impressionistic," phenomenological criticism, the so-called "criticism of consciousness" of Georges Poulet and his associates. Another line, however, antithetical to that one, might be called "allegorical" criticism. This line leads from certain aspects of Ruskin through Pater and Wilde to Proust, and beyond Proust to Walter Benjamin and to the rhetorical or "deconstructive" criticism of our own moment in literary criticism. Jacques Derrida, Paul de Man, and Harold Bloom in their different ways exemplify this.

How Pater could produce such diverse "children," like a genetic pool containing potentially both blue-eyed and brown-eyed offspring, my reading of Pater will attempt to indicate. It must be remembered, however, that the figure of genetic "lines" is a trope. Like all figures it is not innocent; it begs the question it assists in raising. In literature, lines of influence go by leaps and swerves, with gaps and deviations. Sudden unpredictable mutation is the law, not the exception. That all reading is misreading is as true of the traditions of criticism as of literature itself. Influence works by opposition, so that the child is a "white" parody or travesty of the father, a mocking "double" or "second." Pater uses this figure in a curious passage at the beginning of Chapter Two of *Marius the Epicurean* (1885). The red rose, he says, came first, the white rose later, as its pale repetition. White things are "ever an after-thought, the doubles, or seconds, of real things, and themselves but half-real, half-material" (*Marius the Epicurean*, 2 vols. London, 1892. I, 14). The question of the relation between the uniqueness of the individual entity and the way it exists as the recurrence of elements which have already been configured in previous ones is one of Pater's pervading concerns. Pater's own work may provide his interpreter with assistance in formulating his multiple relations to those who came before and after.

The remarkable early pages of *Marius the Epicurean* are half autobiographical no doubt, but autobiography veiled, displaced. Pater's early life is translated figuratively into the life of a Roman boy of the second century after Christ. Among the first things the reader learns of Marius is that the "old country-house, half farm, half villa" (*ME* 5), where he passed his childhood, was famous for a "head of Medusa" (*ME* 21) found nearby. The head was Greek work in bronze with golden *laminae*. An emblem there? The reader also remembers the passage in the essay on Leonardo da Vinci in *The Renaissance* (1873) where Pater cites Vasari's disturbing anecdote of the Medusa "painted on a wooden shield" (*The Renaissance: Studies in Art and Poetry.* London, 1922. 105), which the young Leonardo prepared as a "surprise" for his father. This "childish" work was proleptic, Pater says, of the great Medusa of Leonardo's adult years:

> It was not in play that he painted that other Medusa, the one great picture which he left behind him in Florence. . . . What may be called the fascination of corruption penetrates in every touch its exquisitely finished beauty. About the dainty lines of the cheek the bat flits un-heeded. The delicate snakes seem literally strangling each other in terrified struggle to escape from the Medusa brain. The hue which violent death always brings with it is in the features; features singularly massive and grand, as we catch them inverted, in a dexterous foreshort-ening, crown foremost, like a great calm stone against which the wave of serpents breaks.
>
> (*R* 106)

What Sigmund Freud made of the Medusa one knows from "Das Medusenhaupt," written in 1922 and first published posthumously in 1940. The Medusa, says Freud, is hieroglyph for the fear of castration and for its veiling or supplementary assuaging. The Medusa head is a sign for the discovery of the absence of the maternal phallus. It also offers in the snakey locks of the Medusa frightening yet secretly reassuring proofs for the existence of that phallus. The Medusa's power to petrify, to turn a man into a column of stone, also offers frightening yet secretly reassuring proof of the spectator's masculinity. As Pater says, the Medusa of Leonardo is "the head of a corpse, exercising its powers through all the circum-stances of death" (*R* 106). All of Pater's most characteristic "portraits," including *Marius*, are of gifted young men doomed to an early death which is also somehow a fulfillment. Was Pater "phallogocentric," frozen like Leonardo himself at a Narcissistic or adolescent homosexual stage? Or did he liberate himself, accommodate himself to the absence of the Logos, head or chief source of meaning and power? Such a Logos fathers all later power but also renders it impotent. Did Pater remain fascinated with longing for a lost completeness which can only be obtained metaleptically, replacing early with late, the lost bliss that never was with the death that he imagines over and over for his various *personae*? Is Pater's work centered or acentered, and, if centered, what is its center, its origin, ground, or end?

A cluster of motifs in the early pages of *Marius the Epicurean* reinforces the motif of the Medusa head to form a hieroglyph of Pater's own. This composite emblem gathers many of the elements that recur throughout his work. Marius, the reader is told, had lost his father in early childhood, as did Pater himself. Marius's sorrow was "crossed at times by a not unpleasant sense of liberty, as he could but confess to himself, pondering, in the actual absence of so weighty and continual a restraint, upon the arbitrary power which Roman law gave to the parent over the son" (*ME* 18). Alas, the sense of liberty was only a momentary illusion, for the dead father has become one of the many genii of the place, "a *genius* a little cold and severe" (*ME* 11). The dead father, along with many other local gods, is the object of a religion of fear for Marius. Such a religion of propitiation and superstitious awe is still alive among children today, as in the singsong of urban sidewalk taboo: "If you step on a crack you'll break your mother's back; if you step on a line you'll break your father's spine." "A sense of conscious powers external to ourselves, pleased or displeased by the right or wrong conduct of every circumstance of daily life—that *conscience*, of which the old Roman religion was a formal, habitual recognition, was become in him a powerful current of feeling and observance" (*ME* 5). Conscience becomes *ascêsis*, an instinctive habit of renunciation, a dainty fastidiousness, a willingness to give up, even a masochism, a pleasure in self-imposed suffering, with apotropaic motives. "Had the Romans a word for *unworldly*?" asks the narrator.

> The beautiful word *umbratilis* perhaps comes nearest to it; and, with that precise sense, might describe the spirit in which [Marius] prepared himself for the sacerdotal function hereditary in his family—the sort of mystic enjoyment he had in the abstinence, the strenuous self-control and *ascêsis*, which such preparation involved.
>
> (*ME* 27)

Marius's mother had devoted herself to keeping her dead husband alive in her memory, and the boy Marius loves her devotedly. There is an odd episode, however, at the time of her death, which occurs, as did the death of Pater's mother, while the son is still a schoolboy, the mother going away from home to die. "For it happened," says the narrator, "that through some sudden incomprehensible petulance there had been an angry childish gesture, and a slighting word, at the very moment of her departure, actually for the last time" (ME 45).

Fear of the dead father and a universalization of that fear in an uncanny sense of unseen powers requiring constant propitiation and love for the mother combined with some inexplicable resentment of her—these come together disguised as Marius's fear of snakes. This odd fear is described but not wholly explained. Fear of snakes is the embodiment of Marius's "sense of some unexplored evil, ever dogging his footsteps" (ME 25). Its primal version is in fact a primal scene: "One fierce day in early summer, as he walked along a narrow road, he had seen the snakes breeding, and ever afterwards he avoided that place and its ugly associations, for there was something in the incident which made food distasteful and his sleep uneasy for many days afterwards" (ME 25). The same sense of uncanny distaste recurs when, sometime later in Pisa, Marius sees "an African showman exhibiting a great reptile" (ME 25), and later still in Rome, "a second time," he sees "a showman with his serpents" (ME 26). The motif recurs once more, in case the reader has not already perceived its importance, in Marius's fear of the "great sallow-hued snakes" kept in the temple of the healing god Aesculapius (ME 33).

Why did Marius, or, one guesses, Pater himself, so irrationally fear snakes? And why snakes coupling? Why did this disturb his pleasure in food and sleep? The narrator's answer is oblique:

> He wondered at himself indeed, trying to puzzle out the secret of that repugnance, having no particular dread of a snake's bite, like one of his companions, who had put his hand into the mouth of an old garden-god and roused there a sluggish viper. A kind of pity even mingled with his aversion, and he could hardly have killed or injured the animals, which seemed already to suffer by the very circumstances of their life, being what they were.
>
> (ME 25–26)

The elements associated with the Medusa head recur here and are covertly interpreted. Parents coupling become snakes coupling, viewed with a combination of fascination, aversion, and pity. It is the pity of unawakened sexuality for the burden of the bestiality of sex combined with fear of the absent father and of his power of reprisal. The "unexplored" evil dogging Marius's footsteps becomes embodied in the snakes' breeding. This scene is proof that the phallus is still there, though the father is dead, as with the snakes on the Medusa's head. The phallus is there even as an attribute of the mother, for in the mouth of the old garden-god there is a sluggish viper, as there are snakes surrounding the open mouth and the dead face of the Medusa in the painting in the Uffizi. This repugnant yet somehow pleasurable discovery is displaced from Marius to "one of his companions," who, like Marius, has "no particular dread of a snake's bite." The act of impiety toward the god or of violation of the mother is not performed directly by the hero, except in that moment of petulance and in that slighting word at the time of her death. Presence and absence of an original fathering power, a paternal potency which yet must be an attribute of the mother, presence and absence both feared and desired in the tension of a double double bind—these are the pervasive Paterian elements brought evasively and unostentatiously together in the account of the childhood of Marius.

Is such a reading of a few fragments of *Marius the Epicurean* a clue to the rest of Pater? Is this cluster a valid synecdoche for the whole, standing in the same relation to all his work as, in Pater's own criticism, a representative figure such as Leonardo or Michelangelo stands to the Renaissance as a whole? What relation might there be between this repugnance for the coupling snakes, yet pleasure in rousing the viper in the mouth of the garden god, and Pater's methods as a critic, the themes and ideas which organize his work? Is all his work oriented by the dread and desire for a proof that the lost father is not really lost? Only a reading of the whole work could tell. The complexity and suggestiveness of the bits examined so far indicate that Pater must be read not so much for what he tells the reader about the artists and works he criticizes but as a literary text demanding the same scrupulous decipherment, phrase by phrase, as the texts of Marcel Proust or of Walter Benjamin, two later writers in Pater's line who similarly require interrogation.

Pater's writing offers the same fascination to the reader as that of any major author, the fascination of a complexity which *works*, which hangs together, which may be "figured out" or resolved. His work has that consonance, those unexpected echoes of this passage with that passage, those hidden resonances and harmonies which Pater saw as the ideal of a musical form that would have absorbed all its matter into that form. Nevertheless, if, as Charles Rosen affirms, the basis of musical expression is dissonance, the critic must, in Pater's case, take note also of disharmonies, contradictions, omissions, hiatuses, incongruous elements which precisely do not "work." In such places the words seem to have exceeded the writer's apparent intention. Such dissonances may be the most important aspect of Pater's work, in spite of his claim in "Style" that the fire of a unified "sense of the world" will in the great writers have burned away such *surplusage* (*Appreciations*. London, 1889. 16). In the something too much, the something left over, the odd detail which may not be evened in a musical form, the snake in the mouth of the garden god, the critic may find the clue and loose the thread that will unravel all that fine fabric of Pater's prose, with its decorous echo of pattern by pattern. The secret revealed by this unraveling may be not so much the hidden center of a personality as an enigma exceeding personality, a secret intrinsic to the materials Pater worked with—language and its concepts, figures, and narrative forms, myths or legends, *legenda*, "things for reading."

The apparent beginning of spiritual life for Pater is the moment, the intense and wholly individual instant of experience. As Pater says in the famous passage in the Conclusion to *The Renaissance*, each momentary experience, each "impression," is cut off by virtue of its uniqueness from all moments before and after. It is also entirely private: "Every one of those impressions is the impression of the individual in his isolation, each mind keeping as a solitary prisoner its own dream of a world" (*R* 235). Moreover, each moment lasts but a moment, the blink of an eye, and then is gone. Time is flux, an endless stream "of impressions, unstable, flickering, inconsistent, which burn and are extinguished with our consciousness of them" (*R* 235). The inevitable goal of each sequence is death, a final end anticipated and rehearsed in the little death of each moment as it flies. For Pater, the imminence of death and the intensity of experience are always only two sides of the same coin, "the sense of death and the desire of beauty: the desire of beauty quickened by the sense of death" (*A* 227), as he puts it in the admirable essay on William Morris, "Aesthetic Poetry."

It would seem that the entire program of Pater's criticism follows from these solipsistic premises. Each man must concentrate all his attention on each moment as it passes, for that moment is all there is and all he has. He must purge by that effort of refinement or *ascêsis*, as essential in Pater's procedure as in the lives of those whose portraits he sketches, all impurities in the moment, all irrelevant associations, all false idealisms, such as those which, in Pater's understanding of Coleridge, weakened that great poet-critic's force (see "Coleridge," *A* 64–106). The moment in its uniqueness or the critic in his experience of it may, then, shed all dross, burn with that "hard, gemlike flame" (*R* 236). Criticism is the exact recording of what Pater calls the unique "virtue" of each moment, meaning by "virtue" the power or energy specific to the elements concentrated in that moment. Virtue is "the property each [moment] has of affecting one with a special, a unique, impression of pleasure" (*R* ix), as Pater puts it in the Preface to *The Renaissance*, where such a strategy for criticism is most eloquently and exactly defined.

The function of aesthetic criticism is clear. The true critic has sharper impressions than others. He is more able than other people to discriminate the exact "virtue" of a given personality or work of art. He is also more gifted than others in his power of expression, as gifted, ideally, as the great writers themselves. He uses his gift of expression not to transmit the truth of his own personality, but to translate into his own language the unique virtue of the work or person he criticizes. He thereby transmits to his readers impressions they might otherwise miss, or, rather, he transmits subtly displaced repetitions of those impressions. Far from being, as is sometimes said, at liberty to make the work mean anything one likes, impressionism is rigorously bound by the work it describes. It is bound as much as the work itself by that truth of correspondence to a particular personality which Pater makes his ideal in "Style." The writer must translate accurately his inner vision. The critic must translate accurately that translation, as is done by that ideal translator of Plato who reproduces him "by an exact following, with no variation in structure, of word after word, as the pencil follows a drawing under tracing-paper" (A 11). The goal of this translation, however, is the transmission of the exact flavor or quality of the consciousness behind the work.

The focus of all Pater's writing is personality, the personalities of Botticelli, Michelangelo, Leonardo, Wordsworth, Coleridge, and others in *The Renaissance* or in *Appreciations* (1889), the personalities of fictional characters in *Marius the Epicurean, Imaginary Portraits* (1887), and *Gaston de Latour* (1896), the personalities of mythological figures in certain of the *Greek Studies* (1895). Subjectivity—the self—is, it seems, the beginning, the end, and the persisting basis in all Pater's writings. In Pater's work, as in one important strand of the Western tradition generally, subjectivity is the name given to the *Logos*, paternal origin, goal, and supporting ground. Subjectivity is the measure, *ratio*, or "reason" for all the interchanges of person with person, by means of art, which Pater's work explores. As the word itself suggests, subjectivity, the subject, is what is 'thrown under' and therefore underlies all the fleeting impressions which make up what is. There is, after all, a snake in the mouth of the garden god. Pater's religious moments, for example in *Marius the Epicurean*, are an extrapolation from his positing of personality as a reassuring, ubiquitous *Logos*. His religion is "a sense of *conscious* powers external to ourselves" (ME 5, emphasis added).

The critic's effort to identify precisely the unique virtue of a single impression or personality leads to an unexpected discovery. This discovery makes of Pater's criticism something quite different from what his stress on personality would make it seem to be. The moment, it turns out, though unique, is not single. Each "impression" is in fact "infinitely divisible" (*R* 235). It is divisible because it is self-divided, an *Andersstreben*, or striving to be other than itself, as he calls it in "The School of Giorgione" (*R* 134). The moment is in battle against itself in a way that recalls the Heraclitean flux, cited as an epigraph for the Conclusion, or the Parmenidean *polemos*, cosmic warfare. Perhaps it is also to be associated with that sadomasochistic element so evident in Pater's sense of human life and of relations between people.

The flame produced by the purification of an *ascêsis* is kindled by the bringing together of divided forces which burst into flame by their antagonistic proximity. That flame is "the focus where the greatest number of vital forces unite in their purest energy" (*R* 236). The first example Pater gives in the Conclusion of the intense instant of sensation is "the moment . . . of delicious recoil from the flood of water in summer heat" (*R* 233). Such a conjunction is the locus "of forces parting sooner or later on their ways" (*R* 234), as brilliancy of gifts in an individual arises from "some tragic dividing of forces on their ways" (*R* 237).

The uniqueness of each momentary impression is a result not of its singleness but of its special combination of contradictory forces. These flow into it from the past and are destined to divide again, each to go its separate way into the future. This means that the moment, which was at first seemingly so isolated, is in fact connected by multiple strands to past and future. Pater speaks of this, sometimes using a metaphor of streams meeting and dividing and sometimes of weaving and unweaving. If the moment is the meeting place of divided forces—the forces of a whole life, of an age, or of all the ages in their sequence (as in Pater's celebrated interpretation of *La Gioconda*)—then that moment in all its sensible vividness and uniqueness can stand for the life, for the age, or for all history. It can stand for these because it contains in concentrated essence forces universally distributed in time and space, meeting and dividing and meeting again. The validity of synecdoche is based on substantial participation. This conception of the moment as both individual and representative lies behind a splendid passage from "The School of Giorgione," anticipating both Joyce's "epiphany" and certain passages in T. S. Eliot:

> Now it is part of the ideality of the highest sort of dramatic poetry, that it presents us with a kind of profoundly significant and animated instant, a mere gesture, a look, a smile, perhaps—some brief and wholly concrete moment, into which, however, all the motives, all the interest and effects of a long history, have condensed themselves, and which seem to

absorb past and future in an intense consciousness of the present. . . .
exquisite pauses in time, in which, arrested thus, we seem to be spectators of all the fulness of existence, and which are like some consummate
extract or quintessence of life.

(R 150)

Pater's materialist notion of impersonal forces underlying each
personality involves a specific theory of repetition. This theory denies the
possibility of finding any fixed origin for any person or impression. Such
denial has important consequences for criticism. It means that the critic
can never find an inaugural point for any idea or for any given hieroglyph
of forces. There are no fathers, each apparent father being himself, often
unwittingly, the heir of forces that have come together and then separated
many times in the past. Whatever the critic reaches as an apparent
beginning, a solid ground on which to base an interpretation, dissolves on
inspection into a repetition. It is another gathering of elements of immemorial antiquity. As in Nietzsche, so in Pater, a sense of vertigo is
generated by this infinite regression into the past, each "source" having
another "source" behind it, and so on ad infinitum. No doctrine, no
seemingly unique collocation of elements in a personality can be said to be
a beginning or to have one.

The notion that the singular personality is Pater's version of the
Logos is, it seems, exploded by his concept of repetition. What is, is the
perpetually woven and rewoven anonymous elements or atoms, forces that
have divided and come together for all eternity and that have an eternal
future of rebirth and death. In place of the subject as Logos, Pater seems to
put another equally traditional idea of the metaphysical ground. This idea,
too, goes back to the Greeks, though more to Heraclitus, to the atomists,
to Lucretius, or even to Aristotle than to Plato. The Logos is a ubiquitous
and multiple force, energy, energeia. This energy is that paternal snake at
the originless origin, perpetually born and reborn in the mouth of the god.

Paradoxically, it is apropos of Plato that Pater, in a splendidly
eloquent passage at the beginning of Plato and Platonism (1893), most fully
expresses his intuition of a universe without determinable origin. In such a
universe, atoms are combined and recombined, world without end, in
perpetual repetition in difference. "Plato's achievement," says Pater, "may
well seem an absolutely fresh thing in the morning of the mind's history,"
but "in the history of philosophy there are no absolute beginnings" (Plato
and Platonism. London, 1893. 2, 1). Far from being a beginning, Plato, in
Pater's view, was a decadent, or at least he lived in a decadent world. Its
decadence is defined, in phrases characteristically Paterian in their weary
cadence, as the presence everywhere of already used atoms of thought.

There was a kind of intellectual pollution of the Greek air at the moment of its greatest cultural splendor:

> Yet in truth the world Plato had entered into was already almost weary of philosophical debate, bewildered by the oppositions of sects, the claims of rival schools. Language and the processes of thought were already become sophisticated, the very air he breathed sickly with off-cast speculative atoms.
>
> (PP 2)

Pater uses four different metaphors to express the way these "off-cast atoms" of thought enter into the intimate texture of Plato's language. All these figures express the notion of tiny particles which make the, so to speak, cellular structure of Plato's thought. These are in no sense superficial borrowings which could conceivably be detached. One metaphor is of the grain of stone, another of parchment with multiple layers of writing, another of woven fabric, another of an organic body, but a similar structural image is in question in each case:

> Some of the results of patient earlier thinkers, even then dead and gone, are of the structure of his philosophy. They are everywhere in it, not as the stray carved corner of some older edifice, to be found here or there amid the new, but rather like minute relics of earlier organic life in the very stone he builds with. . . . [I]n Plato, in spite of his wonderful savour of literary freshness, there is nothing absolutely new: or rather, as in many other very original productions of human genius, the seemingly new is old also, a palimpsest, a tapestry of which the actual threads have served before, or like the animal frame itself, every particle of which has already lived and died many times.
>
> (PP 2, 3)

This image of a repetition not exterior but woven into the genetic structure of Plato's thinking leads to a powerful vision of an infinite regression back in time and outward beyond Western culture in an ever wider and deeper unsuccessful search for the beginnings of ideas whose immemorial antiquity deny Plato any status as an origin. Plato was not the inaugurator of an Occidental civilization merely, as Whitehead said, a "footnote" to his work. He was himself already a latecomer, an afterthought. He was a belated footnote to still earlier footnotes, themselves footnotes to footnotes, with nowhere an original text as such:

> The central and most intimate principles of [Plato's] teaching challenge us to go back beyond them, not merely to his own immediate, somewhat enigmatic master—to Socrates, who survives chiefly in his pages— but to various precedent schools of speculative thought, in Greece, in Ionia, in Italy; beyond these into that age of poetry, in which the first

efforts of philosophic apprehension had hardly understood themselves; beyond that unconscious philosophy again, to certain constitutional tendencies, persuasions, forecasts of the intellect itself, such as had given birth, it would seem, to thoughts akin to Plato's in the older civilisations of India and of Egypt, as they still exercise their authority over ourselves.

(PP 2–3)

No element in Plato is new, not one speculative atom. What is new is the way of putting these elements together. In Pater's doctrine of recurrence, repetition is always with a difference. The difference lies in the way old forces are brought together once more in a slightly changed way and under new conditions. Pater's term for this novel way of assembling new materials is "form." Plato's originality lies in his brilliant novelty of form:

> Nothing but the life-giving principle of cohesion is new; the new perspective, the resultant complexion, the expressiveness which familiar thoughts attain by novel juxtaposition. In other words, the *form* is new. But then, in the creation of philosophical literature, as in all other products of art, *form*, in the full signification of that word, is everything, and the mere matter is nothing.

(PP 4–5)

Form is everything, matter nothing. Here is another point of overlapping with Nietzsche, who in the preface of 1886 to the second edition of *Die fröhliche Wissenschaft* (1882) praises the Greeks for stopping at the surface (*bei der Oberfläche*) and for believing in forms, tones, words (*an Formen, an Töne, an Worte*). What is Pater's concept of form? What is his critic to make of the abundance of metaphors which are essential to his expression of his thought—threads, forces, writing, and so on? What is the exact status of these figures, and why does he need more than one to express the "same" idea? In "Style," Pater attempts to deny insofar as it is possible the figurative basis of language. He wants language to be the transparent reflection of a personal thought which preceded it and which could, or so it seems, exist without it. He wants the word to be identical with its meaning or with the thought it transmits. In *The Renaissance*, he several times praises the subjects of his essays for creating images that are saturated with their meaning, so that there is no discernible difference between sign and referent, word and meaning. In Greek art, for example, "[t]he mind begins and ends with the finite image, yet loses no part of the spiritual motive. That motive is not lightly and loosely attached to the sensuous form, as its meaning to an allegory, but saturates and is identical with it" (R 205–06). The material basis of spiritual meaning is wholly sublimated in that meaning.

Nevertheless, the full exploration of Pater's concept of form will deconstruct once more the apparent end point reached in the interpretation of his work. Such an exploration puts in question both the notion that for Pater subjectivity is the *Logos* and the notion that for him material energy is the *Logos*. Alongside those ideas, overlapping them, folded inextricably into them, contradicting them, and yet necessary to their expression is a notion that is properly literary or semiotic. This incipient theory of signs is a thread which will unravel all the fastidiously patterned fabric of Pater's thought. It can hardly be called a fully developed "theory." It is more an implicit assumption in all Pater's practice with words. This "theory" in all its dimensions involves the categories of difference and discontinuity.

Meaning or significance in a personality, in a gem, a song, a painting, a piece of music is always defined by Pater as a force, as the power to make an impression. This power is not single, nor is it a harmonious collocation of energies making a unity. A "virtue" always results from antagonistic forces, sweetness against strength in the case of Michelangelo, strangeness against the desire for beauty in Leonardo, and so on. The meaning is in neither of the two forces separately, nor in their sum. It arises in the space between them, out of the economy of their difference.

The sign thus constituted by two enemy forces does not draw its meaning solely from its own internal differentiation. It also carries within itself the echo, across the gap of a further difference, of earlier similar gatherings of forces. These lateral resonances form that "chain of secret influences" of which Pater speaks in the essay on Leonardo (*R* 116). Each virtue is an assemblage of divided energies, and it draws its meaning from its reference to other virtues of which it is the rebirth. The present moment, which, in the Conclusion to *The Renaissance*, seems, in its evanescence, to be all there is, carries "a sense in it, a relic more or less fleeting, of such moments gone by" (*R* 236). The vestige in the present sign of past signs, as the passage quoted from *Plato and Platonism* confirms, is intrinsic to the form of the present sign. The past is an inextricable part of the meaning of the present. The rejection of fixed origin is a necessary component of this insight. The past moment of which the present moment contains the relics was itself a system of differentiated traces referring back to a still earlier moment of division, and so on.

Another discontinuity in each sign or virtue is the relation of meaning to its material embodiment. Pater always insists, correctly enough, on the necessity of a material carrier for artistic meaning. "All art," he says, "has a sensuous element, colour, form, sound" (*R* 209). In spite of his desire to have this material basis saturated with its meaning, Pater recognizes a perpetual residue of non-saturation in the sign. There is always a margin of incongruity between the meaning and its sensuous embodiment.

This distance reveals itself in various ways in Pater's work. It is present in his occasionally explicit recognition of figure, as in the assertion in "Style" that each word carries its weight of metaphor and so is a displaced expression of its meaning. "A lover of words for their own sake," says Pater,

> to whom nothing about them is unimportant, a minute and constant observer of their physiognomy, [the writer] will be on the alert not only for obviously mixed metaphors of course, but for the metaphor that is mixed in all our speech, though a rapid use may involve no cognition of it. Currently recognising the incident, the colour, the physical elements or particles in words like *absorb, consider, extract,* to take the first that occur, he will avail himself of them, as further adding to the resources of expression.
>
> (A 17)

A word has a virtue, and like any such power it is made of antagonistic particles in combination. These minute forces make up "all that latent figurative texture in speech" (A 17). This *Andersstreben* means that we cannot say what we mean without being in danger of saying something else implicit in the elementary particles or self-contained tropes in the words we use. Pater's own writing is heavily dependent on figures which are obviously figures: the images of the gemlike flame, of woven fabric, of the relics of long-dead minute organic life in stone, and so on. In all such cases, Pater's "literal" meaning is some linguistic or artistic expression, not fire, cloth, or stone at all. In a similar way, all his work depends on the problematic validity of the trope of synecdoche, a momentary confluence of "forces" in Pico, for example, standing for the whole *Zeitgeist* of the Renaissance. Pico is only in figure a "quintessence." Even the apparently objective word "force" is a figure, since there is no energy as such in the innocent black marks on a page of Wordsworth or Hugo.

The discrepancy between embodiment and meaning is also present in Pater's notion that each form of art attempts to transcend itself, to sublimate the matter in which it is forced to work by that striving to be other than itself whereby each form of art borrows from others, "a partial alienation from its limitations, through which the arts are able, not indeed to supply the place of each other, but reciprocally to lend each other new forces" (*R* 133–34). It is through this effort that all art, in Pater's famous phrase, "constantly aspires towards the condition of music" (*R* 135). The condition of music is pure form, the spiritualization of the material substratum so that no referential dimension is left. In music the meaning arises entirely out of the differential relation between note and note, element and element, force and force. In the condition of music, matter has become form, or the form *is* the matter:

> That the mere matter of a poem, for instance, its subject, namely, its given incidents or situation—that the mere matter of a picture, the actual circumstances of an event, the actual topography of a landscape— should be nothing without the form, the spirit, of the handling, that this form, this mode of handling, should become an end in itself, should penetrate every part of the matter: this is what all art constantly strives after, and achieves in different degrees.
>
> (*R* 135)

Nevertheless, insofar as this *Andersstreben* remains an aspiration, not an achievement, as Pater implies it always does, some element of unspiritualized matter remains.

This discrepancy between incarnation and meaning is, finally, present in all those imaginary portraits of men born out of their time, an Apollo or a Dionysus in Christian Europe, as in "Apollo in Picardy" or "Denys l'Auxerrois," a presage of the Enlightenment in still half-barbaric Germany, as in "Duke Carl of Rosenmold." The tragedy of all these figures is in the incompatibility between the meanings they carry and the material conditions within which they are forced to embody them. This incompatibility, as much as the tragic division of forces within them-selves, destines them to obscurity and early death. Their triumph is that they do reenact the old pattern, for the gods in exile are gods still, and the story works itself out anew in the changed conditions. Even so, Pater's portraits are always of those who do not wholly embody their meaning. They are gods born out of their time. This incongruity dramatizes a universal condition of artistic expression in Pater's view of it.

A remnant of non-saturation is always present, a part of the body left over, some matter not wholly absorbed into form. Its existence leads to the recognition that art for Pater is generated only in the interval between forces. This is not that other kind of Logocentrism which sees the Logos as energy rather than as subject. It involves a different notion, more difficult to grasp, in fact ungraspable. It is the ungraspable as such, an ungraspable which for Pater, with his sense for nuance, is essential to literature and to art generally. This notion is ungraspable because it cannot be thematized or conceptualized. It can only be glimpsed fleetingly, out of the corner of the eye, in the interplay between images. This non-conceptual insight, perpetually in flight, is the notion of meaning constituted by difference. Such meaning is not a correlate of force, whether that force is subjective or objective, self or matter. Such meaning is always in excess of the material substratum which embodies it. It appears momentarily in the openings between, and it is always in league with death. Such a notion might be called the uncanny, but it is not the uncanny as the occult presence of some ur-force which has differentiated itself and works as fate. It is the uncanny as the absence of origin. It is the mouth of the garden god with no snake in it.

Is this not that idea of "the disembodied spirit," rather than some more conventional notion of immortality, which Pater formulates in a splendid passage about Michelangelo's "predilection" for those who die young and for all the imagery of death? Here the absence of any definable origin becomes transferred, in a metalepsis, to the absence of any fixable image for that future which is created by life but which lies beyond death. The relation of a dead body to the meaning it contains by not containing it is the most extreme form of that discrepancy between the material image and its meaning which governs all Pater's insight into artistic signs. Here for once Pater is oriented not toward the past but toward the future, though the structure of material signs creating something which exceeds them, a "new body," body not body yet possible only in relation to some body, remains the same. To call Michelangelo's four famous sculptured figures *Night, Day, The Twilight*, and *The Dawn*, says Pater, is far too definite for them. Rather they "concentrate and express,"

> less by way of definite conceptions than by the touches, the promptings of a piece of music, all those vague fancies, misgivings, presentiments, which shift and mix and are defined and fade again, whenever the thoughts try to fix themselves with sincerity on the conditions and surroundings of the disembodied spirit.
>
> (R 95)

Then follows an extraordinary description of the "range of sentiment" in relation to death, of which, says Pater, Michelangelo is "the poet still alive, and in possession of our inmost thoughts" (R 95–96), as if Michelangelo's "new body" were, by some kind of transmigration, our own:

> —dumb inquiry over the relapse after death into the formlessness which preceded life, the change, the revolt from that change, then the correcting, hallowing, consoling rush of pity; at last, far off, thin and vague, yet not more vague than the most definite thoughts men have had through three centuries on a matter that has been so near their hearts, the new body—a passing light, a mere intangible, external effect, over those too

rigid, or too formless faces; a dream that lingers a moment, retreating in the dawn, incomplete, aimless, helpless; a thing with faint hearing, faint memory, faint power of touch; a breath, a flame in the doorway, a feather in the wind.

(R 95–96)

The most fully conceptualized expression of this third aspect of Pater's work, implicit denial and deconstruction of the other two, is a passage in the key essay of *Greek Studies*, "The Myth of Demeter and Persephone." This essay was written in 1875, in the poise between euhemeristic, cosmological, and linguistic theories of myth, in such scholars as Max Müller, and the appearance in 1890 of the first two volumes of Frazer's *The Golden Bough*. Pater's essay is almost exactly contemporary with Nietzsche's *The Birth of Tragedy* (1872). Like Nietzsche's essay it has both a particular interest in relation to the thought of its author and a more general importance as the expression and exemplification of a theory of interpretation. The passage also, by way of its reference to Giotto's frescoes in Padua depicting Virtues and Vices, links itself to a "chain of secret influences" that binds together a series of crucial texts. This series extends from the places where Ruskin discusses those paintings by Giotto through Pater to a passage in Proust, which echoes Ruskin, to critical essays by Walter Benjamin and Paul de Man on Proust.

Pater begins by distinguishing between the abstract personification by modern artists of such entities as "wealth" or "commerce" and the "profoundly poetical and impressive" personifications of Giotto and other early masters. The reader may expect that Pater is going to discriminate between modern concoctions in which there is no intrinsic relation between the meaning and its embodiment, "mere transparent allegory, or figure of speech" (*Greek Studies.* London, 1895. 98), and, on the other hand, genuine symbolism, in which the meaning saturates its material vehicle. Matters are not so simple in this passage. Giotto, or other artists like him in the modern period, Blake or Burne-Jones, or that old artist who designed the stained glass of the Apocalypse at Bourges, produce "something more than mere symbolism" (GS 98). This is achieved by "some peculiarly sympathetic penetration, on the part of the artist, into the subjects he intended to depict" (GS 98). The word "subject" here has an odd and unexpected meaning. It refers not to that "ethical" or "allegorical" theme of the work but to the material carrier of that theme. The artist's sympathetic penetration is into that embodiment in its peculiar relation to its ethical meaning. This carrier is presented literally, with full mimetic specificity. It is pictured as "realistically" as a Victorian novelist copies, with scrupulous fidelity, the details of daily life:

> Symbolism as intense as this is the creation of special temper, in which a
> certain simplicity, taking all things literally, *au pied de la lettre,* is united
> to a vivid pre-occupation with the aesthetic beauty of the image itself,
> the *figured* side of figurative expression, the *form* of the metaphor. When
> it is said, "Out of his mouth goeth a sharp sword," that temper is ready
> to deal directly and boldly with that difficult image, like that old
> designer of the fourteenth century, who has depicted this, and other
> images of the Apocalypse, in a coloured window at Bourges. Such
> symbolism cares a great deal for the hair of Temperance, discreetly
> bound, for some subtler likeness to the colour of the sky in the girdle of
> *Hope,* for the inwoven flames in the red garment of *Charity.*
>
> (GS 98–99)

This admirable passage, like the similar passages in Ruskin, in
Proust, in Benjamin, and in De Man, calls attention to the paradoxical
self-cancelling effects of such literalism in allegorical representation. On
the one hand, as Proust observes, the intense literalism of such allegory
greatly increases the "aesthetic beauty" of the work of art which employs
it.

> [P]lus tard j'ai compris [says Marcel] que l'étrangété saisissante, la beauté
> spéciale de ces fresques tenait à la grande place que le symbole y
> occupait, et que le fait qu'il fût représenté non comme un symbole
> puisque la pensée symbolisée n'était pas exprimée, mais comme réel,
> comme effectivement subi ou matériellement manié, donnait à la signifi-
> cation de l'oeuvre quelque chose de plus littéral et de plus précis.

On the other hand, an exactly opposite effect is produced by taking
literally what is after all "only" a figure of speech, so that a sword literally
goes out of the mouth of the Christ of the Apocalypse or, in the curiously
parallel example Proust gives, Giotto represents Envy with a swollen
protruding tongue like an illustration in a medical text for some ghastly
disease. Whether or not the parallel here would support a claim that
Proust had read the passage in Pater has little importance, but the
examples both give are similar cases of a grotesque literalism incongruous
with its abstract significance. Both examples involve the organ of speech,
that snake in the mouth of gods and men which is the father of lies, that
is, of "figurative expression." In both examples, the realism with which
the figured side of the figure is represented only intensifies the incompatibility between tenor and vehicle in the metaphor. It calls attention to the
fictive or verbal aspect of the expression, even to its absurdity. There is no
substantial similarity between the abstraction and its material embodiment, though they may seem plausibly enough connected in the purely
linguistic expression. The embodiment can be represented. The more

vividly and literally it is pictured, the more beautiful the work of art. Nevertheless, the more literally it is represented, the more it brings into the open the fact that the "ethical" meaning—Temperance, Hope, or whatever—has, as Proust observes, not been represented at all. It has only been indirectly named in a metaphor. This metaphor confesses in its intense literalism to its inability to be anything but itself, a mouth with a sharp sword going out of it, flames, the blue of the sky, the hair of a discreet woman, neatly bound. At best the painter can translate into visual images the equivalents of verbal metaphor, painting flames on the garment of Charity, the blue of the sky on the girdle of Hope. The allegorical meaning vanishes in the realism with which its vehicle is represented. That meaning is shown to exist only as names, as an interplay of displaced words which are the basis of the visual representation.

Even so, Pater returns at the end of the paragraph to the idea of a people for whom the powers governing the universe were seen as real persons. For such a people the false equations of metaphor were literally true. When they talked of the return of Kore to Demeter, for example, they were "yielding to a real illusion; to which the voice of man 'was really a stream, beauty an effluence, death a mist' " (GS 100). Pater's mode of expression here, however, to turn back to the other side once more, demystifies such ways of seeing and returns them to the verbal figures which they take literally. To a vision of such a temper the "illusion" was "real," hence not an illusion. To Pater it is an illusion, a voice not a stream, beauty not an effluence, death only figuratively a mist.

Back and forth between these various contradictory readings of the passage its reader is forced to go. Each reading depends on others which contradict it and it contradicts the others in its turn. The passage, in its insistence that only a "special temper" is capable of the "real illusion" of allegory au pied de la lettre, can be taken as reaffirming Pater's subjectivism. In its suggestion that the stratum below the play of allegorical representation is material forces, flame or sky, the passage may be seen as congruent with Pater's objectivism, his materialism of "inwoven" forces. In its recognition that both of these notions are generated by a play of language, the passage may be taken as congruent with the third reading of Pater I have proposed. The god's mouth is empty or is filled only with that uncanny simulacrum of a snake born and dying and born anew in the interaction of the signs men make. In this third interpretation, the reader is seen as intervening actively in any interpretation. Meaning is produced in an act of deciphering which can never reach the original or intrinsic meaning of any text. An "impression" is as much an act as a passion. It is the stamping of crisscrossing forces with a momentary stillness in one reading. Another critic of another "temper" will produce a different reading of the same text. No judge will be able to arbitrate between them, since the text is "undecidable," incapable of being encompassed in a single total reading.

All three of these readings, and other variations on them, are present not only in this paragraph from "The Myth of Demeter and Persephone" but also intertwined throughout Pater's work as a whole. The last reading sees the subject of Pater's writing as ultimately, whatever its ostensible theme, writing and reading themselves. Reading is a further writing, and all writing is a palimpsest. The critic produces an additional inscription over an earlier inscription in the flesh, that necessary material basis of all art, though art always exceeds its fleshly incarnations. This fact, however, may only be experienced in the flesh, in a literalism which defeats itself. The critic is, like Leonardo da Vinci, *homo minister et interpres naturae* (R 98), but the minister and the interpreter are perpetually caught in a dance of antagonism, each denying the other and yet dependent on him. Pater's writings, like those of other major authors in the Occidental tradition, are at once open to interpretation and ultimately indecipherable, unreadable. His texts lead the critic deeper and deeper into a labyrinth until he confronts a final aporia. This does not mean, however, that the reader must give up from the beginning the attempt to understand Pater. Only by going all the way into the labyrinth, following the thread of a given clue, can the critic reach the blind alley, vacant of any Minotaur, that impasse which is the end point of interpretation.

Pater's work, then, is heterogeneous, dialogical, or antilogical. Dialogical and antilogical come, in fact, to the same thing, since the doubling of the Logos is a sign of its absence. Each reading in the interchange of overlapping voices may be worked out with full cogency, though it is impossible to have all at once. All three cannot be simultaneously "true." Moreover, they may not be related to one another dialectically or in some kind of hierarchy. My necessarily narrative or sequential development falsifies their implications upon one another, just as the apparent historical development in Pater's theory of myth makes, as Pater himself says, a fictitious narrative of what are in fact simultaneous members of a single system. In all its dimensions, in Pater's interest in the impressions made or felt by the "unique" personality, in his art of portraiture, in his essays on sculpture, in his studies of mythical figures and of an allegorical art that is "more than mere symbolism," Pater's work can be defined as an exploration and deconstruction of the problematic trope of personification, that turn of language or art which gathers impersonal forces under a human figure. Is subjectivity a fixed point of origin from which all else follows, or is personality a fragile receptacle within which impersonal energies are momentarily brought together, or are both the person and the forces gathered within it linguistic fictions generated by the interchange of sign with sign in the productive workings of art or literature?

My three readings of Pater's use of the trope of personification may not be reconciled in any way. They form a bewildering oscillation in which each reading will lead to the others if it is followed far enough, though the others contradict and cancel it out, while at the same time being necessary to its expression. To put this in Pater's terms: If the magical appearance of unity to which we give the name "person" is always produced differentially, by the division or combat of contradictory forces, and yet exceeds anything which may be identified as in those forces, as the "new body" exceeds the dead body, then the momentary poise in a personification will always be divided against itself, folded, manifold, dialogical rather than monological. It will always be open, like all the master tropes of the great texts in the Western tradition, to multiple contradictory readings in a perpetual fleeing away from any fixed sense.

GERALD MONSMAN

The Abandoned Text:
"Gaston de Latour"

Although one could never argue that
as an artistic achievement the unfinished *Gaston* has been considered as
significant a work as *Marius*, its individual scenes and intricately reflexive
structure can be shown to be as masterfully planned as those of its
predecessor. In comparison with *Marius*, *Gaston* exhibits a noticeable
change in atmosphere: the violence is no longer quite so hidden under a
tranquil surface, and the ambiguity of motives, the personal regrets, and
especially an abiding sense of guilt are all more prominent. Yet what
primarily distinguishes *Gaston* from *Marius* is Pater's failure, despite repeated efforts, to finish it; and the deducible reasons are pertinent to an
understanding of Pater's art generally. In order to explain why *Gaston* was
still largely unfinished at Pater's death in 1894, it is necessary first to turn
one's attention to its structure and to the psychological urgencies that
build up within it.

Pater had begun work on *Gaston* shortly after or possibly even
before finishing *Marius*. The first five chapters appeared serially in *Macmillan's Magazine* from June to October of 1888, and one additional chapter
(entitled "Giordano Bruno. Paris: 1586") came out as an independent
article in the *Fortnightly Review* for August 1889. After Pater's death,
C. L. Shadwell edited the six published chapters (the Bruno essay had been
revised by Pater for inclusion in *Gaston*) and one new chapter from

unpublished drafts. As projected by the overly fastidious Shadwell (who withheld considerable material as insufficiently polished), *Gaston* would seem to be a rival to the love elegies of Sir Benjamin Backbite, envisioned by their author "on a beautiful quarto page, where a neat rivulet of text shall meander through a meadow of margin." Conjectures as to why the novel remained unfinished have pointed variously to problems with characterization or with the historical setting or with Pater's own frenetic schedule. As to characterization, it is suggested that either Pater lost interest in his hero or that certain embarrassing emotional themes cropped up (homosexuality, sadism) thwarting the completion of his scheme for Gaston and others. The second supposition alleges that the scope of the work with its complex historical background was just too broad to be distilled fictionally; and with a post-Reformation setting, Pater could not have solved quite so deftly as in *Marius* the problem of a theologically reasoned assent. Finally, other critics suggest that Pater began serialization of the work prematurely and that in the light of his other commitments he overestimated his ability to compose a chapter a month. Admittedly, all of these factors may have contributed in some degree to his faltering pace in 1888, but they do not account for his failure to finish in the 1890s.

Although Shadwell presumably had little detailed knowledge of motives when he conjectured that Pater became "dissatisfied with the framework which he had begun, and . . . deliberately abandoned it," this opinion is supported by the *Athenaeum* reviewer (T. Bailey Saunders) who writes of *Gaston:* "Only a part of it had been given to the world; and that part—with which, as Mr. Shadwell suggests, and as the present writer can from his own knowledge affirm, Pater was dissatisfied—had been deliberately abandoned, or rather, perhaps, put aside for future reconsideration." The Shadwell-Saunders "dissatisfied" does not quite suggest simple over-commitment, indicating that the mere press of having to meet serial deadlines did not alone contribute to the termination of its run. The agonizingly slow pace of composition after 1888 indicates a more basic thematic or structural problem. Arthur Symons reported that in 1889 Pater thought he needed two or three years to finish; and in 1890 Herbert Horne told "Michael Field" that Pater had announced to him his intention of sacrificing his vacations in order to complete the novel. As Pater's library borrowings indicate, he seems to have been actively researching the historical background as late as the spring of 1893 when, for the seventh time, he borrowed volumes of Pierre de Brantôme's works from the Taylorian Institution.

Doubtless the fact that Pater intended *Gaston* to be second in a trilogy of which *Marius* had been the first accounts in large measure for his selecting the complex age of the Valois for its setting. As *Marius* had been set in the period of transition from paganism to Christianity, so *Gaston* is located in the time just following the Reformation, in the transition from Catholicism to Protestantism. Though the sixteenth century in France was an age of crisis, Pater focuses on history as filtered by memory and emotions, dissolving the action so radically that Gaston seems merely to have read about what happened all around him. In *Marius*, the thread of personal narrative is strongest in the closing chapters (book 4), although the use of Marius's journal in the place of direct dialogue still mutes his dramatic presence. Gaston as a dramatic figure may be only marginally more shadowy than Marius, but most readers will feel that the thread of narrative in *Gaston* is strongest in the *opening* chapters and is retained still in the first of the three finished portraits (that of Ronsard) but that it reappears only rarely in the essay on Montaigne and disappears entirely in the chapter on Bruno. In the chapter with the greatest potential for dramatic action, the penultimate "Shadows of Events," Pater dissolves the drama (marriage, betrayal, massacre, escape, childbirth) by a kind of retrospective distancing or temporal blurring of word and deed. The unpublished chapters carry forward the narrative thread only minimally. For example, nearly the whole of chapter 9 takes place within the single moment of Gaston's ascent of the staircase leading to the boudoir of Queen Margot; and in chapter 11 Pater apologizes for dwelling "at length on what was visible in Paris just then, on the mere historic scene there, forgetful it might seem of the company of Gaston, but only because I do suppose him thoughtfully looking on with us all the while, as essentially a creature of the eye, even more likely than others to be shaped by what he sees." This emphasis upon the protagonist's processes of perception and the personification of culture, rather than upon the direct imitation of life, is central to the novel's artistic self-consciousness.

Pater's Gaston begins as a rather conventional Victorian lad, a "romantic" type questing for a spiritual home within the tangible world of the senses, for an ideal not in opposition to the actual but in harmony with it: "Two worlds, two antagonistic ideals, were in evidence before him. Could a third condition supervene, to mend their discord, or only vex him perhaps, from time to time, with efforts towards an impossible adjustment?" And again: "Was there perhaps somewhere, in some penetrative mind in this age of novelties, some scheme of truth, some science about men and things, which might harmonise for him his earlier and later preference, 'the sacred and the profane loves,' or, failing that, establish, to his pacification, the exclusive supremacy of the latter?" Like his fellow countryman du Bellay, of whom Pater had written in *The*

Renaissance, Gaston is a dreamer longing for the harmonies of the unfallen world of childhood. His birthplace, the old château of Deux-manoirs, embodies in the unusual doubleness of its plan the attachment of brothers who did not want to be separated by their marriages. This fraternal affection recalls Pater's description of its earlier French example, the friendship of Amis and Amile. There Pater had commented on "that curious interest of the *Doppelgänger*, which begins among the stars with the Dioscuri." Young Gaston's tranquil home, embodying the fraternal unity of self and Other, is not unlike Marius's White-nights or Hippolytus's Eleusis—a world ideally balanced between sense and spirit, not yet lapsed into either impassioned sensuality or cold formalism. But if childhood enjoys a perfect rapport between the self and the sensuous world, "inward and outward being woven through and through each other into one inextricable texture," maturation, on the other hand, reveals an emphatically decentered identity: "that continual vanishing away, that strange, perpetual weaving and unweaving of ourselves." Gaston's problem, specifically, is the emerging spirit of relativism, expressed for him in the Renaissance by Montaigne's or Bruno's teachings and for Pater in the nineteenth century by Darwin, Mill, and Spencer.

Yet, for a time at least, Gaston's "simple old-fashioned faith, was blent harmoniously" with the desire of beauty, "two neighbourly apprehensions of a single ideal." Within this harmonious framework young Gaston assumes clerk's orders in the family chapel of Saint Hubert. Although it is a step which seemingly will end the race of Latour, Gaston being the last of his line like Marius, Duke Carl, or Sebastian van Storck, yet it is an act which testifies to a belief in relationships that transcend the physical family. In a passage that recalls Pater's earlier "purpurei panni" (the phrase is Wilde's), Pater juxtaposes the warm, sunny landscape of La Beauce with the cool, shadowy interior of Saint Hubert's, suggesting that the lad Gaston fuses outward sense and inner vision:

> Yes! there was the sheep astray, *sicut ovis quae periit*—the physical world; with its lusty ministers, at work, or sleeping for a while amid the stubble, their faces upturned to the August sun—the world so importunately visible, intruding a little way, with its floating odours, in that semicircle of heat across the old over-written pavement at the great open door, upon the mysteries within. Seen from the incense-laden sanctuary, where the bishop was assuming one by one the pontifical ornaments, La Beauce, like a many-coloured carpet spread under the great dome, with the white double house-front quivering afar through the heat, though it looked as if you might touch with the hand its distant spaces, was for a moment the

unreal thing. Gaston alone, with all his mystic preoccupations, by the privilege of youth, seemed to belong to both, and link the visionary company about him to the external scene.

Like the impressionistic painter's initial dissociation of pure color tones which recompose in the eye of the beholder only at a distance, the colors and shapes of La Beauce are rendered by Pater with pictorial richness. Pater's statement in "Giorgione" that a great picture in its primary aspect "has no more definite message for us than an accidental play of sunlight and shadow for a few moments on the wall or floor: is itself, in truth, a space of such fallen light, caught as the colours are in an Eastern carpet, but refined upon, and dealt with more subtly and exquisitely than by nature itself" finds here its descriptive equivalent.

That outer world of La Beauce, so like the impressions of the perpetual flux described in the Conclusion to *The Renaissance*—"unstable, flickering, inconsistent"—is seen "intruding a little way" through "the great open door" toward the mysterious interior of the church. The open door forcefully recalls such other visionary moments as Florian's encounter through the open garden gate with the hawthorn and its summer perfume. The "quivering" unreality of La Beauce encircling the "incense-laden sanctuary" constitutes Gaston within Saint Hubert's after the fashion of the human image described in the Conclusion: "a design in a web, the actual threads of which pass out beyond it." Here the "web"—Mona Lisa, elsewhere, had "trafficked for strange webs with Eastern merchants"—is a carpet, an image which turns us back to the eastern carpet in "Giorgione." And in the "many-coloured carpet" of La Beauce, the design of the child in the church is confirmed as the scenic center by the dramatic foreshortening which makes it seem "as if you might touch with the hand" the distant spaces of the landscape. (Much the same foreshortening occurred, for much the same reason, in Marius's vision at the shrine of Aesculapius where, looking through a cunningly contrived panel, he supposed he saw "Pisa.—Or Rome, was it? asked Marius, ready to believe the utmost in his excitement.") In this context it is not without significance that another Gaston de Latour had undergone a similar ritual a century before: the flux which continuously modulates toward new centers has now again reconstituted the religious center, reanimated the past. Further, a heritage not physical only but also spiritual is manifest in "the old over-written pavement at the great open door," anticipating a similar image of continuity for Emerald Uthwart at school, who sits "at the heavy old desks, carved this way and that, crowded as an old churchyard with forgotten names."

Although the doubleness of Deux-manoirs echoes Gaston's harmonious balance of inner and outer worlds—faith and beauty—yet on occasion certain "inward oppositions," even in his idyllic world of childhood, "beset him." The condition of fraternal unity, expressed by the brothers Latour and later echoed for Gaston in Montaigne's friendship with the "incomparable" Etienne de la Boetie (" 'We were halves throughout, so that methinks by outliving him I defraud him of his part. I was so grown to be always his double in all things that methinks I am no more than half of myself' "), must ultimately become for Gaston a thing of the past. Even before he leaves home, the wild and bloody world of experience enters in the form of King Charles, benighted on the hunt: "a madman—*steeped* in blood." This wild, Dionysian figure is a foreshadowing of the Saint Bartholomew's Day massacre and the strife of the religious wars into which Gaston gradually moves. Also, the quarreling brothers Gaston encounters one night are in contrast to his ancestral brothers and their bond of familial devotion (and the affection of Ronsard and du Bellay or Montaigne and de la Boetie as well): "with a sudden flash of fierce words two young men burst from the doors of a roadside tavern. The brothers are quarrelling about the division, lately effected there, of their dead father's morsel of land. 'I shall hate you till death!' cries the younger, bounding away in the darkness; and two atheists part, to take opposite sides in the supposed strife of Catholic and Huguenot." As the Saint Bartholomew's Day massacre, Pater notes, would come to be used to settle personal quarrels, so this private quarrel also finds its fulfillment in public strife. Through this public-private correspondence, the ancestral devotion of the Latour brothers is meant to be seen in nostalgic contrast to the looming conflict of the religious wars.

Paradoxically, as Gaston moves as a page into the cloistered life of the episcopal household at the cathedral of Chartres, the past is supplanted by the secular present—a present embodied in the "precocious worldliness" of his fellow acolytes: "they had brought from their remote old homes all varieties of hereditary gifts, vices, distinctions, dark fates, mercy, cruelty, madness." Like Pisa and Marius's friend Flavian, Chartres displays a "strange mixture of beauty and evil," a discord characteristic of Ronsard's poetry also, which Gaston shortly thereafter discovers. Prior to his poetic awakening, the winter of 1567, the coldest in a half-century, brought the siege of Chartres by the Huguenots, imprisoning Gaston and his grandparents among others within the city. In a curious detail obviously included for thematic purposes, Pater narrates Gaston's brush with death in a collapsing church "under a shower of massy stones from the *coulevrines* or great cannon of the besiegers," which is so similar to Marius's escape from the falling rock of a landslide that one is tempted to apply to Gaston's story the meaning of Marius's experience. Marius's sense "of hatred against him, of the nearness of 'enemies' " shakes his Epicurean commitment to a life of the senses; Gaston's commitment, on the other hand, had been to a clerical calling which now in turn he abandons. Pater additionally connects Gaston's brush with death with a second powerful motive for change (he being an orphan): the death of his grandmother in the midst of the siege. "That broken link with life seemed to end some other things for him," that is, his vows and tonsure. There is also here a connection with "The Child in the House," for just as the empty house from which Florian rescues his trapped bird "touched him like the face of one dead," so here Gaston gazes upon the cathedral of Chartres "as he had gazed on the dead face" of his grandmother. But in contrast to Florian's homesickness, Gaston has "no keen sense of personal loss" when the cathedral is despoiled by war because that childhood "link" between the church and the outer world—Saint Hubert's filled with the visionary company in contrast to Chartres emptied of its accumulated treasure—has now been "broken."

At this crucial juncture in the preceding novel, Marius is introduced to Cornelius and experiences a foretaste of the resolution of his problem; Gaston, on the other hand, encounters a new profane religion. He visits Ronsard, having already made the acquaintance of his odes. His court days and his creative days over, Ronsard in middle age and failing health was nonetheless not only lay superior of the Priory of Croix-val but also the high priest of the worship of physical beauty and liberty of heart and imagination. "Modernity" begins with a submerged analogy between Gaston's relation to his physical environment and his relation to literature. After long confinement by siege, he is released into an open countryside still charged with the peril of warfare; so, too, the literature of the past—"chained to the bookshelf, like something in a dead language, 'dead, and shut up in reliquaries of books' "—is released by Ronsard's Odes and Amours into a literary springtime charged with moral peril. The landscape and the odes are related through the common imagery of springtime—flowers, larks, fruit, heat, blossoms, freshness—and both pose perils for the young and impressionable Gaston. This movement of the chapter outward from the "circle" of siege which shut up Gaston and the others like "prisoners" into the perilous, impassioned, and troubling landscape is repeated in the visit to Ronsard. First, Gaston crosses the "outer ring of blue up-lands"; next, the poet appears within "the high espaliered gardenwall, . . . visible through the open doors." The open doors of the church of Saint Hubert and of Ronsard's "enchanted castle" promise escape (actual or illusory) from the solipsism of the self "ringed round, . . . each mind keeping as a solitary prisoner its own dream of a world."

Often, in Pater's description of the development of his characters, a literary discovery is suddenly the textual prelude to their maturer manhood: Winckelmann's sudden, fervent awakening to the glory of antiquity through surreptitious reading of his master's Greek classics or Emerald Uthwart's and the English poet's leap of intellectual awakening. Sometimes this passion for an aesthetic, intellectual, or emotional ideal is effected by a single book: Apuleius's *Metamorphoses* with Marius or Duke Carl's accidental unearthing of Conrad Celtes's *Ars versificandi*. So too the eighteen-year-old Gaston, fresh from the cathedral school at Chartres, discovered for the first time the excitement of contemporary poetry in Ronsard's recent *Odes*. In his Postscript to *Appreciations*, Pater spoke of the periodic revitalization of classic forms by the romantic impulse, which in *Marius* he depicted as accomplished by the Frontonian revival and which in *Gaston* Ronsard effected for Virgil. Pater notes that Ronsard's *Odes* "took possession of Gaston with the ready intimacy of one's equal in age." Since Ronsard published his *Odes* two years prior to Gaston's birth, the text has just that slight discrepancy in years as does Gaston's double, Charles; but unlike the antagonistic doppelgänger, Gaston enjoys a fraternal unity with the poems and hence a filial relation with Ronsard, the textual father. Just as in the essay on Michelangelo Pater had found that artist-poet to be "in possession of our inmost thoughts," so analogously Ronsard "seemed but to have spoken what was already in Gaston's own mind." Looking up from his reading of Ronsard's unfinished manuscript, the *Franciade*, Gaston is suddenly himself read as a "legible document" by the poet who becomes "paternally anxious" for his furtherance.

Although Ronsard's poetry offers a renewal and freedom, it asks too steep a price by demanding that Gaston sever ties completely with his heritage of Deux-manoirs. In this, Ronsard's book of poetry is closest to Apuleius's Golden Book, for Gaston can no more be satisfied with Ronsard than Marius had been with Apuleius. Perhaps because he could not truly reconcile faith with art, Ronsard had failed to keep alive the fires of the fresh modernity of his youth, its romanticism, and so Gaston must push on. At Ronsard's recommendation, Gaston goes further south to the Gironde to visit Michel de Montaigne in his tower-library by the Dordogne. When about 1569 Gaston visited Montaigne, the *Essais* were unwritten, but Pater has Montaigne weave a cento of their contents in a nine-month discussion with his guest. As Ronsard had been the equivalent to Apuleius in *Marius*, so Montaigne the skeptic (as did Emerson, Pater overemphasizes Montaigne's skepticism) corresponds to Lucian. Lucian would have agreed with Montaigne that the "priceless pearl of truth" does not inhere in any theory man can invent, for diversities of opinion are "themselves ultimate." Indeed, Lucian suggests that those looking for some basic ground of truth are like temple guards searching among a host of secular cups, flagons, and diadems for a missing sacred vessel—neither shape nor material known, and unfortunately not inscribed with the name of its divine owner. And to the young Pater's insistence in "Coleridge's Writings" on the inevitable failure of all efforts to label and so identify that cup/dogma for all time, both Lucian and Montaigne would have subscribed: "Theology is a great house, scored all over with hieroglyphics by perished hands. When we decypher one of those hieroglyphics, we find in it the statement of a mistaken opinion; but knowledge has crept onward since the hand dropped from the wall; we no longer entertain the opinion, and we can trace the origin of the mistake." Lucian still harbors a wistful longing after the impossible dream of discovering the cup, of deciphering the inscription, and finding the god: "And we too desire, not a fair one, but the fairest of all. Unless we find him, we shall think we have failed." Montaigne's "undulant" philosophy, on the other hand, seems to rest content with the ultimacy of diversity. "But could one really care for truth, who never even seemed to find it?" Gaston asks himself concerning Montaigne. Perhaps, Gaston concedes (and Pater subtly puns on "ground" of being), "there was some deeper ground of thought in reserve; as if he were really moving, securely, over ground you did not see."

In effect, Montaigne demonstrates as illusory or as merely provisional the possibilities implicit in Ronsard's verse for revitalization through a celebration of sensuous experience. Extending Ronsard theoretically, Montaigne is unable to suggest for the diverse world of thought and experience either an extrinsic or an intrinsic power of organization such as Gaston had known at Deux-manoirs; and the peril of Ronsard's poetry becomes explicit in Montaigne's tower: "How imperceptibly had darkness crept over them, effacing everything but the interior of the great circular chamber, its book-shelves and enigmatic mottoes and the tapestry on the wall,—Circe and her sorceries, in many parts,—to draw over the windows in winter. . . . Was Circe's castle here? If Circe could turn men into swine, could she also release them again?" The darkening circular chamber, the windows of which are covered by the tapestry of Circe's castle on the wall, possesses a host of thematic filiations: with the encircled "solitary prisoner" of the dreaming mind, with Ronsard's "enchanted castle," with Marcus Aurelius's nearly "window-less" audience chamber, with Apuleius's discourse in the darkness after the banquet. The moral diversity inherent in Ronsard's pursuit of the sensations of beauty and evil becomes in Montaigne's tower no longer a liberating landscape but leaves one in an imprisoning circle, "walled up suddenly, as if by malign trickery, in the open field."

This ultimate failure of sensuous experience is a function of the growing self-consciousness of western culture:

> In the perplexed currents of modern thought, . . . the eternal problem of culture—balance, unity with one's self, consummate Greek modelling . . . [—]could no longer be solved . . . by perfection of bodily form, or any joyful union with the external world: the shadows had grown too long, the light too solemn, for that. . . . The chief factor in the thoughts of the modern mind concerning itself is the intricacy, the universality of natural law, even in the moral order. For us, necessity is not, as of old, a sort of mythological personage without us, with whom we can do warfare. It is rather a magic web woven through and through us, like that magnetic system of which modern science speaks, penetrating us with a network, subtler than our subtlest nerves, yet bearing in it the central forces of the world. Can art represent men and women in these bewildering toils so as to give the spirit at least an equivalent for the sense of freedom? . . . Natural laws we shall never modify, embarrass us as they may; but there is still something in the nobler or less noble attitude with which we watch their fatal combinations.

If, since a web is a tapestry, we couple that "magic web woven through and through us" with the tapestry of Circe and, further, if modern man, caught in the "bewildering toils" (bewilder: AS *be* + *wild* + *deōr* to be covered with the wild beast; toils: MF *toile* net, fr. L *tela* web, fr. *texere* to weave) of natural laws, is connected with Circe's victims trapped in swine—if so, then Montaigne's tower has become the modern castle of Circe. What Pater is dramatizing in the circular tower-library is the emerging modern equivalent (Montaigne's skepticism "does but commence the modern world") to the antique and mythical form of entrapment. When the windows of Montaigne's darkening chamber ("the shadows had grown too long" for "joyful union with the external world") are covered in winter by the pictured castle of Circe ("a sort of mythological personage without us, with whom we can do warfare"), the tapestry portrays on the mythological level of an external battle of wills what by the covering of windows it also depicts on the symbolic level of an internal bondage. In effect, then, the double scene of Circe's castle on the wall of Montaigne's tower brilliantly depicts by complex equivalences the progress of western consciousness (particularly evident in the tower-library with "more books upon books than upon any other subject") from the Greeks to the Renaissance. To dramatize further the significance of this elaborate tableau, Pater has Gaston finish the chapter by playing at dice with Montaigne's young wife, enacting in play the role of mankind watching the "fatal combinations" of natural laws—and with Montaigne declining to join them because, as he explains, " 'play was not play enough, but too grave and serious a diversion' "!

Although the transition from Montaigne's Circean tower to the bloodshed of 1572 constitutes a three-year jump in the life of Gaston, thematically it represents a mere shift from the game of dice to the "fatal combinations" of Saint Bartholomew's Eve. The circular tower of the modern Circe who thought diversities were ultimate is replaced by the city, which resembles "a prison or a *trap*":

> Delirium was in the air already charged with thunder, and laid hold on Gaston too. It was as if through some unsettlement in the atmospheric medium the objects around no longer acted upon the senses with the normal result. Looking back afterwards, this singularly self-possessed person had to confess that under its influence he had lost for a while the exacter view of certain outlines, certain real differences and oppositions of things in that hotly coloured world of Paris (like a shaken tapestry about him) awaiting the Eve of Saint Bartholomew.

In the "shaken tapestry" of Paris the "quivering" carpet of La Beauce reappears, yet in the unsettled atmosphere attending the royal nuptials of Henry and Margaret the moral distinctions, the design or "outlines" manifest within the sanctuary of Saint Hubert, are missing in the Louvre-castle-tower-city of Circe's malign paradise: "Charles and his two brothers, keeping the gates of a mimic paradise in the court of the Louvre, while the fountains ran wine—were they already thinking of a time when they would keep those gates, with iron purpose, while the gutters ran blood?" By enthrallment to sensual passion (or, since opposites meet, by allegiance to some outworn dogma), the tapestry can lose its central human design which opens from the narrow circle of the present into that larger spirit of humanity and can become an "issueless circle" that traps the soul like a bird (in the stone vaulting, the web between the ribs, of Saint Vaast's in contrast to Saint Hubert's) or can become what in the unpublished chapters Pater calls an ever-revolving circle such as may be found, for example, in mazes revolving perpetually into themselves as the one on the cathedral floor at Chartres. Need one note that this reference to Chartres again contrasts it with Saint Hubert's?

In Gaston's marriage to the Huguenot Columbe, the factional causes of Catholic and Protestant seek a private reconciliation, just as the two feuding houses in the portrait of Denys had been reconciled by marriage. But Gaston's marriage represents a potential for harmony that is almost immediately frustrated by public events; and, by being painted against the background of Gabrielle de Latour's story, his tragedy has been sharpened. Gabrielle, watching at her window ten years for the return of her husband, had touched the sleepy world of Deux-manoirs with "one of those grand passions, such as were needed to give life its true meaning and effect." In the Conclusion to *The Renaissance*, Pater spoke of "great passions" and the "ecstasy and sorrow of love" which give one a "quickened sense of life." Although such a "great" or "high" passion had also forcibly moved Sebastian van Storck meditating on Grotius's wife, Gabrielle's story approximates more closely the Ceyx-Halcyon legend and the myth of Cupid and Psyche as they formed themselves in Marius's imagination. This constancy of Gaston's ancestor was a test of fidelity to an ideal as strict as anything Psyche endured; and like Psyche's bower of bliss, Gabrielle's chamber, expressive of that "great passion of old," was for Gaston a "magic apartment." Much as Prior Saint-Jean, gazing longingly from his window, had died upon the final permission to return to the valley of the monks, Gabrielle had "died of joy" at that "wonderful moment" of her husband's return. Gabrielle's felicity of a hundred years before may have been planned to be repeated in Gaston's life where "against all expectation" he too, perhaps, may have been reunited, not with Columbe, his dead wife, but with his lost child.

As his grandmother's death, which counterpoints and personalizes the mass deaths at Chartres, coincides with his quitting the clerical vocation, so that "quiet double-holiday morning" on which Gaston's aged grandfather peacefully dies finalizes the irretrievable loss of harmony. The doubleness of this holiday is only in one sense that of Sunday, 24 August, Feast of Saint Bartholomew; figuratively, it is the contrast of deaths peaceful and violent, the fragmentation of wholeness into the antagonistic doppelgänger. Elsewhere in Pater's fiction this slaughter of Saint Bartholomew's massacre and the death of Columbe is echoed in Denys's death following a marriage, in the marriage-martyrdom of the Gallic Christians in *Marius*, and most closely in the obliteration of Duke Carl and his bride after the death of the old grand duke of Rosenmold. One feels that long, leisurely lives with scarcely perceptible endings are not going to be numerous among Gaston's acquaintances, as the Triumvirate's encounter with their bloody doubles foretells. In the master trope of the tapestry, the fate of Gaston's young friends is forecast: "Reappearing, from point to point, they connected themselves with the great crimes, the great tragedies of the time, as so many bright-coloured threads in that sombre tapestry of human passion. . . . Threads to be cut short, one by one, before his eyes, the three would cross and recross, gaily, pathetically, in the tapestry of Gaston's years; and, divided far asunder afterwards, seemed at this moment, moving there before him in the confidential talk he could not always share, inseparably linked together, like some complicated pictorial arabesque."

The fraternal double, no longer that of the brothers Latour, has been reembodied now in the violently quarreling brothers by the roadside tavern. And just as the antagonistic brothers are an emblem on the private level of a public division, so a correspondence of private to public exists in the fraternal opposition of the priestly Gaston to the royal Charles IX. That the pathetic, blood-crazed Charles is Gaston's opposing doppelgänger on the national level is evident from a number of analogues. Charles was born in 1550, Gaston in 1552; thus, both are of an age (the slight discrepancy in years is suggested by the myth of the Dioscuri and recurs in Pater's other pairings). Both undergo a ritual; as Gaston is made a clerk in orders, "far away in Paris the young King Charles the Ninth, in his fourteenth year, has been just declared of age." The reference at this point to the parallel *rites de passage* specifically stresses the association between royal and priestly careers. Most significantly, Charles, soaked in blood from his hunting expedition, stops at Deux-manoirs and sleeps for some hours in the love chamber of Gabrielle de Latour, the favorite haunt of Gaston. Charles's presence there suggests a reanimation of Gabrielle's antagonistic doppelgänger within Gaston's marriage-to-be—her sorrow for the absent mate will now become that of Gaston.

As a madman hunter, an effeminate winter Dionysus, bloody Charles (animal blood, not yet that of humans) significantly foreshadows the massacre of Saint Bartholomew's Eve and Gaston's guilt in it; for, paradoxically, the "madness" and "delirium" of Paris on Saint Bartholomew's Eve belong as much to the hunted (Gaston-Columbe) as to the hunter (Charles, who literally had come to Deux-manoirs as a hunter):

> In the conception of Dionysus . . . a certain transference, or substitu-
> tion, must be made—much of the horror and sorrow . . . of the whole
> tragic situation, must be transferred to him, if we wish to realise in the
> older, profounder, and more complete sense of his nature, that mystical
> being of Greek tradition to whom all these experiences—his madness,
> the chase, his imprisonment and death, his peace again—really be-
> long. . . . Dionysus *Omophagus*—the eater of raw flesh, must be added to
> the golden image of Dionysus *Meilichius*—the honey-sweet, if . . . we are
> to catch, in its fulness, that deep undercurrent of horror which runs
> below, all through this masque of spring, and realise the spectacle of that
> wild chase, in which Dionysus is ultimately both the hunter and the
> spoil.

Madness, chase, imprisonment, death—these also describe Paris and the massacre of 1572. And like Denys with "his contrast, his dark or antipathetic side, . . . a double creature, of two natures, difficult or impossible to harmonise," Gaston now has become both hunter and hunted. By his predisposition to regard his own interfaith marriage as a "mere mistake" or "unmeaning accident," Gaston is linked morally both to the "illicit and inauspicious" public nuptials of Protestant Prince Henry and Catholic Margaret and to the ensuing, nearly accidental, marriage slaughter on Saint Bartholomew's Eve: "not the cruelty only but the obscurity, the accidental character, yet, alas! also the treachery, of the public event seemed to identify themselves tragically with his own personal action, . . . had made him so far an accomplice in their unfriendly action that he felt certainly not quite guiltless, thinking of his own irresponsible, self-centered, passage along the ways, through the weeks that had ended in the public crime and his own private sorrow," leaving with him the sense "for the rest of his days of something like remorse." Columbe's belief that she has been treacherously deserted doubtless echoes Aliette's death in Pater's 1886 critical portrait, "Feuillet's 'La Morte.' " There the husband, Bernard, exclaims: "She died believing me guilty! . . . And she will never, never know that it was not so; that I am innocent." Bernard's grief brings him to his deathbed on which he is converted from unbelief to the religion of his wife—a pattern possibly to be repeated in Gaston's turn to the Huguenot belief of Columbe.

Pater allows fourteen years to elapse after the 1572 massacre before resuming the thread of his narrative in the next and, as the novel now stands, final chapter. If from Montaigne the skeptic Gaston learned of the relativity of values and the diversity of opinions, afterward from Giordano Bruno, who came to Paris in 1579 and is lecturing at the Sorbonne in 1586, he is initiated into an idealism that preached the spiritual unity of creation. But just as Ronsard's enthrallment to physical sensation turns out to have much in common with the intellectual skepticism of Montaigne, so Montaigne's skepticism also has much in common with Bruno's religious mysticism. Good and evil are still perilously allied: "If God the Spirit had made, nay! was, all things indifferently, then, matter and spirit, the spirit and the flesh, heaven and earth, freedom and necessity, the first and the last, good and evil, would be superficial rather than substantial differences." But juxtaposed with the massacre in which Gaston suffers the personal loss of his wife and child (not to mention the more general loss of life), Bruno's refusal to recognize the reality of evil is powerfully condemned. In this respect, Bruno's refusal to see evil is much like Marcus Aurelius's moral blindness, for just as Aurelius sponsored the "Manly Amusement" of the amphitheater and the martyrdom of the Gallic Christians, so Bruno is—retrospectively— the intellectual sponsor of the massacre of Saint Bartholomew's Eve. Although the pluralism of Montaigne's diverse entities which negate any Absolute Spirit is supplanted by the monism of Bruno's Spirit who negates finite reality, the common *practical* result (always the touchstone for Pater) of their theoretical indifference or inconclusiveness is the immorality of Gaston's Paris.

In the unpublished chapters, Queen Margaret of Navarre—Margot of the *Memoirs*—is explicitly presented as a Renaissance Circe whose palace is the Louvre and whose enchanted island is Paris. In his chronicles, Brantôme, a disciple of Montaigne's and Bruno's seeming license to accord aesthetic values pride of place over moral values, eloquently portrays Margot as the femme fatale of her age. Not just the Circe on Montaigne's wall but the idolized ladies of Ronsard's verse had prefigured Brantôme's sorceress: the pagan goddess Minerva took the place of Our Lady in Ronsard's apartment, "bringing the odd, enigmatic physiognomy, preferred by the art of that day, within the sphere of religious devotion"; and on the walls of Ronsard's study his ladies "might have been sisters, those many successive loves, or one and the same lady over and over again." Circe, Minerva, Ronsard's loves: Margot's multiplicity is not unlike that of Mona Lisa, and her face seems to haunt the art of her age, not as the priceless pearl of truth as her name would suggest but as the visible form of an unseen force of cruel love. After the fashion of Circe's Ulysses, Gaston is enthralled by the spectacle of Margot's exotic religion of carnal beauty. Our Lady of Chartres of his consecrated youth has become the temptress of the Louvre, a modulation from innocence to corruption reminiscent of Demeter's daughters as Pater had described them in *Greek Studies.* As amanuensis, Gaston serves Margot much as Marius had served Marcus Aurelius, although Aurelius's lofty spirituality lay at the opposite extreme from Margot's sensual disavowal of the spiritual realm. This narcissism is initially evident to Gaston in the house of Margot's lover, Jasmin, in which a decorative pseudoclassicism fails to capture the true classical harmony of sense and spirit (that problem of balance no longer to be solved by any mere "perfection of bodily form"). A volume of the *Meditations* of Marcus Aurelius causes Gaston to sense that in Jasmin's empty house not only is the human form absent (as it was in Circe's swine) but its spirit also has been destroyed by being enthralled to sensuality. (Ironically, Aurelius had been presented in *Marius* as a despiser of the body, his empty palace revealing a moral isolation as disastrous in its way as the elaborate but lifeless "aestheticism" of Jasmin's mannered dwelling.) Only in the painted glass of Jean Cousin, who rejuvenates the old Gothic under the influence of the Italian style, and in the work of the modern Italian masters themselves, such as da Vinci, does Gaston find a power capable of "linking paternally, filially, age to age." Their portraiture reconstitutes the living human form absent among the elaborately balanced harmonies of Jasmin's empty house.

Montaigne's tapestry of the flux has no central design; diversity is ultimate. Bruno's tapestry has centers everywhere; none is preeminent. But that paternal-filial linking of age to age so evident in the ritual at Saint Hubert's and in the emphatically historical existence of Deux-manoirs from the Middle Ages to the Revolution suggests there can be an ongoing human center perpetually reconstituted from age to age. Yet, if one interprets the idea of family in Pater's work to include all who feel ties of a spousal, parental, or fraternal nature, one notices that his writings are positively haunted by the theme of the divided family, of severed ties; and, indeed, a corresponding quest for reunion constitutes the central plot suspense (though *suspense* is too strong a term) for *Gaston de Latour* as a whole. Although Columbe has definitely died, Pater evidently intended Gaston's search for his lost child to culminate in a reunion at his death. Many of Pater's heroes, questing after that reunion which symbolizes the reintegration of sense and spirit, find themselves reliving ritual or mythic patterns, finally sacrificing their very lives to their foreordained roles. Even mythic instances of spousal or paternal-maternal reunion, as in the tale of Cupid and Psyche or the story of Demeter and Persephone, involve a descent into the underworld; more emphatically among mortals, this reunion, as Duke Carl's return to Gretchen, is sealed by death.

Seemingly, only by sacrificing the physical continuity of the Latour family in the ritual at Saint Hubert's is Gaston able to reconstitute the ideal human image within the tapestry. Analogously, at the Christmas Mass in *Marius*, the past is reanimated only by the crucified Christ, who "seemed to have absorbed, like some rich tincture in his garment, all that was deep-felt and impassioned in the experiences of the past." The deeply dyed vesture of Christ and the "many-coloured carpet" of La Beauce appear also in the "strange dyes, strange colours" of the flux as caught for a few moments in those "strange webs" for which Mona Lisa traffics, webs produced, she knows, by "that strange perpetual weaving and unweaving of ourselves." "Strange," because the design in the web is at once new and wonderful but, also, latent with "the fatality which seems to haunt any signal beauty." All of these images center in the master symbol of the blood on the arena's sand in which the human form, that "design in a web," is redeemed from death by its reenactment in the present. As Pater notes in *Plato* (substituting cultural history for Wordsworth's clouds of glory): "we come into the world, each one of us, 'not in nakedness,' but . . . clothed . . . in a vesture of the past, nay, fatally shrouded, it might seem, in those laws or tricks of heredity which we mistake for our volitions." And one of those small acts of devotion that Gaston recollects when he hears of Montaigne's seemingly pious end—one of those concessions to "a certain great possibility, which might lie among the conditions of so complex a world," that takes Montaigne one step beyond the ultimacy of diversity—is his wrapping himself in "an old mantle that had belonged to his father. Retained, . . . in spite of its inconvenience, 'because it seemed to envelope me in him,' it was the symbol of a hundred natural, perhaps somewhat material, pieties. Parentage, kinship, relationship through earth,—the touch of that was everywhere like a caress to him."

Owing to Pater's concept of identity as expressive of the composite experience of history—the self ceaselessly traversed by codes of meaning like threads through a tapestry—any given moment in time represents a "retracing" or "reminiscence" of previously existing moments. Thus Gaston, lodged in Abelard's quarter, "all but repeats Abelard's typical *experience*" since, like Abelard and Hélöise, Gaston and Columbe are tragically divided. Repetition or "Imitation:—it enters into the very fastnesses of character; and we, our souls, ourselves, are for ever imitating what we see and hear, the forms, the sounds which haunt our memories, our imagination. We imitate not only if we play a part on the stage but when we sit as spectators, while our thoughts follow the acting of another, when we read Homer and put ourselves, lightly, fluently, into the place of those he describes." One might note the numerous references to stage plays in *Gaston* as elaborating this motif of the reenactment of the past within the present, but the most pervasive instance of "imitation" in Gaston's experience and the one which best illuminates Pater's projected design for his unfinished romance is the Homeric account of Ulysses' journey home from Troy to Ithaca. Possibly Charles Lamb's *Adventures of Ulysses*, which unlike typical nineteenth-century translations presented realistic characters who also signified "external force or internal temptations," encouraged Pater to adapt Homer's epic for his own symbolic ends.

Since for Pater both the self and its repetitions are multiform, *Gaston*'s parallels with *The Odyssey* move on several historical planes simultaneously and are modified by a large number of non-Homeric correspondences from literature and history. If Queen Margot is Circe and Gaston Ulysses, Gabrielle de Latour, who lived a century before, plays the part of (a) Penelope: "Here certainly she had watched, at these windows, during ten whole years, for the return of her beloved husband from a disastrous battle in the East, till against all expectation she beheld him crossing the court at last." Of course, Gabrielle is not only Penelope—no one is merely *one*—and the fact that she "died of joy" upon her husband's return owes less to Homer than to Pliny's "Roman lady who died for joy to see her son return alive from the rout at Cannae" (to quote—appropriately, considering Gaston's own experience—Montaigne's "Of Sorrow"). Given such an interweaving of sources, one might worry about "overreading" Homeric echoes were it not that the episode of Gabrielle connects itself forcefully with another event so that, combined, they present an inescapable Odyssean parallel. At Chartres, Gaston beholds "a strange maritime personage, stout and square, returned, contrary to all expectation, after ten years' captivity among the savages of Florida," whose matted hair and outlandish hands and face suggest tenure as one of Circe's swine. Not only was Ulysses a "maritime personage," but the echo of "against all expectation" in "contrary to all expectation" leaps the gap of a century to fuse Gabrielle's belated warrior with Gaston's captured sailor into a single Homeric archetype. Finally, the decade common to both episodes corresponds precisely to the interval Ulysses wandered after the fall of Troy.

This Homeric correspondence would have provided a major level of meaning for the completed text with Gaston's return to Deux-manoirs. Excluded, of course, would be a final Homeric-style shoot-out and triumphant reunion; for in Pater's projected version of the tale, Penelope-Columbe (or her equivalent, the missing child) symbolizes Gaston's lost wholeness. As both the seeker and the one sought, she is the goal of Gaston's quest to overcome his divided and conflicting self, that inner antagonism which is externalized in the general warfare of the age. From this angle, Penelope's deferred choice of a suitor in Ulysses' absence is akin to Montaigne's "suspended judgment" or to Lucian's skeptical refusal to accept any particular scheme as possessing final truth. Like Lucian, she too longs not for a fair one, "but the fairest of all." Additionally, that famous Web of Penelope, "never ending, still beginning," would lead inevitably back to the master trope of the tapestry, Penelope (like the web-trafficking Mona Lisa) being an embodiment of "that eternal process of nature, . . . the 'Living Garment,' whereby God is seen of us, ever in weaving at the 'Loom of Time.' " Clearly Gaston-as-Ulysses can never hope to find Columbe-as-Penelope within the plot of the novel because she herself is the eternal process both of weaving and of all things woven, including that ultimate symbol of the web, the text (L texere to weave) itself. The real drama of Gaston's quest for Columbe has shifted from the plot to the next frame out; and on this level the text dramatizes the act of artistic creation. Gaston, now the collective mind of his age, has become a textuality in search of an author.

Clearly Homer's tale came too close to the conventional historical romance and had to be reconstituted by Pater in such a way that Ulysses' triumphant reunion with Penelope would dramatize the immediate act of its own recomposition. *The Odyssey* reflected the unself-conscious mind of the Greek who supposed man's will to be limited by "a sort of mythological personage without us, with whom we can do warfare," but the growing self-consciousness of western culture will not permit an art built upon such assumptions: "That naïve, rough sense of freedom, which supposes man's will to be limited, if at all, only by a will stronger than his, he can never have again. The attempt to represent it in art would have so little verisimilitude that it would be flat and uninteresting." Pater rejects low-mimetic "formal realism" because it fails to recognize the limits of documentary or naturalistic description. To treat the categories of time, space, matter, and identity as if they were static falsifies the actual character of experience, which is a continuous, changing process grasped only in terms of the subjective perceptions of the individual. Only by substituting autobiographical processes and problems of perception for the external actions of conventional fiction can an elusive outer reality be replaced by a self-sustaining imaginative reality. As Pater writes: "all true knowledge will be like the knowledge of a person, of living persons, and truth, . . . to the last, something to *look* at," adding that "human persons and their acts" are visible representations "of the eternal qualities of 'the eternal.' " In conventional fiction there is no consciousness opening itself to the reader, no mental or personal reality which, reembodied by the innermost self of the reader, can summon back into life the author's feelings and ideas. Authors who produce realistic novels share Hermotimus's quixotic aspiration to find Lucian's inscribed cup, to find and fix an objective truth within the flux. And yet Hermotimus's hope is ironically undercut as he sits among those "sepulchral inscriptions" on the Appian Way. Like theological truths among funereal "hieroglyphics" or originality in "reliquaries of books," the design isolated from the vitality of the web is merely a lifeless textual husk—epitaph, hieroglyphic, or reliquary. What the visionary text does, however, is perpetually return the design to the life of the web, allowing it to escape final formulation as it slips back into that larger flow of personality through time from which it originally came. Although such a text cannot catch external reality in its net of words, as the realistic novel purports to do, it can approach the structure of reality asymptomatically through an ongoing dialectic between consciousnesses. Within the scope of the plot, Gaston can never adequately recapture his lost wholeness; that wholeness can be reestablished only through the interplay of his story with the next frame out—the authorial level of inscription.

    Pater's notion of the textual Other in which the author seeks "deliverance from mortality" is brilliantly worked out in terms of the

Homeric theme of Telemachus and Ulysses, each in search of the other. Pater, as author and orphaned son longing for a father, and his specular double within the text, Gaston, as the father questing for his son, jointly constitute that lost paternal-filial wholeness which only the dialectic between inner and outer levels of self and Other can restore. In the preexisting texts that he reweaves imaginatively from the culture of the sixteenth century, Pater finds his father. But just as Telemachus and Ulysses are absorbed into and idealized by the figure of Penelope and her eternal weaving and unweaving, so Pater begets, simultaneously with the recovery of his own father, a nineteenth-century textual son which in its (his) turn will quest as a father for a vitalizing reunion with some future son. Not only is "the old over-written pavement" at the great open door of Saint Hubert's literally a record of fathers and sons, but as a palimpsestic web it symbolizes the eternal *textual* creation of the filial present by the paternal past and the corresponding re-creation of the now filial past by the paternal present. The bloody Charles IX, whose last words "had asserted his satisfaction in leaving no male child to wear his crown," represents a failure to recognize this centrality of the paternal-filial design within the web of history, and his sentiment contrasts sharply with, for example, the Latours' sense of family life being "like a second sacred history" or that saving instinct which enveloped Montaigne in the vesture of his paternal mantle. Circe's prison of low-mimetic formal realism, of that "false impression of permanence or fixity in things," can be escaped not by discovering "some scheme of truth . . . in some penetrative mind" outside one's own perceptions but rather by locating truth in the subjectivities of seeing itself, which by the act of writing become objectified, like the returned Ulysses, as "something to *look* at." What would not Pater as a child have given to have heard with Telemachus the words: "I am that father whom your boyhood lacked and suffered pain for lack of. I am he." Pater the adult both heard and himself uttered these words every time he wrote.

PERRY MEISEL

The Chemistry of the Crystal

T hat Pater is remembered best for his mannerisms as a stylist suggests not only how lightly we take his powers as a theoretician of art and culture, but also how little serious attention we tend to afford a writer's, particularly a critic's, fundamental materials—his personal brand of language, his distinctive rhetoric and vocabulary, and the distinctive kinds of knowledge they combine to produce. In order to disengage the Paterian thread from the fabric of Woolf's criticism in a specific way, of course, we shall in any case need an inventory of Pater's characteristic figures. By means of a catalogue of the recurrent tropes at work in his prose both early and late, we can in fact isolate some of the significant units in his eminently peculiar and recognizable rhetoric, and so try to gauge on the level of language itself just how precise the contours of his vision may be, especially if there is still some need to countermand Eliot's judgment that Pater is "incapable of sustained reasoning." That Pater's vision is discordant at key moments in its itinerary will concern us only later on, although to begin by taking at his exact word even the customary Pater, the Pater we already know, will prepare us for the task ahead.

Expressiveness, of course, is the manifest focus of Pater's vision of art, and with it comes an attendant concern for the extent to which the work reveals what is peculiar or particular to the temperament or personality of the artist who has made it. In fact, "all knowledge," says Pater in *Plato and Platonism*, is to be understood on the model of "knowing a

From *The Absent Father: Virginia Woolf and Walter Pater.* Copyright © 1980 by Yale University.

person," much as, in *Gaston*, even Bruno's "abstract theory" becomes a "visible person talking with you." Following from such a focus is Pater's sense of perfect art as an ideal kind of "integrity" or "unity with one's self," as he calls it in the portrait of Winckelmann, in which the artist's "every thought and feeling," like Giorgione's, is "twinborn with its sensible analogue or symbol." In fact, the "profound expressiveness" that characterizes the ideal work may be ascribed to the "magnetic" quality by which thought and feeling on the one hand, and the artist's medium or material on the other, are drawn together in such a way as to grant their union an almost natural status.

To this rather traditional notion of fusing form and content into the ideal transparency of a perfect work of art, however, Pater adds his own special variation. The celebrated "gemlike flame" signifies not only the successful arrest of the privileged moment in all its apparent immediacy; it also signifies a particular kind of artistic competence that solders manner and matter together by means of what is really a prescriptive regimen that establishes for Pater a normative and synchronic measure of achievement for the history of art as a whole, and that functions as a principle of evaluation for Pater the practical critic.

In the "Preface" to *The Renaissance*, Pater's project of critical self-definition is already formulated as a desire "to disengage" the "active principle" of "genius" or aesthetic "virtue" from its particular historical manifestations so as to examine it for its timeless components or constituent parts—for its "elementary particles" or "golden pieces," as Pater will call them in *Appreciations*. "Few artists," he writes, "not Goethe or Byron even, work quite cleanly, casting off all *débris*, and leaving us only what the heat of their imagination has wholly fused and transformed." The figure of the "chemist" earlier in the "Preface" suggests that what Pater really has in mind here is a kind of chemical process (he even uses the surprising word "formula" at the start of the "Preface," retaining it as late as the 1892 essay on Raphael) by which the force of genius is, quite literally, the "heat" by which "all impurities," as he says of Giorgione, are "burnt out of it, and no taint, no floating particle of anything but its own proper elements allowed to subsist within it." Thus the artist's "form" or "mode of handling" his subject "should penetrate every part of the matter," just as matter or "motive" should "saturate" and be "identical with" form. Hence the celebrated opinion that "all art constantly aspires towards the condition of music," since in music alone is "the constant effort of art" to "obliterate" or interfuse the distinction between "matter" and "form" already realized by the medium itself.

It is, then, the "gemlike flame" that is the agent of this process of "refinement" by which all that is alien to the work—all "residue," or "surplusage," as Pater will call it in *Appreciations*—is fired out or burnt away. With its sadomasochistic implications informing a view of the artist here as an exemplary sufferer or martyr who must "sacrifice . . . a thousand possible sympathies" in his pursuit of the perfect work, the figure of the chastening flame is at the center of Pater's notion of *ascesis*, that renunciative and self-restraining discipline by which an artist like Leonardo reaches "perfection . . . through a series of disgusts." Thus the "ideal art, in which the thought does not outstrip or lie beyond the proper range of its sensible embodiment," is the product of a "happy limit" or "narrowing" imposed by genius upon itself.

Virtually all of Pater's historical heroes practice this regimen of self-curtailment (it is the imaginary heroes, by contrast, who are usually found in ruins), whether it is the classicist Winckelmann, the anonymous creators of Greek sculpture, perhaps above all Flaubert, the focus of the essay on "Style." Here the apparently "natural economy" that allows the exemplary Flaubert to search out an almost "pre-existent" attraction between "a relative, somewhere in the world of thought, and its correlative" —anticipating but also reversing Eliot in advance—"somewhere in the world of language" is really the product of a hard-won "self-restraint, a skilful economy of means" rather than a natural one, "*ascesis*." Such an artistic program requires that "every component element" in any art "will have undergone exact trial," and that the artist " 'may be known,' " says Pater in a citation from Schiller, " 'by what he *omits*.' "

As a constant standard of evaluation, Pater's "formula" can be used to account for an artist's shortcomings as well as for his successes. Thus Pater measures the imperfections in Wordsworth as a deviation from the familiar norm that otherwise signifies the poet's strength: "When the really poetical motive worked at all," says Pater, "it united . . . the word and the idea; each, in the imaginative flame, becoming inseparably one with the other, by that fusion of matter and form, which is the characteristic of the highest poetical expression." Had "the writer himself" also "purged away" the "alien element" or "residue" that is nonetheless to be found elsewhere in his poetry—that which is merely "conventional, derivative, inexpressive"—then the imperfections in his work would have been entirely consumed, leaving Wordsworth's achievement far cleaner than it is. Indeed, even the distinction between classic and romantic formulated in the "Postscript" to *Appreciations* tends to vanish when the romantic artist manages, "by the very vividness and heat of [his] conception," to "purge away . . . all that is not . . . appropriate to it," eventually achieving a "form" which "becomes classical in its turn." By "refinement," then,

Pater means a rather precise kind of artistic combustion or "alchemy" by which manner and matter, form and content, coalesce into the willed perfection of an ideal work of art, or indeed, an ideal personality like Thomas Browne's, which earns Browne the measure of a "high and noble piece of chemistry."

The chemical metaphor even extends to Pater's notion of the structure of the perfect work, which is habitually described, in another celebrated figure, as a "crystal" whose symmetry and proportion bespeak "the perfect identification of matter and form" of which it is the product. Among the figure's variants are to be included gems like the "diamond," with which Pater represents the perfection of "Platonic aesthetics," and the quality of luminous whiteness attributed to such perfect aesthetic structures by the Paterian representations which denote them. Thus a "white light" seems to be "cast up" on Botticelli's madonnas, much as the "white flame" of Isabella's emotion "leaps" into her "white spirit" in *Measure for Measure* without spoiling, in an almost overdetermined use of the figure, her "cloistral whiteness" at the start of the play. In such moments the artist's "power of refraction, selecting, transforming, recombining the images it transmits" to "realise" a "situation" has been tried to such a degree that even "in a chill and empty atmosphere"—whether Shakespeare's courtroom or Botticelli's "wan," "abject," and even "cheerless" spirituality—he will "define," as always, "the focus where rays, in themselves pale and impotent, unite and begin to burn."

Like the moment, the ideal of the crystal, too, emerges at the very start of Pater's career in the 1864 "Diaphaneitè." Here the characteristic "blending and interpenetration" of the perfect work of art is already figured as, or embodied in, the "clear crystal nature" of genius in all its historical manifestations, present as it is in "the eternal outline of the antique" as well as in modern luminaries like Goethe or Carlyle.

This crystalline art and the fusion of which it is the product—that interpenetration wherein "the term . . . becomes, in a manner, what it signifies"—remain the constant ideal and evaluative standard in Pater's work as a whole, and may be traced through it accordingly. Thus, in *Marius*, for example, where religion is above all else an exercise in aesthetic perfection, even the proper worship of Isis is "itself a flame, of power to consume the whole material of existence in clear light and heat, with no smoldering residue." Indeed, in *Marius* the discipline of *ascesis* and the chemical figures that describe it are applied to life in all its variety. Hence the " 'labor of the file,' " which enriches the artistic work proper "by far more than the weight of precious metal it removed," is also to be found in the "military hardness, or *ascesis*" of a Roman officer like

Cornelius, whose craft of "selection" and "refusal" accounts as well for the composure and "freshness" of his personal demeanor and transmits to Marius himself "the clear, cold corrective, which the fever of his present life demanded" during his first years in Rome.

Indeed, there is no sphere of existence that cannot be viewed through, and elucidated by, the interrelated figures of fusion and *ascesis*, denoting as they do the necessary preconditions for the production of perfect work in art and life alike. Even the "exquisite conscience" of Stoic morality, says Pater, is a "mode of comeliness" or "purely aesthetic beauty," a product as it is of the same "management" that would erect in the sphere of social government an ideal polity whose aesthetic perfection also resembles the New Jerusalem implicit in the "scrupulous . . . love" of Marius's aesthetic Christianity. Christ himself conforms to the pattern of Paterian virtue, too, the image as he is of one who gives up or renounces "the greatest gifts" according to the same renunciative pattern that distinguishes all of Pater's successful artists and aesthetic personalities. Even Falsehood, according to Lucian in the "Conversation Not Imaginary" late in the novel, reflects the structure of Christ's perfection since, like Christianity, Stoicism, and art, falsehood, too, is "conscious of no alloy within." Hence Pater leaves us with the provocative paradox that perfect Falsehood is the result of its being, as it were, true to itself.

The ideal of fusion also goes by the name of "fitness" in *Marius* as well as in *Plato and Platonism*. In both cases the term manifestly refers to the way in which fusion, in an almost literal kind of way, represents a perfect match or fit between sensibility and whatever plastic medium it chooses in order to express itself, whether Marius's "daintily pliant sentences," "the fine arts" of Greece and "the art of discipline" in "the lives" of its citizens, even the " 'seamless' unity" of "the City of the Perfect" itself, Plato's Republic. Moreover, "aesthetic fitness" carries with it a latent reverberation or murmur of significant religious meaning as well. If the term denotes a uniform kind of aesthetic harmony in both Greek polytheism and primitive Christianity, it also connotes a more specific kind of Protestant morality and perfection suggested not only by the implicit identity between Marius's quest and the quest for "A paradise within thee, happier far," but also by his feeling that the proper choice of philosophy and conduct in life is a sign for what Pater calls "instinctive election." *Ascesis* allows of a more specifically Christian reading in this context, too, certainly in the sense of the trial that Pater's artist-heroes must undergo in a manner reminiscent of questing Protestant pilgrims like Spenser's, Milton's, or Bunyan's, although also of the Catholic kind that Pater himself was drawn to by identifying, with qualifications to be sure, the renunciative discipline of both the artist and the polity of Lacedaemon with "the monasticism of the Middle Ages," and by describing Marius's "close watching of his soul" as "a foresight of monasticism itself in the prophetic future." From this point of view, even the figure of the flame carries with it the specifically Christian variant of the " 'divine spark' " in the essay on Browne.

Moreover, the figure of fitness also stands for its own fitness as a figure, capable as it is of sounding a number of meanings or references at once without perceptible residue or surplusage. That the various levels or layers of life gathered under the tropes of fitness and *ascesis*—art, morality, politics, conduct, religion—share the same structure of articulation in Pater's rhetoric suggests that Pater's own work, in its apparent textural consistency from early to late, possesses as crystalline and transparent a structure as do the various isomorphic contexts it describes. Indeed, Pater's obvious delight in pagan polytheism, together with his virtual polymorphous perversity in the realm of the senses, suggests an equivalent delight in the polyphony of contexts to which his chemical rhetoric refers.

Of course, the figure of the artist as industrious and industrial (in both cases, read Victorian) chemist recalls, too, what is for Pater the paradigmatic beginning of art in the "perfectly accomplished metal-work" of early Greek sculpture. The precise link here is the figure of Hephaestus, "the god of fire," who becomes at this period in Greek life "representative of one only" of the "aspects" of fire, "its function, namely, in regard to early art." The god "becomes," in short, "the patron of smiths, bent with his labour at the forge, as people had seen such real workers." This is a notion of the modern artist that reappears, of course, in the Paterian Stephen of Joyce's *Portrait*, who will, in the celebrated words, "forge in the smithy of [his] soul the uncreated conscience of [his] race," and so render the Paterian artist an exemplary ironworker as well as a hieratic visionary. Indeed, metallurgy is the most persuasive historical source and model Pater has for the chemical fusion of medium and sensibility, and it provides his rhetoric with a working link to the genius the Greeks apparently had for "joining the parts together, with more perfect unity and smoothness of surface."

Early Greek art, then, is "the art of soldering" ("coupled" as it is here with "the name of Glaucus of Chios," it recalls, too, the "Yeux Glauques" fashioned by the hammer work of Pound's "medallions" in the *Mauberley* sequence), and it is for Pater the first kind of art to "perfect . . . artistic effect with economy of labour." Most important, however, is that the successful laying of the foundations of art here in the ironworker's forge is followed directly by the birth of personality itself in Greek art and culture, prepared for as it is in the stage of the smith, and remaining the buried model for artistic production in subsequent ages. Indeed, even the figure of temperament itself may be read with an accent on the tempering or combusting of hard metal or steel, much as it may also be read with an accent on the tempering of a musical instrument in order to insure the sweetness of its harmonies.

In addition to the chemical figure of the crystal, of course, Pater also uses the figure of the house or dwelling to generate a second vocabulary with which to describe the well-wrought work of art and the well-wrought personality. Carrying almost as much Protestant resonance as the ideal of fitness and the necessity of trial, the recurrent figure of the house gathers under itself a set of images that range from the Bunyanesque "*House Beautiful*," "which the creative minds of all generations—the artists and those who have treated life in the spirit of art—are always building together, for the refreshment of the human spirit," to the rather humbler but equivalent one of the "house" of his "thoughts" that Marius wishes to put in order. Here, too, we should include the Château of Deux-manoirs in which Gaston passes his childhood and which is the "visible record of all the accumulated sense of human existence among its occupants"; the cathedral at Chartres to which Gaston journeys in youth and which begins to suggest that Pater's unfinished romance is in fact organized by its buildings; and, indeed, the cathedral that structures "Apollo in Picardy," as well as those that give their names to "Vézelay" and "Notre-Dame d'Amiens."

Like the chemical crystal, the figure of the house or dwelling—"the airy building of the brain," as Pater puts it in his essay on Wordsworth—is a cipher for a notion of cultural achievement whose derivation is to be understood in the murmuring Freudian sense implied by Pater's occasional proleptic use of the terms "sublimation," "sublimes," and "sublimates" as synonyms for the activity of *ascesis* itself. As a product of the fierce antinatural discipline required of genius on both the level of individual achievement and the level of civilization as a whole, both ciphers for culture, crystal and dwelling alike, bespeak the denial of instinct embodied in the "girding of the loins in youth" which characterizes all of Pater's successful culture workers and which is precisely what is lacking among those dreamier members of his imaginary contingent who fail to achieve what is expected of their youthful promise.

Pater's use of the figure of the house is especially evident in the abundant species of "intellectual structure" to be found in his work: the "sanctuary" of Florentine painting; the "literary architecture" presented in "Style" and in the portrait of Browne; the "edifice" and "theoretic building" of Plato's philosophy; the religious house of Cecilia in *Marius*; the village church in the imaginary portrait "Denys L'Auxerrois"; even the "wall" and "chamber" of personality and mind that emerge in the "Conclusion" to *The Renaissance*. Indeed, Pater uses the figure to describe the structure of the individual as often as he uses it to describe the various cultural edifices of which the individual forms a part. Hence it provides the overarching metaphor of the personal "habitation," "material shrine," or "house of thought" into which Florian Deleal fashions himself in "The Child in the House," as well as the rich image for thought as a whole of "the house within" in *Plato and Platonism*, with "its many chambers, its memories and associations, upon its inscribed and pictured walls."

Included, too, is the activity of "building," whether Florian's "brain-building" in "The Child in the House"; the "word-building" that Marius learns from the rhetoricians; or the building of the cathedral in "Denys." Of crystalline genius itself, Pater calls it the "basement type" of cultural life as a whole in "Diaphaneitè," rendering the figure a foundation in its own turn for the house of Pater's own thought insofar as his work aspires to be an expression of the virtues and requirements of civilization, too.

Moreover, much in the same way that Pater can judge Wordsworth negatively by the measure of fusion and fitness, so can he also use the figure of the house to picture genius in ruins. Here one recalls in particular those decayed and dilapidated houses in the imaginary portraits, where Pater's protagonists are often at as much of a loss to repair themselves as the figures with which they coincide. Hence the "desolate house" in which Sebastian van Storck loses his unfulfilled life; the "burnt or overthrown" grange in which the unhappy Duke Carl perishes with his bride-to-be; the sturdy but nonetheless "irregular . . . ground-plan" of Gaston's hereditary château; even the neglected and half-ruined family mausoleum which Marius, in an almost graphic psychoanalysis, must rebuild in order to complete and compose the unfinished business of his life.

With the figure of the house or dwelling, too, comes the early feeling and the later desire, so important to Marius, to Florian, and to Emerald Uthwart all alike, for "a peculiar ideal of home." Tangled in a matrix of associations that links a pagan spirit of place or sense of "local sanctities" with a Wordsworthian one, the Paterian ideal of "home" is a plea for a sense of ground or attachment to a "visible locality and abiding-place, the walls and towers of which" a character like Marius "might really trace and tell." Indeed, in *Gaston*, "those who kept up the central tradition of their house" feel always bound to "the visible spot, where the memory of their kindred was liveliest and most exact."

From this desire for ground follows another of Pater's characteristic tropes for aesthetic competence and production, although it is one that begins to threaten the unity of the Paterian ideal we have seen so far. This third way of talking about art lies in a vocabulary of the natural whose most recurrent figure is that of flowers, especially the rose that W. H. Mallock took as a pejorative emblem for Pater's achievement as a whole, and with whose image Wilde opens *The Picture of Dorian Gray*.

In Pater's first book, the entire "mythology of the Italian Renaissance" is figured as a "new" and "strange flower" in the sketch of Pico. Within the period itself, collective achievements like the poetry of the Pleiad constitute a "special flower," too, just as individual works like Du Bellay's *Regrets* are called "pale flowers" in their own right. Indeed, cultural conditions themselves are gathered under the trope of "sacred soil" in the portrait of Winckelmann, thus providing a ground or field of understanding for both Michelangelo's "blossoming" and Leonardo's "strange blossoms and fruits hitherto unknown."

In *Appreciations*, these tropes of the natural are to be found at work with the same consistency, with Coleridge's organicism functioning as a kind of touchstone for figures like the "flowers" of Rossetti's "poetry" or "the sudden blossoming" of Coleridge's own genius. Even the high discipline of conduct in the Lacedaemon of *Plato and Platonism* is a "perfect flower," just as the Republic itself is envisioned as a "perfect flower" in its own right, both of them examples of the late blossoming of "seeds" dropped by the "flower" of earlier philosophers like Pythagoras. In *Marius*, of course, the abundance of flowers of all kinds in the pageantry of Marius's native religion bespeaks its "spontaneous force" and remains a sign for the "undiminished freshness" of youthful impressionability throughout the novel. In young manhood, Marius "was always as fresh as the flowers he wore," while, even as he progresses in years, his sensibility remains fresh enough to be figured as "his . . . Epicurean rose-garden."

Such an alliance between these figures of nature and "direct sensation" is perfectly apt here, since Pater wishes to use his tropes as a means of identifying the crystalline perfection of genius with the "transparency," as he puts it in "Diaphaneitè," "of nature" itself. To match the idea or matter of a work or a personality with its perfect sensible embodiment means making "the term . . . what it signifies" and so constituting a full and transparent sign in which the idea and its sensible vehicle become fit or fused in "a veritable counterfeit of nature" itself; "painted glass," as Pater puts it in *Gaston*, "mimicking the clearness of the open sky."

Indeed, art and culture seen as "natural objects" coincide in Pater's mythology with those periods of history in which subjectivity itself is paramount, whether in "the natural objects of the . . . Pointed style" of the Gothic cathedral, whose recapturing of nature and of freshness gives it a precedence for Pater over the Romanesque style which it supersedes in the late cathedral pieces included in *Miscellaneous Studies*; or, indeed, in the supposed original for all the renaissances in history, the civilization of Greece, "springing as if straight from the soil." Hence Gaston's notion of "modernity"—of renaissance—is the same as Pater's: "for a poetry, as veritable, as intimately near, as corporeal, as the new faces of the hour, the flowers of the actual season." It is formalized best by Bruno, the "vigour" of whose "doctrine" is "like some hardy growth out of the very heart of nature."

Accompanying these kinds of figures and their attendant vision of man's genius as a product of nature is a theology of the work of art as "half-sacred," as Pater puts it in the essay on Coleridge in *Appreciations*, and which puts us only a step away from the Religion of Art of the 1890s. More important, however, is that the notion of art as a sacred object carries with it a vestige, retrieved in Pater's pagan Wordsworth, of the "natural or half-natural objects" that constitute the "relics" of early Greek religion in which the "visible idol" was "conceived" as "the actual dwelling-place of a god." Much, then, as the modern notion of the artist as ironworker can be linked to the beginnings of Greek sculpture, so the modern and quasi-religious notion of the artist's voice speaking through his work can be linked in turn to the "sacred presence" of a god in a pagan artifact or a particular spot of ground, and linked in *Gaston*, in a mono-theistic and less persuasive revision, to "the indwelling spirit" apprehended by Bruno in life as a whole.

It is these natural qualities that constitute the transcendent mode of discourse to which the Paterian artist aspires, a privileged style of language which is undissociated and which carries with it both an ideal and an understanding of art that Frank Kermode has characterized as a verita-ble "physical presence"—in Joyce's Catholic terms, as the word made flesh. For Pater himself, of course, such an aesthetic ideal remains Greek in its constant attempt to regain those "Homeric conditions," as he calls them in *Plato*, under which "experience was intuition, and life a continu-ous surprise." Here, too, "every object," like the object created by modern art, is "unique," and "all knowledge" a knowledge of "the concrete and the particular, face to face," in another Christian echo or anticipation, "delightfully."

Such natural transparence and presence, then, are the chief proper-ties of genius's "eternal outline" as early as "Diaphaneitè" and as late as *Plato*, where "the eternal outline" of all perfect achievement is asserted to be "a definition of it which can by no supposition become a definition of anything else." The work of art, in other words, is an object for which no substitutions are possible, an object, as we are accustomed to seeing it, that is original and unique. It is, of course, precisely this kind of modern—and Greek—originality that is signified by the privileged moment's ideal of "immediate vision" and the autochthony it bestows upon its beholder, although it is also autochthony that is signified by the figure of the gemlike flame itself, at least in the Promethean profile of fire adduced by Bachelard, for example, who places together "under the name of the Prometheus complex all those tendencies which impel us to know as much as our fathers, more than our fathers, as much as our teachers, more than our teachers." Hence the gemlike flame and the autogenesis with which it is linked represent, too, the wishful priority of modernity itself, engaged as it always is, in all its renaissances, in an attempt to achieve "the advantage of having no past."

Given Pater's quest for the personality of the artist as it shows forth in his work, it is hardly unusual that he seeks the form of perfection in a language of "organic wholeness," as he calls it in his essay on Lamb. What remains disturbing, however, is the degree to which the crystalline consistency of Pater's own vision is put into question by the presence of this language of nature within a constellation of figures that is, as we have seen, otherwise ruled by a language whose vocabulary is concerned with the willful discipline of culture. Is the artist an almost passive or unconscious flowering or growth in a natural rhythm of human history? Or is he a Flaubertian martyr of *ascesis*, the product of a rigorous discipline of repression and eventual sublimation, an emblem for civilization itself? Having constructed a language that bespeaks the conquest of nature by means of *ascesis* and its attendant achievements of fitness and the home or abode of sensibility, Pater also wishes to naturalize his account of culture by speaking of it through this second or covering language of organicism and natural growth. His remark in "Style" that "the house" an artist "has built is rather a body he has informed" focuses and magnifies this discontinuity by showing us how Pater's rhetoric wishes to ground its originating principle of expressiveness in the soil of a nature that is itself subdued or repressed by the very exercise of the powers it is supposed to signify.

Such a difficulty in making continuous or coincident the figures of chemical fusion and *ascesis* with those of flowers, blossoms, and other kinds of natural growth suggests that there is a "residue" or "surplusage" in Pater's transparent vision after all. We can even locate a set of hybrid figures in which Pater means either to ignore or to reconcile this discontinuity by using both figural languages in tandem, as though their presuppositions were coterminous. In *Marius*, for example, the votive rites to Isis include the display of gold and silver ornaments simultaneously with "real fruit and flowers," an equivocating double image like the "gem or flower," "flower or crystal" with which Pater means to figure alike the object of philosophical discourse and comely manners in *Plato*. Both examples suggest the kind of discontinuous assumptions that are particularly manifest in a similar but extended cluster of figures in *Plato* meant to describe the Pythagorean elements in Plato himself:

> Ancient, half-obliterated inscriptions on the mental walls, the mental tablet, seeds of knowledge to come, shed by some flower of it long ago, it was in an earlier period of time they had been laid up in him, to blossom again now, so kindly, so firmly!

Much as *ascesis* and the doctrine of fitness fall under the machinery of culture rather than under the rhythms of nature, so the "inscriptions" on "the mental tablet" here require an implicit understanding of the history of philosophy as a history of writing, and an understanding of the history of culture in turn as an edifice or construction. Such presuppositions, of course, are far different from the ones that emerge in the second group of figures at work in the passage, and that tacitly require us to translate the cultural categories of writing and building into the natural ones of "seeds," "flower," and "blossom." Indeed, in the essay on Lamb the same discontinuous tropes are to be found as well, with "men's life as a whole" described at one moment as an "organic wholeness" and, at another, as "the whole mechanism of humanity."

The trick is to resolve these two ways of talking, but the difficulties are formidable. How can a single model for culture accommodate the requirements of sublimation on the one hand and those of organic presence on the other? How can the artist as smith be reconciled with the artist as natural or hieratic visionary? How, in short, can self-expression be identified with self-curtailment?

We can at least see our way to a tentative resolution by noting, as Pater's gardenly figures should have suggested already, that the language of the natural is, after all, really a language of cultivation. Marius's "undiminished freshness" may well be represented by the figures of "seeds," "blossoms," and so on, although with the caveat that these are but elements in his "Epicurean rose-garden," in that circumscribed plot of a paradise within by which, for Pater at least, nature is already begotten by nurture. Moreover, cultivation is also a polite word for colonization, and suggests the achievement of sensibility to be similar to the annexation of territory in an imperialist line of reasoning that turns out to be a natural part of industrialization itself, at least in the Victorian context that gives the metaphor its contours.

Where nature is, there nurture already was, we might say of the organic in Pater. Nature appears only as representation, that is, in figures so blunt—"blossoms," "seeds," and so on—that they call attention to themselves as figures even as Pater himself reminds us, albeit with nostalgia for the illusion of a prelapsarian age of presence, that "experience, which has gradually saddened the earth's colours for us, stiffened its motions, withdrawn from it some blithe and debonair presence, has quite changed the character of the science of nature, as we understand it." To be sure, Pater here goes on to valorize "the suspicion of a mind latent in nature," although it is of the Hegelian kind whose focus is properly that of culture in Pater's own sense of the term, with nature clearly reduced to a metaphor, perhaps in evidence of that very dissociation lamented by Pater in his modernist myth of a lost golden age of presence and immediacy.

Such a formulation nonetheless maintains the irreducibility of the opposition between nature and culture, with the supposed "freshness" of Pater's heroes and their work coexisting uneasily with their status as exemplary sufferers. Indeed, the tension is in some ways a classically Victorian one between science and religion, reason and affection, which Pater reinterprets and brings to bear as tropes on questions of art and culture in his attempt to achieve a higher level of argument capable of resolving contradiction, or at least of dismissing some of the factors that contribute to it. With the chemistry of the crystal suggesting that theological organicism is one of Pater's least persuasive dialects, the language of nature remains largely a covering language in his texts, a language that tries to substitute for the renunciative labor of culture the appearance of spontaneous growth and visionary power in order to recompense the artist for his toil by granting him the conviction that he has found his way to something divine.

In the following essay, the page citations given for Pater's "Conclusion" refer to "Poems by William Morris," *Westminster Review* 90 (Oct. 1868): 309. All other page citations for Pater's works refer to the *New Library Edition of the Works*, London: Macmillan, 1910.

BILLIE ANDREW INMAN

The Intellectual Context
of Walter Pater's "Conclusion"

For eight years before Pater wrote the conclusion to "Poems by William Morris," the first version of the "Conclusion" to *The Renaissance*, his mind had been selecting and storing ideas, images, and techniques that would come together in the composition of this work. Readings in philosophy and Goethe dating 1860–3, readings in aesthetics and Renan dating 1863–5, and recent readings in belles lettres and contemporary science—all came to bear upon this brief conclusion.

The immediate inspiration for the "Conclusion" was very likely Morris' *Earthly Paradise*, Parts I and II of which (March–August) had appeared in April of 1868 and which Pater was reviewing. On its face, in its original context, the "Conclusion" is a defence of Morris' new, un-utilitarian poetry. Moreover, the comprehensive theme of the "Conclusion" could have been derived from *The Earthly Paradise*. As a reviewer, Pater discerned in this work a dominant theme that he was able to empathize with, and which he expressed in the review in one of his very best phrases: "the desire of beauty, quickened by the sense of death." The "Conclusion" is his own elaboration upon this theme: the first half evokes the sense of death, the second half the desire of beauty quickened by the sense of death. In addition, the persona in the "Conclusion" is in some respects like the Wanderers in Morris' poem, who learn from their long wandering that the earthly paradise they have sought does not exist and

From *Journal of Prose Studies* 4, no. 1 (May 1981). Copyright © 1981 by Frank Cass & Co., Ltd.

that they cannot escape death. At the end of the quest, a remnant of these men arrive at "a nameless city in a distant sea." After describing many of their experiences for the Elders of the city, their spokesman states their primary discovery—that "the lot of all men should be ours / A chequered day of sunshine and of showers / Fading to twilight and dark night at last." As the Wanderers contemplate the remainder of their lives, it is as if they say, as Pater does in the last paragraph of his review, "we have an interval and then we cease to be"; how can we "make as much as possible of the interval?" (312). Like Pater's "wisest" people, they choose to spend the interval, in part, "in art and song," retelling stories from their native lands, but with an awareness of death that makes every pleasure exquisitely melancholy. In other words, the dilemma of the persona in the "Conclusion" and the resolution of the dilemma echo the dilemma of the Wanderers and its resolution. The Apology of *The Earthly Paradise* recommends to readers, who are assumed to be in a similar dilemma, a similar resolution:

> But rather, when aweary of your mirth,
> From full hearts still unsatisfied ye sigh,
> And, feeling kindly unto all the earth,
> Grudge every minute as it passes by,
> Made the more mindful that the sweet days die—
> —Remember me a little then I pray,
> The idle singer of an empty day.

Pater's "Conclusion" might be called a brilliant elaboration upon Morris' theme—"Grudge every minute as it passes by / Made the more mindful that the sweet days die." But the appeal for readers of Pater is not so much in the theme itself as in the texture of the elaboration and the rich and complex intellectual context that informs it, the context that this paper proposes to elucidate.

The first half of the "Conclusion" (the first four paragraphs in the 1868 version), which creates the sense of death, is not a continuous argument. It is two discourses, each with its beginning and end, the first derived from contemporary science and the second from sceptical philosophy. Anyone who approaches the first half as if it were one argument and begins a close analysis of its logic will soon discern a central inconsistency: the persona speaks authoritatively in the first paragraph about the constitution of the physical world and the unity of humanity with the physical world; but in the second and third paragraphs, he denies knowledge of the physical world and proclaims the isolation of the individual person. For example, the most recent critic to analyze the 'argument,' Perry Meisel, soon discovers "blindness" and "deception" in Pater's mind. Summarizing the logical problem, he states:

If experience is ringed round by personality, where is the 'without' from
which forces are supposedly to pass through it? Indeed, nothing at all is
supposed to be able to pierce the individual ringed round in his 'isolation',
even though such a claim requires for its own coherence some notion
of an inside and an outside clearly separated from one another. Pater's
solipsism, in other words, is erected on a spatial metaphor whose truth
he is here intent to deny as he requires it in order to deny it.

What Meisel does not see is that Pater is representing "modern thought"
in the first half of the "Conclusion," as he says in the first sentence. He is
saying that whether we "begin with that which is without," as modern
science does, or "begin with the inward world of thought and feeling," as
modern philosophy does, we become equally disillusioned, because neither
gives us any basis for metaphysical certainty. Both approaches cast us into
flux, depressing us with the sense of death. In short, Pater is saying that
whether we turn to science or philosophy, however different their assumptions and approaches may be, we do not find an assuring presence.

I have three reasons for saying that Pater was influenced by contemporary science in the writing of the first paragraph of the "Conclusion." First, he refers to science by name in the text, twice. Second, he
imitates the style of scientific demonstration, using the imperative "Let us
begin" and "Fix upon it"; the second person plural pronoun; the present
tense of verbs; and many common concrete nouns. All of these techniques
had been used together repeatedly in scientific writing from Bacon's to
Tyndall's. Third, the concept developed in the first paragraph was one of
the leading conclusions of biological scientists working in the late 1860s,
the physical basis of life, or the absence of any force but chemical forces in
all of life's processes, including thought. This concept was powerfully
presented by George Henry Lewes in an article that appeared in the
avant-garde *Fortnightly Review* at the beginning of the month in which
Pater completed his review on Morris, July 1868. It was the third part in a
four-part essay entitled "Mr. Darwin's Hypotheses." Although there is no
external evidence that Pater read this article, the issue of the *Fortnightly* in
which it appeared also contained Swinburne's "Notes on Designs of the
Old Masters at Florence," which nobody doubts that Pater read. Lewes
had informed himself about cell life by reading Max Schultze and other
German cytologists, and in the first several pages of this essay he discusses
their findings. His opening sentence must have been fascinating to contemporary readers: "The simplest form of organic life is not—as commonly
stated—a cell, but a microscopic lump of jelly-like substance, or protoplasm" (61). But his biggest news was that a cell is " 'a nucleus with
surrounding protoplasm' " (61). Earlier in the nineteenth century proto-

plasm had been associated with cells, but that it was the essential environment of the nuclei of all cells had not been assumed. Lewes summarizes the leading scientific conception of existence in nature, stating: "Every individual object, organic or inorganic, is the sum of two factors:—first, the relation of its constituent molecules to each other; secondly, the relation of its substance to all surrounding objects" (62). He explains that every cell has a life cycle of its own: "it is born, is developed, and decays" (62). After discussing cells in relation to lower forms of life, he turns to higher forms, using the following web image, somewhat similar to Pater's "strange perpetual weaving and unweaving of ourselves" (311): "Rising still higher, we see animal forms of which the web is woven out of myriads upon myriads of cells, with various cell-products, processes, fibres, tubes" (62).

If Pater read Lewes' article in July 1868, it could have acted as a prompter, but it probably did not introduce him to the idea that the physical constituents of the human body are constantly changing and that they are integral to a larger physical system. Herbert Spencer had already expressed these ideas in *The Principles of Biology*, 1864–7, although he was apparently unaware of the significance of protoplasm to cell life. It is uncertain whether Pater read Spencer, but the conceptual and verbal parallels between Spencer's text and Pater's make it seem likely that he did. Spencer discusses at length the chemical elements that compose organic matter; he discusses "the unceasing change of matter which oxygen and other agents produce throughout the system"; and he discusses "certain molecular re-arrangements of an unstable kind." He summarizes his description of organic change, as follows:

> Thus we have growth, decay, changes of temperature, changes of consistence, changes of velocity, changes of excretion, all going on in connexion; and it may be as truly said of a glacier as of an animal, that by ceaseless integration and disintegration it gradually undergoes an entire change of substance without losing its individuality.

Spencer's very assurance that individuality is preserved in spite of change might have implanted a fear that inspired Pater's image, in the fourth paragraph, of a person "losing even his personality, as the elements of which he is composed pass into new combinations" (311).

At one point the verbal similarity between Pater's text and Spencer's is striking. In the sixth sentence, Pater states: "Our physical life is a perpetual motion of them [elements in process]—the passage of the blood, the wasting and repairing of the lenses of the eye" (310). Spencer's

Chapter 4 in Volume I is entitled "Waste and Repair," and one lengthy paragraph is concerned with the eye, or specifically the simultaneous waste and repair of vision. Another verbal parallel, "from moment to moment," occurs in passages that deal with heat. Pater states:

> This at least of flame-like our life has, that it is but the concurrence renewed from moment to moment of forces parting sooner or later on their ways.
>
> (310)

Spencer had stated:

> There can be no doubt that this thermal re-action which chemical action from moment to moment produces in the body, is from moment to moment an aid to further chemical action.

If Pater did not read Lewes and Spencer, it is plain that he had acquired scientific information like theirs somewhere, and it is interesting to observe that in handling scientific matter, he was careful to follow a principle enunciated by Hegel in the *Ästhetik*, which he had borrowed from the Queen's College Library, 28 April–23 May, 1863. In the *Ästhetik*, Hegel distinguishes between the scientist's mode of thinking, and the artist's, stating, "the beauty of art is presented to sense, feeling, perception, and imagination: its field is not that of thought, and the comprehension of its activity and its creations demands another faculty than that of scientific intelligence." Pater had applied Hegel's distinction previously. In "Coleridge's Writings," he praises Wordsworth for expressing as a sentiment his conception of an intelligence in nature, in a manner "which perfect art allows" (in other words, which perfect art allows, according to Hegel), while criticizing Goethe for expressing a similar idea in "Gott and Welt" in technical, scientific language, which he says is "something stiffer than poetry." He was to apply it again, in 1869, in "Notes on Leonardo da Vinci," in saying: "Goethe himself reminds one how great for the artist may be the danger of over-much science . . . he did not invariably find the spell-word, and in the second part of *Faust*, presents us with a mass of science which has no artistic character at all." True to Hegelian principle, Pater, in the first paragraph of the "Conclusion," avoids Goethe's 'mistake': his technique is to hold scientific detail to a minimum and to use a maximum of metaphor, even though he is stating scientific conclusions and suggesting the authoritative style of scientific demonstration.

As Pater turned inward in the second paragraph of the "Conclusion," he was, as far as sources are concerned, moving backwards in time.

The undergraduate register at the Queen's College Library shows that Pater pursued a self-formed course of reading in philosophy beginning in November 1860 and ending in December 1863. The first philosophical book borrowed was Volume II of Fichte's *Werke*, containing *Darstellung der Wissenschaftslehre (The Science of Knowledge)*, *Die Bestimmung des Menschen (The Vocation of Man)*, and other works. He proceeded from Fichte to Hobbes, to Ritter's *History of Ancient Philosophy* in Alexander J. W. Morrison's translation, to Hume, Kant, Schleiermacher, Reid, Berkeley, Bacon, Locke, Hegel, Lucretius, Plato's *Theætetus*, Fichte again (this time, Volume V of the *Werke*, including *Versuch einer Kritik aller Offenbarung (Essay toward a Critique of All Revelation)*, *Die Anweisung zum seligen Leben (The Way towards the Blessed Life)*, and other works), *Theætetus* again, and, finally, Eduard Zeller's *Die Philosophie der Griechen*. In his reading Pater encountered a number of times the sceptical argument stated in the "Conclusion." That it had an impact upon him is indicated in "The History of Philosophy," unpublished manuscript No. 3 in the collection at the Houghton Library, Harvard University. In this manuscript, Pater explains the effect that reading philosophy has on a young truth-seeker. He states that the first step in the intellectual quest is always scepticism, and as philosophers who introduce the neophyte to scepticism, he lists Fichte, Berkeley, Spinoza, and Kant, in that order. At another point in the manuscript he lists as milestones of modern scepticism "Berkeley's Theory of Vision, Kant's Criticism, and Fichte's _____." That Pater did not remember the name of Fichte's book is not very significant, since he often left blanks where names and specific examples were needed. What is significant is that Fichte appears, with Berkeley and Kant, in both lists. Add to this prominence the fact that Fichte came first in the order of reading in 1860, and it is easy to conclude that Pater made his first step in the philosophical search, the step toward scepticism, while reading Fichte. Internal evidence also points to Fichte as the primary influence. Pater's explanation of the sceptical argument in the second and third paragraphs of the "Conclusion" bears more resemblance to Fichte's in *The Vocation of Man* than to that of any other philosopher. The book as a whole follows the course of one neophyte's quest for truth, from the first stirring of the philosophic impulse to the final resolution in faith. It is divided into three parts: "Doubt," "Knowledge," and "Faith." The theme of the perpetual flux is developed in "Doubt," with an emphasis, like Pater's, on moments that pass so rapidly that they can never be said to *be*. For example, Fichte has his neophyte say: "Nature pursues her course of ceaseless change, and while I yet speak of the moment which I sought to detain before me it is gone, and all is changed; and in like manner, before I had fixed my observation upon it, all was otherwise." Near the end of the section called "Knowledge," Fichte explains the impossibility of knowing anything by empirical means. The first sentence states the main theme of the second and third paragraphs of the "Conclusion," and even suggests the organization of the first half of the whole:

> There is nothing enduring, either out of me, or in me, but only ceaseless change. I know of no being, not even of my own. There is no being. I myself absolutely know not, and am not. Pictures are:—they are the only things which exist, and they know of themselves after the fashion of pictures:—pictures which float past without there being anything past which they float; which, by means of like pictures, are connected with each other:—pictures without anything which is pictured in them, without significance and without aim. I myself am one of these pictures: —nay, I am not even this, but merely a confused picture of these pictures. All reality is transformed into a strange dream, without a life which is dreamed of, and without a mind which dreams it;—into a dream which is woven together in a dream of itself. Intuition is the dream; thought,—the source of all the being and all the reality which I imagine, of my own being, my own powers, and my own purposes,—is the dream of that dream.

The idea here that nothing exists but pictures in the mind is paralleled by Pater's "swarm of impressions," "unstable, flickering, inconsistent, which burn, and are extinguished with our consciousness of them" (310); his idea that the pictures float is paralleled by Pater's "race of the midstream" and his image of an impression as "a tremulous wisp constantly reforming itself on the stream"; and the dream imagery is paralleled by Pater's famous idea that each mind keeps "as a solitary prisoner its own dream of a world" (311). Fichte's description of the solipsistic mind is enhanced by the following additional statement: "Not immediately from thee to me, nor from me to thee, flows forth the knowledge which we have of each other—we are separated by an insurmountable barrier". In Pater's text the barrier is called "that thick wall of personality through which no real voice has ever pierced on its way to us, or from us to that, which we can only conjecture to be without" (310).

That the sceptical argument had a peculiar fascination for Pater is suggested by the fact that when explaining scepticism in *The Vocation of Man*, Fichte was trying to discredit it. To him the solipsistic state to which scepticism led was so absurd as to prompt a new approach to the whole question of truth, which he pursued in "Faith." Whether Pater was initially persuaded by Fichte's basis for faith is an open question, but that he rejected it at some point is obvious from statements in "The History of

Philosophy." In this manuscript Pater says that even though scepticism seems fantastic to most people, it is "the dominion of the common sense for all really instructed minds." And, further, "The mind which has once broken the smooth surface of what seemed its self-evident principles can never again be as natural as a child's, nor perhaps will it ever find an equivalent for its earlier untouched healthfulness in that rationalised conception of experience, and man's relation to it, by which it is the ambition of philosophy to replace it."

Less pervasive influences on the second and third paragraphs of the "Conclusion" than Fichte's very likely came from Hume, Berkeley, and Plato. Hume's influence can be seen in Pater's repeated use of the term *impressions*, instead of Berkeley's *sensations*, and Fichte's *pictures*. The term *infinitely divisible*, used in the third paragraph of the "Conclusion," perhaps also came from Hume. Pater states: "Analysis goes a step further still, and tells us that . . . each of them [impressions of the individual] is limited by time, and that as time is infinitely divisible, each of them is infinitely divisible also" (311). This seems to be what Pater understood from Hume's Sections I and II in Part II of Book I of *A Treatise of Human Nature*, entitled "Of the Infinite Divisibility of Our Ideas of Space and Time" and "Of the Infinite Divisibility of Space and Time," respectively. If these two chapters were the source, however, Pater misinterpreted Hume or disagreed with him. Hume had taken up the subject of infinite divisibility of time in order to deny it, assuming that time had to be made up of indivisible parts, or there could be no progression. He states: "For if in time we could never arrive at an end of division, and if each moment, as it succeeds another, were not perfectly single and indivisible, there would be an infinite number of co-existent moments, or parts of time; which I believe will be allow'd to be an arrant contradiction." For Hume, infinite divisibility was identical with "a total annihilation," which he rejected. Of course, Pater could simply have been presenting the point of view of Aristotle, who said in the *Physics*: "every line is divided *ad infinitum*. Hence it is so with time." It is important to note, however, that Pater absorbed Hume's distinctive and central idea (recreated derisively by Fichte in his rendering of the sceptical stance) that the mind is only a collection of perceptions, in constant motion. Hume states in the *Treatise*: "But setting aside some metaphysicians of this kind [who maintain that they perceive something simple and continuous that they call themselves], I may venture to affirm of the rest of mankind, that they are nothing but a bundle or collection of different perceptions, which succeed each other with an inconceivable rapidity, and are in a perpetual flux and movement."

Berkeley's influence can be seen specifically in the following passage: "when reflection begins to act upon those objects [which surround the perceiver] they are dissipated under its influence, the cohesive force is suspended like a trick of magic, each object is loosed into a group of impressions, colour, odour, texture, in the mind of the observer" (310). Although Hume referred to senses other than sight in a general way, it was Berkeley who repeatedly referred to sensations from the other senses, as well as to colour in visual sensations.

Plato influenced the "Conclusion" in two ways, the first of which was indirect. Reading Plato's *Theætetus*, with marginal summaries and copious notes in Lewis Campbell's eloquent English, in March 1863, must have been an awakening experience for Pater. Here, in this ancient text, he found concepts that he had thought to be modern: such as, relativity, the perpetual flux, and the subjectivity of knowledge. The Pythagorean argument detailed in this dialogue must have seemed like a review of the sceptical ideas that he had previously found in modern sources. He concluded, as he states in "History of Philosophy," that "successive metaphysical systems have been, in fact, little more than so many recombinations of the pieces which Plato had long ago placed, once for all upon the board." The indirect influence of Plato's *Theætetus*, then, was to confirm sceptical ideas that Pater had already absorbed from other sources. One passage in the "Conclusion," however, which seems not to have been anticipated in any of the other sources that Pater had read, could have been inspired directly by a passage in *Theætetus*. Pater refers to objects, not "in the solidity with which language invests them, but of impressions unstable, flickering, inconsistent" (310). The reference seems to echo the following passage from Section 157 of *Theætetus*:

> there arises a general reflection, that there is no one self-existent thing, but everything is becoming and in relation; and being must be altogether abolished, although from habit and ignorance we are compelled even in this discussion to retain use of the term. But great philosophers tell us that we are not to allow either the word 'something,' or 'belonging to something,' or 'to me,' or 'this' or 'that', or any other detaining name to be used; in the language of nature all things are being created and destroyed, coming into being and passing into new forms; nor can any name fix or detain them.

Thus, what appears to be in Pater's text an anticipation of an idea current in modern semantics—that language creates an illusion of solidity and certainty—could easily have been derived from Plato, who regarded it as already established by other philosophers.

In sum, in the first half of the "Conclusion" Pater shows that modern science can only integrate the human being into the chemical universe and that philosophy, when it presumes to convey truth and is "sincere" ("William Morris," 309), can only consign the human mind to a solipsistic isolation. These are the "truths" that "the modern world is in possession of," to which Pater had referred contemptuously in the paragraph preceding the conclusion to "William Morris"—truths that do not make the spirit free but overwhelm it with the sense of death. In the second half of the "Conclusion" Pater tries to circumvent science and philosophy by simulating a return to an earlier mental state, or, as he calls it in "The History of Philosophy," an "unreflecting" and "unsuspecting receptivity of mind." He has accepted the idea of eventual dissolution, the truth of science, and the subjectivity of knowledge, the truth of philosophy; but he endeavours to compensate for them through intensity of consciousness, and he subdues philosophy to his own purpose by making it an agent in the process of perceiving.

Pater knew at the time he was writing *Marius the Epicurean* that the experiential stance, which he had created in the second half of the "Conclusion," did not necessarily follow from the metaphysical propositions of the flux and the subjectivity of knowledge, which he had laid down in the first half, and he probably knew this when he wrote the "Conclusion." Two philosophers with whom he was familiar had preceded him in assuming an experiential ethic after stating a sceptical philosophical position—David Hume and Aristippus of Cyrene, Hume by simply circumventing scepticism of the senses and Aristippus by apparently "deducing" the experiential ethic from the sceptical base. It is significant that Pater did not list Hume in "The History of Philosophy" among the philosophers who led the neophyte into scepticism, even though he must have known that Hume was recognized in the history of philosophy as a leading sceptic. The philosophers who seemed to him to strengthen scepticism were, as he indicates in this manuscript, those like Fichte, Berkeley, and Kant, who tried to reconstruct philosophy upon metaphysical bases but failed to convince him of the validity of these bases. Hume, of course, made no such attempt; after reasoning his way into solipsism, he simply went on living, considering sceptical doubt of external reality to be a malady that he could never be entirely cured of, but that he could control by not dwelling too much in the mind. Hume ends Part I of *A Treatise of Human Nature* by vowing not to be ruled by philosophy:

> Most fortunately it happens, that since reason is incapable of dispelling these clouds [questions and anxieties into which his philosophy has thrown him], nature herself suffices to that purpose, and cures me of this

philosophical melancholy and delirium, either by relaxing this bent of mind, or by some avocation, and lively impression of my senses, which obliterate all these chimeras. I dine, I play a game of back-gammon, I converse, and am merry with my friends; and when after three or four hours' amusement, I wou'd return to these speculations, they appear so cold, and strain'd, and ridiculous that I cannot find [it] in my heart to enter into them any farther.

Here then I find myself absolutely and necessarily determin'd to live, and talk, and act like other people in the common affairs of life.

Pater states in "The History of Philosophy," that Hume, with his scepticism "of the supposed inherent judgment of the understanding" cleared away metaphysical cobwebs and returned the mind to "the corrective experience of the senses." In the same manuscript he says that realizing the impossibility of proving metaphysical ideas or even of knowing "the mental substance of ourselves" can help one relax philosophically, or, more precisely, "bring us back with a great sense of relief after the long strain of a too curious self-inquiry to the phenomena of the superficial natural world."

Thus, the great Scottish philosopher could have set the example for Pater's turn toward sensuous appreciation in the second half of the "Conclusion." Pater could also have been familiar with the straightforward injunction of the sceptical Aristippus of Cyrene to appreciate the moment. Pater had had the opportunity, upon borrowing Zeller's *Die Philosophie der Griechen* from the Queen's College Library in December of 1863, to read a synopsis of the philosophy of Aristippus. He might have encountered it again in 1868. A review of Oswald J. Reichel's translation of Zeller's *Socrates and the Socratic Schools*, the part of *Die Philosophie der Griechen* including the section on Aristippus, appeared in the *Saturday Review of Politics, Science and Art* on 18 July, 1868 (93–5). This anonymous review either anticipates several of the ideas that were to become identified with Pater, or it was written by Pater himself. However that may be, it is a matter of record that Pater had Zeller's book in his hands in 1863, and that Zeller gives a clear and complete summary of the philosophy of Aristippus, from the subjectivity of knowledge—

Perceptions, being sensations of a change within ourselves, do not supply us with the least information as to things in themselves

to the experiential ethic—

The only rule of life is to cultivate the art of enjoying the present moment. The present only is ours.

It is possible that Pater, not only when writing *Marius*, but also when writing the "Conclusion," considered the basic 'argument' in the "Conclusion" to be Cyrenaic.

There is a double irony in the idea that opens the second half of the "Conclusion": "The service of philosophy, and of religion and culture as well, to the human spirit, is to startle it into a sharp and eager observation." The first irony is that here philosophy is enlisted in an endeavour that seems antithetical to it—enriching observation without reflection; and the second is that the name of Novalis is associated with the endeavour. On the surface, Pater's idea, stated in the second sentence, seems just an explanation of the preceding statement, a quotation from Novalis: "To philosophize is to dephlegmatize—to vivify." But in Fragment No. 15 in the "Logologische Fragmente," from which the idea is taken, Novalis did not mean that philosophy should vivify by sharpening the eye. Fichtean in orientation, he meant that it should vivify by creating awareness of the unifying principle of consciousness in oneself and in all living things. Pater simply disregarded the context of Novalis' statement and imposed his own; or perhaps when quoting he did not even remember the context.

It is very likely Ernest Renan who breathes beneath the misleading name of Novalis. Although Renan was not to appear in the library borrowings until 1883, when Pater borrowed *Mélanges d'histoire et de voyages*, he was referred to three times in "Coleridge's Writings" (111, 122, 131). The absence of borrowings of Renan's early works, coupled with Pater's demonstrated familiarity with some of them, suggests that Pater owned some of these works in the 1860s. The fact that five volumes of Renan's early works were in Pater's library at the time of his death strengthens the likelihood. *Averroès et l'Averroïsme*, an early work by Renan that Pater was to paraphrase a passage from in "Pico della Mirandola," is one that he was probably familiar with when he wrote "Coleridge's Writings" and the "Conclusion." This work could have helped Pater relate philosophy to spectacle, by maintaining that the history of philosophy was valuable as a spectacle. Renan develops this idea, as follows, in his Preface to *Averroès et l'Averroïsme*:

> from the moment when one admits that the history of the human soul is the greatest reality open to our investigations, all research to throw light on a corner of the past takes on a significance and a value. It is, in a sense, more important to know what the human spirit has thought on a problem than to have an opinion on that problem; for, even though the question is unsolvable, the work of the human spirit to solve it constitutes an experimental fact which always has its interest; and in supposing

that philosophy should be condemned to always be only an eternal and vain effort to define the infinite, one cannot deny at least that there is in this effort, for curious spirits, a spectacle worthy of the highest attention.

Pater had been very close to this humanistic, historicist statement of Renan's in "Winckelmann" when he had said: "Philosophy serves culture not by the fancied gift of absolute or transcendental knowledge, but by suggesting questions which help one to detect the passion and strangeness and dramatic contrasts of life." Here, in the "Conclusion," he differs only in emphasizing concrete rather than abstract spectacles.

The emphasis in the middle sentences of the fifth paragraph on observation of concrete details suggests the experiential stance that Pater had attributed to Goethe in "Coleridge's Writings," when he stated: "The true illustration of the speculative temper is not the Hindoo, lost to sense, understanding, individuality; but such an one as Göthe, to whom every moment of life brought its share of experimental, individual knowledge, by whom no touch of the world of form, colour, and passion was disregarded" (108). In this essay Pater also calls Goethe, as well as Renan "a true humanist," and one who "holds his theories lightly" (111). Like Hume and Renan, Goethe had helped to liberate Pater from the tyranny of philosophy.

Pater closes his fifth paragraph with a scientific image: "How may we pass most swiftly from point to point, to be present always at the focus where the greatest number of vital forces unite in their purest energy?" (311). The source of this image could be John Tyndall's "On the Relations of Radiant Heat to Chemical Constitution, Colour, Texture," the lead essay in the *Fortnightly Review* on 15 February, 1866. There is no proof that Pater read this article, but the least that can be claimed is that it is a scientific source that can explain the image. In his essay Tyndall reports several experiments conducted with flames. In one he presents to the imagination of the reader an experiment with lightless rays from an electric lamp. He collects these "dark rays" by means of a black liquid that separates them from the luminous rays. He states: "I bring these invisible rays to a focus at a distance of several feet from the electric lamp; the dark rays form there an invisible image of the source from which they issue. By proper means this invisible image may be transformed into one of dazzling brightness." He emphasizes that at the focus where the rays converge there is no light and the air is "just as cold as the surrounding air," since the ether, the transmitting medium, is "detached from the air." He adds dramatically:

> But though you see it not, there is sufficient heat at that focus to set London on fire. The heat there at the present moment is competent to

raise iron to a temperature at which it throws off brilliant scintillations.
It can heat platinum to whiteness and almost fuse that refractory metal.
It actually can fuse gold, silver, copper, and aluminium. The mo-
ment, moreover, that wood is placed at the focus it bursts into a blaze.

Pater had used imagery strikingly like Tyndall's in "Winckelmann," composed just a few months after Tyndall's essay appeared, in writing an
analogy to explain how Browning was able to take characters unremark-
able in themselves (like the invisible dark rays, one may say) and put
them into a situation that 'glorifies' them. He states: "To realize this
situation, to define in a chill and empty atmosphere [like Tyndall's cold
air, separate from the ether] the focus where rays, in themselves pale and
impotent, unite and begin to burn, the artist has to employ the most
cunning detail, to complicate and refine upon thought and passion a
thousand-fold" (99–100, 214). It seems that Tyndall's invisible rays also
inspired the image in the "Conclusion" of the focus where "vital forces
unite in their purest energy."

The first sentence of the sixth paragraph presents the most famous
image in Pater's works: "To burn always with this hard gem-like flame, to
maintain this ecstasy, is success in life." In context, it seems that this
flame is the same as that in the preceding sentence, the flame at the focus
of the pale rays. But why does Pater call it gem-like? Which gem does he
have in mind? Why does he call the flame hard? I think it possible that in
his memory Pater had conflated two images of flame described in Tyndall's
essay. At another point Tyndall describes the oxyhydrogen flame which,
like the pure flame from the dark rays, would be invisible in a clean
atmosphere. He says that its temperature is 6000 degrees Fahrenheit and
that 2000 degrees is hot enough to fuse cast iron. He adds: "When this
flame impinges on a piece of lime, we have the dazzling Drummond light."
In other words, heating calcium oxide in the flame of an oxyhydrogen torch produces calcium hydroxide; and, according to the New Columbia Encyclopedia, during this reaction "much heat is given off and the solid
nearly doubles its volume"—and the dazzling, white Drummond light, or
limelight, radiates forth. Thus Tyndall calls to mind the brightest light
known to nineteenth-century eyes, blazing from lime turned crystalline. If
Pater had this light in mind when he wrote "a hard gem-like flame," the
gem is a diamond—hard and radiant. This image relates the "ecstasy" of
the "Conclusion," which seems the summum bonum of earthly life, to
"the supreme moral charm of the Beatrice of the Commedia," referred to
in "Diaphaneitè," of which Pater states: "It does not take the eye by
breadth of colour; rather it is that fine edge of light, where the elements of

our moral nature refine themselves to the burning point." When this generalized refining fire, as well as the generalized "clear crystal nature" of Diaphaneitè (253), are remembered, it is easy to see why Pater would have been struck by Tyndall's heat and light images. The focus of the purest rays, the heat hot enough to fuse metals, and the dazzling diamond-like limelight gave him exactly the scientific, imagistic detail he could use to individualize his rather conventional general concepts. This imagery was to persist in his works. In "Dante Gabriel Rossetti," he says of Dante Alighieri: "To him, in the vehement and impassioned heat of his conceptions, the material and the spiritual are fused and blent: if the spiritual attains the definite visibility of a crystal, what is material loses its earthiness and impurity." And in "The Genius of Plato," he states: "For him [Plato], as for Dante, in the impassioned glow of his conceptions, the material and the spiritual are blent and fused together. While, in that fire and heat, what is spiritual attains the definite visibility of a crystal, what is material, on the other hand, will lose its earthiness and impurity." The gem-like flame, thus, is associated with white light, the perfect fusion of material and spiritual elements, and Dantean ecstasy.

The implication in the remainder of the sixth paragraph is that what passes for life is often death-in-life, or, to use Pater's image, sleeping before evening. Pater's dominant message is *Wake up and look*: "While all melts under our feet, we may well catch at any exquisite passion, or any contribution to knowledge that seems by a lifted horizon to set the spirit free for a moment, or any stirring of the senses, strange dyes, strange flowers and curious odours, or work of the artist's hands, or the face of one's friend" (311). Pater had long been familiar with the idea that art lifts one above the enslavement of the world. In the *Ästhetik*, Hegel discusses at length the power of poetry to create a sense of freedom. To Hegel art was superior to nature because it proceeded from creative mind, whereas nature was bound by laws of necessity. He states: "what we enjoy in artistic beauty is just the *freedom* of its creative and plastic activity. In the production and contemplation of these we appear to escape from the principle of rule and system." Art also, according to Hegel, gives one something to cling to in the flux: "The individual living thing . . . is transitory; it vanishes and is unstable in its external aspect. The work of art persists." And it was probably Hegel who introduced Pater to the idea of the expanded moment, as it relates to painting. For Hegel it was painters who were to seek expansion of the moment, because painting can embody only one moment in time. Pater had already extended the concept to poetry in a reference in "Winckelmann" to Browning's expanded moments. In the "Conclusion," he simply takes the concept a step further, extending the expanded moment to perceptions of the real world.

In spite of his indebtedness to Hegel, Pater is quite un-Hegelian in grouping impressions from life and art together, as he does, for example, in the phrases the "work of the artist's hands, or the face of one's friend." Hegel assumed that the perceiver and the perceived work of art were both autonomous: "He [the perceiver] suffers it [the art object] to exist in its free independence as an object." But Hegel did not assume that people could treat other people as if they were autonomous works of art. In "Diaphaneitè" Pater removed the distinction between life and art, recommending that people be treated "in the spirit of art," or, in other words, like autonomous works of art. And here, in the "Conclusion," he writes compellingly about observing and perceiving works of art, live hands and faces, hills—without making any distinction between what is expected from art objects, live objects, and natural scenery. This tendency to obliterate the distinction between life and art is the most startling element in the "Conclusion," because it makes life, like art, something, not to be participated in, but simply to be appreciated. To treat life in the spirit of art is to create stasis. It is true that there is one expression in the sixth paragraph of the "Conclusion" that seems to move the persona from the spectator's stance into participation. Pater states: "gathering all we are into one desperate effort to see and touch, we shall hardly have time to make theories about the things we see and touch." Touching, here, however, seems to be merely a mode of perception, as it was to Berkeley, who wrote extensively about seeing and touching, especially in *A New Theory of Vision*, Sections XLV–XLIX. For Berkeley, it was necessary to touch a tangible object in order to perceive it fully.

Near the end of the sixth paragraph Pater asserts the right to explore impressions and opinions eclectically, without allegiance to any system that would restrict vision or choice. In selecting Comte and Hegel as thinkers whose "facile orthodoxy" he will not submit to, he is divorcing himself from the two chief, opposing schools of philosophy at Oxford in his day, the positivist and the transcendental. (Hegel's aesthetic philosophy is probably not at issue here.) He thus is claiming for himself the widest range of choice, in terms that his readers will understand. A surface reading of the next passage would suggest that Pater was indebted to Victor Hugo for the idea that philosophy is an instrument for enlarging and diversifying one's experience, since he quotes Hugo's statement from *Les Misérables* ("Jean Valjean," Bk. II, ch. 2) that "philosophy is the microscope of thought." But as in the case of Novalis, Pater sets the quotation from the source into a context that places a new interpretation upon it. In Hugo's context the statement has nothing to do with eclectic appreciation; it means that nothing can escape the upright moral eye of philosophy—no evil, equivocation, or falsehood. Beneath Pater's eclectic manifesto, as beneath the related quotation from Novalis, we find the presence of Renan. In "The Religions of Antiquity" (1857), which appears to have been Pater's principal source of ideas on religion in "Coleridge's Writings" and "Winckelman," Renan states:

> Eclecticism is . . . the obligatory method of our age. . . . Schools are in science what parties are in politics: each one is right by turns; it is impossible for an enlightened man to shut himself up in one of them so exclusively as to shut his eyes to what the others hold to be reasonable.

Thus, even in asserting eclectic independence, Pater likely was following a precursor, Renan.

The final paragraph of the "Conclusion" opens with Pater's mistaken reference to the sixth book of Rousseau's *Confessions*. Pater uses the reference to enhance the main thrust of the paragraph, his advocacy of intellectual excitement. Although in Book VI Rousseau describes, as Pater says, the onset of what he thought to be a "mortal disease," he does not, as Pater says, determine that the remainder of his time can best be spent "by intellectual excitement, which he found in the clear, fresh writings of Voltaire." As Gerald Monsman has pointed out, Voltaire is not mentioned in Book VI. Also, Rousseau does not seek intellectual excitement, to expand the interval before death. He resolves to make the most of his time by employing his mind "in more noble cares, as anticipating those I should soon have to attend, and which I had till then much neglected." His studious and religious reading lead to intellectual excitement, but have not been undertaken for it.

Pater next generalizes the idea of the interval before death by referring accurately to Victor Hugo's statement, "we are all condamnés," although he did not remember the exact source of the statement or did not want to clutter his text with it. As Marcel Françon has observed, the source is *Le Dernier Jour d'un condamné* (*The Last Day of the Condemned*), a story in which a prisoner condemned to death keeps a journal of his thoughts and feelings until almost the moment of his execution. At one point he consoles himself with the idea that all people are condemned to death, although some with an "indefinite reprieve."

In concluding the "Conclusion" with a straightforward assertion that the best way to spend the interval before death is in intellectual excitement, or multiplied consciousness, and the best way to achieve this state is by the love of art for art's sake, Pater suggests the influence of Baudelaire, as well as that of Morris. There is no certain link between

Pater and Baudelaire at this time; Pater does not mention Baudelaire by name until 1876, in "Romanticism." But it would have been difficult for the alert man of letters and reader of Swinburne that Pater was in 1867 and 1868 not to have been familiar with Baudelaire's works. In "Charles Baudelaire: *Les Fleurs du mal*," in the *Spectator*, on 6 September, 1862, Swinburne had associated Baudelaire with the idea that "the poet's business is . . . to write good verses, and by no means to redeem the age and remould society" (998). In *William Blake* (1866) he had used the term *art for art's sake* in a passage in which he had also referred to Baudelaire as "a living critic of incomparably delicate insight and subtly good sense, himself 'impeccable' as an artist." On 1 January, 1868, his elegy on Baudelaire, "Ave atque Vale," appeared in the *Fortnightly Review*. Pater had been aware of Swinburne ever since he had caught a glimpse of him in the autumn of 1858 walking near Headington, and he owned copies of *Chastelard* and *Atalanta in Calydon*. He probably learned the term *art for art's sake* and its association with Baudelaire from Swinburne.

From internal evidence it appears that the idea of "multiplied consciousness" came from Baudelaire's "Le Poème du haschische," in *Les Paradis artificiels*. Baudelaire explains in this work the rewards of drug-induced acuteness of consciousness:

> If you are one of these souls [the modern *homme sensible*], your innate love of form and color will initially find great pasturage in the earliest developments of your intoxication. Colors will assume unaccustomed strength, and will enter your mind with triumphant intensity. . . . Craggy countrysides, receding horizons, city vistas whitened by the ghastly lividity of a storm, or lit by the dense heat of setting suns . . . the first sentence that hits your eyes, if they should happen to fall upon a book; in short, everything—the whole universality of existence—rises before you with a new and hitherto unsuspected glory.

Of course, Baudelaire does not recommend smoking hashish; he calls it "slow suicide." But he does regard the heightened state of mind as paradisical, an ultimate value. As one can see in the following passage, he condemns the means, not the end of intoxication:

> But man is not so forsaken, so deprived of any *honest* means of reaching heaven, that he should be obliged to turn to pharmacy and witchcraft; he need not sell his soul to pay for the intoxicating kisses and affection of the Houri.

And what honest means does Baudelaire suggest? In a word, art. To epitomize the divine intoxication he pictures a man on "the lofty summit of Olympus"; "all about him the Muses of Raphael or Mantegna compose their sublimest dances to solace him for his long fastings and constant prayers. . . . Divine Apollo, master of every art . . . gently sets his bow to the most vibrant strings." In contrast to the "false happiness" resorted to by the poor creatures of the earth who need drugs for excitement, he sets the true happiness of artists: "we, the poets and philosophers, have regenerated our souls through constant work and meditation; through the conscientious use of our Will, and the enduring loftiness of our Purpose, we made ourselves a garden of true beauty." Pater could have borrowed from Baudelaire not only the idea that the artist holds an advantage in the pursuit of multiplied consciousness, but also the idea that passionate devotees of other ideals may achieve the state. In his famous prose poem "Enivrez-vous," he advises: "Lest you be martyred slaves of Time, intoxicate yourselves, be drunken without cease! With wine, with poetry, with virtue, or with what you will." This pronouncement finds its parallel in Pater's statement that "High passions give one this quickened sense of life, ecstasy and sorrow of love, political or religious enthusiasm, or the 'enthusiasm of humanity.' Only, be sure it is passion."

And so, beneath the surface of Pater's text, the muses hum—Goethe, Renan; Fichte, Hume; Spencer, Tyndall; Hegel, Aristippus, Plato; Morris, Baudelaire. I do not mean that Pater's "Conclusion" is a pastiche of other writers' ideas, but that throughout an eight-year period, by selective reading, Pater accumulated ideas to which he felt affinities, assimilated them, and on a brilliant occasion expressed them in the "Conclusion." His originality is in the unique synthesis and the compelling expression.

In the course of this essay, I have used certain abbreviations that Gerald Monsman has used before me in his *Pater's Portraits:* The ten volumes of the standard Macmillan edition are abbreviated in the text as follows: *The Renaissance:* R; *Marius the Epicurean:* ME, I or II; *Imaginary Portraits:* IP; *Appreciations:* Ap; *Plato and Platonism:* PP; *Greek Studies:* GS; *Miscellaneous Studies:* MS; *Gaston de Latour:* GdL; and *Essays from the "Guardian":* EG. The 1889 edition of *Appreciations* is cited as Ap (1889), the *Uncollected Essays* I have abbreviated UE, and the *Imaginary Portraits* edited by Eugene Brzenk is rendered *IPB*. The numbers following the abbreviations refer to the page numbers.

JAY FELLOWS

"Abysmal Dilemmas": Pater's Withdrawing Ground

It's the same cry again: a yell possibly of terror, or of acute pain, or of feverish agitation; somewhere very close the same long-drawn-out, searing cry, quickly dying away as a distant groan, suddenly pierces the night and the silence. Sitting up in bed with a start, supporting myself on both arms held out behind me amid a tangle of damp sheets, head cocked, ears straining, I listen to the silence again, falling back

—ROBBE-GRILLET, Coda, *Topology of a Phantom City*

Paterian liturgical diction is, often, that of the "many-sided"—this, despite an apparent appeal to Apollonian centrality. As such, he is not a man of happy altitude, as of, say, Newman's "True Centre." Towers, as in "Sebastian van Storck," are suspect, though they provide the ability to look into the oblivion of his own nothingness, his own zero. But it should be pointed out that Sebastian, with his tower of oblivion, is only a Paterian "portrait" of the oblique, just as Gaston de Latour, a man, or rather *the* Paterian man, of the felicitous tower is himself part of Pater's textualized autobiography of consciousness only at Emerald's "diagonal influence." But ground level—and the search for grounding that is so important to Pater—is an activity that is, almost always, carried out on ground level. What Pater would do—attempts to do—is surround altitudinous logocentricity, its command-ing metaphysics, by his vantage points of "many-sidedness."

But the exception to this condition occurs in a quotation to *The Renaissance*, not to be dismissed, when there is a condition of "unity," of a "general elevation," "centralised, complete":

> The fifteenth century in Italy is one of these happier eras, and what is sometimes said of the age of Pericles is true of that of Lorenzo:—it is an age productive in personalities, many-sided, centralised, complete. Here, artists and philosophers and those whom the action of the world has elevated and made keen, do not live in isolation, but breathe a common air, and catch light and heat from each other's thoughts. There is a spirit of general elevation and enlightenment in which all alike communicate. The unity of this spirit gives unity to all the various products of the Renaissance. . . .
>
> (R, 14)

But this can be so because of the multiplicity inherent in the Renais-sance's vantage points—or, even as they are with the lateral Goethe, "siderealized" (R, 181), whether of an hour angle or minute, which is to say whether of a 360 degree circumscription or a divided, sixtieth part of an hour about four minutes shorter than the solar day of "frost and sun." Still, what for Ruskin is a sign of fragmentation is for Pater a strategy for prolonged coherence. Pater describes the plurality of Renaissance sides in a diction that becomes swiftly liturgical. In a variety of ways, Pater will say, as he does from almost the beginning, "For us the Renaissance is the name of a many-sided unified movement . . ." (R, 2).

The divided mastery of the elevated yet circumferentially perceived, "many-sided" Renaissance is Pater's solution to the kind of altitudinous and centered absolutism of a Coleridge ("appreciated," with important qualifications, from a distance) and a Ruskin (ignored in proximity)—a solution, circumferential in its many-sidedness, that in practice is, ironi-cally, as defensive as the Center of a shield of concentric superimposition. If perceived mastery must be divided, Pater himself often avoids that act by focusing on the less than conclusive, the less than masterful. Faced with the ultimate, he would see instead the "ante-penultimate." Discuss-ing Greek sculpture, he chooses to analyze—and make a case for—what is prior to "final mastery":

> The very touch of the struggling hand was upon the work; but with the interest, the half-repressed animation of a great promise, fulfilled, as we now see, in the magnificent growth of Greek sculpture in the succeeding age; which, however, for those earlier workmen, meant the loins girt and

the half-folded wings not yet quite at home in the air, with a gravity, a discretion and reserve, the charm of which, if felt in quiet, is hardly less than that of the wealth and fulness of final mastery.

(GS, 250)

As a strategy to deal with "final mastery," the "absolute"—what is signified by Derrida's "transcendental signified"—the flexible agility implicit in the "many-sided" is contrasted specifically to the intensity of the perception of a single-sidedness that Pater, despite his own instincts toward surgical penetration, sees as a limitation. His Wincklemann, although himself of penetrating mind, is not "one-sided": "Penetrating into the antique world by his passion, his temperament, he enunciated no formal principles, always hard and one-sided. Minute and anxious as his culture was, he never became one-sidedly self-analytical" (R, 220). The Paterian Winckelmann's procedure provokes the useful distinction that Richard Rorty makes between "Great systematic thinkers [who] are constructive and offer arguments," as opposed to the "Great edifying philosophers [who] are reactive. . . ." To be "one-sided," as well as to achieve the synoptic, is to indulge in a "taste for metaphysics," which is an "absolute or transcendental knowledge" that is the enemy of a modern philosophy and culture that asks questions rather than making assertions:

Every one who aims at the life of culture is met by many forms of it, arising out of the intense, laborious, one-sided development of some special talent. They are the brightest enthusiasms the world has to show: and it is not their part to weigh the claims which this or that alien form of genius makes upon them. But the proper instinct of self-culture cares not so much to reap all that those various forms of genius can give, as to find in them its own strength. The demand of the intellect is to feel itself alive. It must see into the laws, the operation, the intellectual reward of every divided form of culture; but only that it may measure the relation between itself and them. It struggles with those forms till its secret is won from each, and then lets each fall back into its place, in the supreme, artistic view of life. With a kind of passionate coldness, such natures rejoice to be away from and past their former selves, and above all, they are jealous of that abandonment to one special gift which really limits their capabilities. It would have been easy for Goethe, with the gift of a sensuous nature, to let it overthrow him. . . . to the larger vision of Goethe, this seemed to be a phase of life that a man might feel all round, and leave behind him. Again, it is easy to indulge the commonplace metaphysical instinct. But a taste for metaphysics may be one of those things which we must renounce, if we mean to mould our lives to artistic perfection. Philosophy serves culture, not by the fancied gift of absolute or transcendental knowledge, but by suggesting questions which help one to detect the passion, and strangeness, and dramatic contrasts of life.

(R, 229–31)

More "sides," an increased number of vantage points, is anodyne to a "taste for metaphysics." The "many-sided" continuum contains enough circumferential extension for Pater's decahedral "Voices" that, in exile, speak for a winter Dionysus and a daemonic Apollo displaced in Picardy, who would subvert the authoritative source—and perhaps even the "respectability" of the public, almost biographical, Pater. The more points of view, the less investment in an "undivided Intelligence" that, after all, becomes divided in perspectivism. It is as if the logocentricity of a metaphysics of unmitigated presence had been surrounded, perhaps attacked, in an effort to bring down that authoritative, synoptic and abstract altitudinous Center—a Center that is, in fact, significantly different in degree from the Apollonian Center that, instead of dominating the Circumference, with centrifugal spheres of excessive influence, attempts to achieve a sane—and "sanitary"— coherence of centripetence.

Towers, while extant in Pater and to be found in both "Sebastian" and "Gaston," though they differ in their performances considerably, are, as the architecture of a metaphysics of presence, hardly typical. Yet if altitudinously synoptic authority is to be brought down by the circumferential division of perception, those "many-sided" vantage points, dependent upon the reciprocity of what they see (the Paterian symbiotic relation, or informing and enforcing oscillation, between vantage and focal points are, of course, their own "paired opposites" that have yet to be undone), are themselves in a process leading to an imbalance or disequilibrium that is not itself safe. We already know that, in Paterian landscape, hollows, as of chambers for echoes, are everywhere ("There was a pool. . . ."). The ground is not firm, as if being stealthily "withdrawn" from beneath one's feet: "Surface, we say; but was there really anything beneath it?" (PP, 15). This is the Heraclitean dilemma, if it is that (and not the free-falling "abîme" of options), of an incertitude that almost appears to be "for its own sake": "Those opinions too, coming and going, those conjectures as to what under-lay the sensible world, were themselves but fluid elements of the changing surface of existence" (PP, 14). This problematic of topology is especially true on the Circumference of "many-sides," where relativity or perspectivism is close to "mid-stream." It is the territory of the exile and outlaw, the autobiographical territory of "distanced intimacy."

When the encompassing vantage points that surround the logocentric, the "transcendental signified" with its implications of metaphysical presence, have divided that "final mastery" to the point of disintegration, the many sides of the surrounding vantage points, with a major reason for their being gone, themselves tend toward a condition of decomposition. A figure that is as ironic as it is appropriate for this disintegration into the domain of echoes, or repetitions neither past nor future but of a compounded present that might, for a moment, sound like that thunder which has been awaited, the repetition of a previous thunder that has itself been predicted by the light of the "lyric glow"/lightning—that figure is the understandably "giddy earth" in the "Anima Naturaliter Christiana" chapter from *Marius*. It is as though, as a new faith arrives, abysses—the "abysm of its [the world's] own atmosphere—had been left," "under this sunless heaven," even as the old gods will be driven from their "abiding places" of efficacious presence into circumferential exile. Their legacy is only the echo, the trace. Yet in Pater that is often the case:

> Surely, the old gods were wroth at the presence of this new enemy among them! And it was no ordinary morning into which Marius stepped forth. There was a menace in the dark masses of hill, and motionless wood, against the gray, although apparently unclouded sky. Under this sunless heaven the earth itself seemed to fret and fume with a heat of its own, in spite of the strong night-wind. . . . He could have fancied that the world had sunken in the night far below its proper level, into some close, thick abysm of its own atmosphere. . . . For a moment Marius supposed himself attacked with some sudden sickness of brain, till the fall of a great mass of building convinced him that not himself but the earth under his feet was giddy.
>
> (ME 2, 211)

Yet potential fragmentation will also be delayed in another way. As with his study of Greek sculpture, Pater will choose to observe the *less* than imposing. If his recessional space accommodates distance, the distance necessary for nostalgic return, the sublime is not part of his optical repertoire. He would focus his attention, like a "sincere learner in the school of Pythagoras," "not as with the ancient Eleatics, nor as with our modern selves too often, in the 'infinite,' those eternities, infinitudes, abysses, Carlyle invokes for us so often—in no cultus of the infinite . . . but the finite . . ." (PP, 59). More precisely, Pater might be considered one of the "cultus of the minute." In fact, the relativism—"that for you, this for me"—that Gaston comes to understand in the chapter, "Suspended Judgment," is based on a perception of minute particularity:

. . . the priceless pearl of truth . . . [lies], if anywhere, not in large
theoretic apprehension of the general, but in minute vision of the
particular; in the perception of the concrete phenomenon, at this particular moment, and from this unique point of view—that for you, this for
me—now, but perhaps not then.

(GdL, 93)

The imminent departure of the immanence of the "old gods," with
their earthquake of anger, is a geographical version of the decomposition
that follows the division of a "final mastery" that is itself like the
deconstruction of the "transcendental signified"—a decomposing of vantage points that Pater would delay indefinitely by shoring up the remaining foundations both by the repetition implicit in the willful experience of
déjà vu that seeks antecedents for what would be the "jaded eye" of an
optics of familiarity and the repetition of "after-thought[s]" that provides
imaginative support from the future. He would attempt to prop himself up
by himself being in that "between" condition of antitheses that are always
close, with Pater, to being reversals of each other, as in a mirror—
reversed theses that are initially hierarchically equivalent, or in this
case, antithetical tenses that participate in the inversions of Pater's
metalepsis, where what is prior indeed has priority until the inevitable
shift of oscillation.

The "minute vision of the particular," its truth, its consequences,
in this autobiography of textualized consciousness that is of anticipation
and recollection, past and future repetitions (with a difference, doubtless,
though one awaits with increasing impatience the light, "lyric" or otherwise, the thunder), carries us back not so far as Vaughan's "The Retreat"
but to Emerald's divided literary landscape of "vignettes," which is a
topology of division. Pater's "appreciated" Sir Thomas Browne, whose
judgment may be more divided in "half" than "suspended" (as a man of
two worlds), if he can accommodate a "cultus of the infinite," is moved
more by what is "small." Though the "loose sally" or "*little trench*" is not
the genre of Browne's "literary architecture," the landscape of his special
sympathy might be Emerald's "vignettes." For Browne, "the world is but a
spectacle in which nothing is really alien from himself, who has hardly a
sense of the distinction between great and little among things that are at
all, and whose half-pitying, half-amused sympathy is called out especially
by the seemingly small interests and traits . . ." (A, 128).

With more conviction than a whole "interest" that is divided half
into pity and half into sympathy, there is Charles Lamb, who, amidst
overt disequilibrium far greater than Pater's, shares Pater's predilection for

the diminutive—a concern for the small which is almost erotic—that is a substitute for metaphysical considerations:

> Unoccupied, as he might seem, with great matters, he is in immediate contact with what is real, especially in its caressing littleness, that littleness in which there is much of the whole woeful heart of things, and meets it more than half-way with a perfect understanding of it. What sudden, unexpected touches of pathos in him!—bearing witness how the sorrow of humanity, the *Weltschmerz*, the constant aching of its wounds, is ever present with him: but what a gift also for the enjoyment of life in its subtleties, of enjoyment actually refined by the need of some thoughtful economies and making the most of things! Little arts of happiness he is ready to teach to others. The quaint remarks of children which another would scarcely have heard, he preserves—little flies in the priceless amber of his Attic wit—. . . .
>
> (A, 110)

Undeniably, there is that prevailing sense of *multum in parvo.* Complexity would be reduced in size without a loss of elaboration. In *Gaston,* a reduced world in miniature emerged from a few books: "Like their elders, they [the half-clerical pages] read eagerly, in racy, new translations, old Greek and Latin books, with a delightful shudder at the wanton paganism. It was a new element of confusion in the presentment of that miniature world" (GdL, 37). Diction of the inverted sublime proliferates. Pater's is a vocabulary of the microscope. What is "dainty" is perceived and expressed. If the Paterian world is in miniature, so is Aphrodite's "architecture . . . of dainty splendour": ". . . [Aphrodite's] connexion with the arts is always an intimate one. In Cyprus her worship is connected with an architecture, not colossal, but full of dainty splendour—the art of the shrine-maker, the maker of reliquaries; the art of the toilet, the toilet of Aphrodite. . . ." But even Homer—the "true Homer"—is full of that "dainty splendour," "delight in which we have seen to be characteristic of the true Homer" (GS, 219). Early Greek art, informed by the Asiatic, is of a "delicacy," a "daintiness of execution": ". . . that [Asiatic] spirit of minute and curious loveliness, follows the bolder imaginative efforts of Greek art all through its history, and one can hardly be too careful in keeping up the sense of this daintiness of execution through the entire course of its development" (GS,222). And if that "daintiness" carries over to a "life-sized Venus of Melos," for example, it is particularly apparent in the elaborately diminutive, where line itself is "*multum in parvo.*" There is, especially, the "minute object of art, the tiny vase-painting, intaglio, coin, or cameo, [which] often reduces into the palm of

the hand lines grander than those of many a life-sized or colossal figure . . ."
(GS, 222–23).

Influenced by Dante, Pater's Michelangelo, in his role as poet, is
of Pater's cultus of the finite-minute. He learns "to dwell minutely on the
physical effects of the presence of a beloved object on the pulses of the
heart" (R, 88). Dwelling minutely, a poetic Michelangelo is not much
different from Pater's Leonardo, whose preferred lens is no less explicit:
"In this return to nature, he was seeking to satisfy a boundless curiosity by
her perpetual surprises, a microscopic sense of finish by her *finesse*, or a
delicacy of operation, that *subtilitas naturae* which Bacon notices" (R,
109–10). A finish that is no ending but a "microscopic sense" of "perpetual surprises" is like the divided interval of the "moment," which is also
the "infinitely divisible" middle of *means* in place of an *end*, the "final
mastery" of which would only be hypothetical.

Pater, in the essay on Coleridge, considers the nature of what he
calls the "modern spirit" (A, 66), which, in the collapsed space of self-
consciousness, combines the narcissist's mirror with the scientist's
microscope—the modern mind that, like the sublimated, displaced/projected
and then reflexively examined "distanced intimacy" of Pater's own
metamorphosizing mind, is itself precisely "so minutely self-scrutinizing . . ."
(A, 98). The "fugitive" and "relative" spirit of a science of observation would view with an exactitude that necessarily encompasses as little
as possible in the found or "given" moments of Heraclitean mutability.
The perception brought by the microscope would divide, lower, and
minutely analyse the generalizations of synoptic altitude, as if to make a
"theory or idea or system" (R, 237) more specifically accurate, and, at the
same time, less burdensomely livable. Truth is found not from the True
Centre but in weightless, "dainty," and "furtive detail." It is as if Western
metaphysics were being undermined by Eastern, or Asiatic exactitude:
"The growth of those sciences consists in a continual analysis of facts of
rough and general observation into groups of facts more precise and
minute. The faculty for truth is recognized as a power of distinguishing
and fixing delicate and fugitive detail" (A, 66–67).

The perceptions of science are reflected in the way one writes. At
once creating and erasing before the creative/erasure of "white memory,"
the writer, in "Style," must earn the reader's "minute consideration" by
an editorial process that accompanies inspiration. There must be a "sense
of self-restraint and renunciation, having for the susceptible reader the
effect of a challenge for minute consideration; the attention of the writer,
in every minutest detail, being a pledge that it is worth the reader's while
to be attentive . . ." (A, 14). Like his Flaubert, Pater, with a mind that

is representative in that it is indeed "modern," if not "post-modern" in its indeterminacy, will be a "minute and constant observer" (A, 20), searching for that much *in* little, if he is not in fact merely content, for a while, making much *of* little—a tempest in a teapot of, say, Charles Lamb's blue china. Many minute sides are also many temporal minutes, and aspects of the "many-sided" Renaissance predict that "modern mind" of Paterian perception, his shaping claustrophilia that is not entirely shared by the post-structural critical consciousness which would do partial, or "erased," combat with "closure" (the allure, as well as fear, of the "*abîme*," beneath the "giddy earth," the options for "freeplay" in freefall), while Pater would for a time attempt to regard the fleeting interval of the present as an enclosing, small white room to be returned to, as an "after-thought," in an act of the phenomenologically impelled, nostalgia of "white memory."

With Pater, even the Pater of endless interiorities, the "modern mind" is new, and the new is small and weightless, if not in fact childish—though if relative optics are "innocent," the more characteristic sight of a Pater, who would find some measure of what Derrida terms a "reassuring certitude" amidst the "substance 'in vacuo' " (PP, 41) of a dismantled metaphysics, is the jaded sight of repetition. It is as if a proportionate world might be seen from a doll's house. Views of the Outside, as we have come to understand, are most comfortable when "framed": the liminality and topology of a framing window, domesticating Euclidean space, tend toward both the picture frame that may, as it does with Sebastian van Storck, hold a miniaturized replica of the Outside, and the temporal frame, behind which (after "return"), there is, along with the "pre-eminently childish" (R, 173) "furniture" of toys, a remembered Outside—an Outside remembered from within what may be one of those "sacred places" (GS, 133) of recovered anteriority and problematic origins, an Outside which would subvert, in diminution and returned-to earliness, the tentatively final conclusion of the "Conclusion" that is the "evening," after a "short day" ("siderealized" or solar?) of death's "final mastery."

Unsurprisingly, Pater is more "at home" in an early Inside than in a late Outside, with the retrospective miniature than the prospective sublime, the microscope than the telescope—and home, if not a doll's house, is where he wants to be both initially, as the Child, and then, finally, as an adult with both experience of the world and the fact and memory of intense nostalgia, an adult who may well be Florian Deleal, having earned his name in necessary, perhaps "Asiatic," centrifugal individuation and "freeplay" that may be of extraordinary intricacy. He would prefer, perhaps require, the myopia of relativism to an ironically youthful prolepsis, with its authoritative, sometimes transcendental judgments that an optics of distance would make both inevitable and of dubious comfort.

Pater, characteristically, finds the modern in the past, or at least the seeds of the modern at a convenient distance. Often, "historically," as well as in the "distanced intimacy" of his autobiography of textualized consciousness, he would talk about immediacy at a distance, the present tense in the past. Paterian philosophy, which is the " 'microscope of thought,' " may be written in a discourse that, advertising the passion of the present, is not, in fact, close enough for the comfort of the "home-body." Still, Pater seems to speak most easily of the present—and the specificity of that present's mutable moment—in the past, and, seemingly, the further back that past-located present the better. (One senses that the incompleted *Gaston*, as opposed to the more historically distanced *Marius*, is creeping up on Pater; further, one is beginning to speak of an anterior present, relinquishing its anteriority as well as an anterior presence.)

Pater, who is quick to point out that Plato himself said nothing new (history as organic unoriginality of occasionally new conjunctions), finds the modern "fugitive" spirit of infinite refinement that is an important component of the relative in the work of Giorgione, which is itself reminiscent of a previous model, Plato's, that would amplify the "smallest interval of musical sound, the smallest undulation in the air." Pater's perception of what is essentially modern is based upon previous repetitions of "reassuring certitude" that "effectively" go back to Plato, and then "beyond . . . unconscious philosophy, again, to certain constitutional tendencies, persuasions, forecasts of the intellect itself" (PP, 7), presumably disappearing into the amorphous anteriority of problematic origins. As depicted in the work of the school of Giorgione—a passage perhaps anticipated by Plato—sound joins Pater's phenomenology of the little, as "life itself is conceived as a sort of listening" (R, 151) in paintings that are themselves about hearing. Reading, one looks to listen to those microscopic moments of sound, "perfect moments of music itself" which are epiphanic, that might be the sound of a gem-like flame flickering:

> It is towards the law or condition of music, as I said, that all art like this is really aspiring; and, in the school of Giorgione, the perfect moments of music itself, the making or hearing of music, song or its accompaniment, are themselves prominent as subjects. On that background of the silence of Venice, so impressive to the modern visitor, the world of Italian music was then forming. In choice of subject, as in all besides, the *Concert* of the *Pitti* Palace is typical of everything that Giorgione, himself an admirable musician, touched with his influence. In sketch or finished picture, in various collections, we may follow it through many intricate

variations—men fainting at music; music at the pool-side while people fish, or mingled with the sound of the pitcher in the well, or heard across running water, or among the flocks; the tuning of instruments; people with intent faces, as if listening, like those described by Plato in an ingenious passage of the *Republic,* to detect the smallest interval of musical sound, the smallest undulation in the air, or feeling for music in thought on a stringless instrument, ear and finger refining themselves infinitely, in the appetite for sweet sound; a momentary touch of an instrument in the twilight, as one passes through some unfamiliar room, in a chance company.

(R, 150–51)

Again, this time in "A Prince of Court Painters," Pater writes about seeing the "small" that is, or will be, the subject of painting. Before Coleridge's "distant vision" of absolute transcendence, Pater's first person, in a diary entry dated "August 1717," discusses the arrival of a new era, the subject matter of which for Watteau will be, among other things, an "infinite littleness" that would be later, perhaps especially, appropriate *after* Coleridge's sublime, though burdensome, "views"—optics and thoughts appropriately joined: to see *should be* at least to provoke thought, if not form an opinion " 'unmixedly' " or otherwise:

And yet! (to read my mind, my experience, in somewhat different terms) methinks Antony Watteau reproduces that gallant world, those patched and powdered ladies and fine cavaliers, so much to its own satisfaction, partly because he despises it; if this be a possible condition of excellent artistic production. People talk of a new era now dawning upon the world, of fraternity, liberty, humanity, of a novel sort of social freedom in which men's natural goodness of heart will blossom at a thousand points hitherto repressed, of wars disappearing from the world in an infinite, benevolent ease of life—yes! perhaps of infinite littleness also.

(IP, 33)

In the infinity of the little that is Pater's present tense—the microscopic moment, which, "infinitely divisible" (R, 235), seems longer than that "short day" which is in fact a life-time that would, in an act of diurnal self-cannibalization, perhaps be Pater's answer to the problem of how to experience "vital forces . . . in their purest energy"—resides precisely in the "uncalculated present." Paterian "perspectivist" success is the failure to form habits (with freedom implicit that, nevertheless, does not include the abyssal freefall of the Sublime Below)—a failure that nevertheless permits the limited, if not minute, focus of the one "particular and privileged hour" (ME 2, 68) that Marius experiences in the chapter, "The Will as Vision." If Paterian *déjà vu* is another expression of the "Will as Vision," with its *willed* or forged "first sight" that permits the

desirably experienced "second sight" or "afterthought," the repetition of
"one privileged hour" (ME 2, 71), can occur again in an unforging or
authentic present whose only *will* is mnemonic, the opposite of that active
forgetfulness which is more often a translated "creative/erasure":

> Himself—his sensation and ideas, never fell again precisely into focus as
> on that day, yet he was richer by its experience. But for once only to
> have come under the power of that particular mood, to have felt the
> train of reflections which belong to it really forcible and conclusive . . .
> left this one particular hour a marked point in life never to be forgotten.
>
> (ME 2, 71)

Pater's present is largely a tense of interrogation or speculation—of
edification theorizing about the efficacy of not having theories. But Marius will make a case, at least for a while, for a virtually microscopic "apex"
that may, in the minute particularity of an interval expanded as much as
possible, provide the only security available in a world where the decomposing ground, perhaps revealing nothing beneath, becomes a vanishing
point: ". . . what is secure in our existence is but the sharp apex of the
present moment between two hypothetical eternities, and all that is real
in our experience but a series of fleeting impressions . . ." (ME 1, 146).
The Pater whose present tense of the "Conclusion" is an "infinitely
divisible" *little infinity* has perhaps become the Marius of the securely
"sharp apex," a present tense surrounded by "eternities" that, if "hypothetical," are not the enclosed dimensions of the Paterian claustrophile
whose extensive dimensions would be framed. Certainly, this is not the
Marius who would shore up his condition of "between" by anterior and
prospective repetitions, the useful "illusion" of *déjà vu* or even the equally
useful illusion of "*déjà vu* inverted." But then the time of the "sharp apex"
is not known for its staying power, its endurance. What is "secure in our
existence" would seem to require all the help, even all the fictions, it can
get.

A young Marius, especially one who is the age of the Marius of
the "New Cyrenaicism," may of course be not much younger than the
writer of the "Conclusion," but with Marius and Pater perpetually shifting
stances in the process of a temporally vacillating education—or education
in which attitudes toward time vacillate—the "sharp apex" of assumed
security is at best a dubious temporal perspectivism pointing to blurred
"fleeting impressions." Still, Marius will announce—and this, as if to
convince either himself or one aspect of Pater—the banishment of those
extensive, if not eternal, tenses of both "regret and desire," as Pater
himself presents or discovers, by proxy, a landscape of presence-in-absence,

oddly enough, given the historical context of the book, of an America that is not only *"here"* but *"now"*—*"here, or nowhere"*:

> And so the abstract apprehension that the little point of this present moment alone really is, between a past which has just ceased to be and a future which may never come, became practical with Marius, under the form of a resolve, as far as possible, to exclude regret and desire, and yield himself to the improvement of the present with an absolutely disengaged mind. *America is here and now—here, or nowhere:* as Wilhelm Meister finds out one day, just not too late, after so long looking vaguely across the ocean for the opportunity of the development of his capacities.
>
> (ME 1, 139)

If the objections of perspectivism that Pater raises against the metaphysical, the undialogized authoritative, are an answer, a solution, they can only be so for a time. "Many-sides" eventually yields too many sides, too many vantage points, and the ground beneath the ground-level that is supposed to save, itself, of necessity, becomes eroded—or a condition very much like the groundlessness of Heraclitus, "stealthily withdrawing the apparently solid earth itself from beneath one's feet" (PP, 15). Then, despite Pater's interest in the penetration of surfaces, there must follow the dream of the abyss, its groundlessness that is like a nightmare. The subversion of the metaphysical must lead to the subversion of the surrounding "many-sides."

With Pater, *"nowhere"* may be no discernible time, no focused time. The present tense that Marius will improve is elsewhere discussed in terms that range from the simple assertion of the almost infinite potential of its existence to the perhaps more convincing uncertainty of its groundless and essentially subjunctive condition: "If he [Marius] could but count on the present. . . ." In fact, the "sharp apex" of the present, which is itself an example of the "Will as Vision," speaks of a kind of bravado in the face of a shattered metaphysics, a defined and willed tense that is supported—or rather exists—because of what surrounds it, the various repetitions of various differences. Far from giving himself over to the present, Pater, whose world is organized about the "before" and "after," about what is "deferred" until later and what later is "belated," is obsessed with those tenses of "regret and desire," the traffic back and forth between them, as with the crossings and recrossings over Euler's seven bridges of Koenigsberg, beneath which once "dark under-current[s]" may have emerged into sunlight.

Time—as of an "awful brevity"—has been seen to be a problematic entity, dependent upon cross-references and metalepses for support. Paterian ground, or *place*, presents many of the same problems: its infirmity. The

Paterian abyss—enjoyed by certain post-structuralists—requires the maker of bridges or the protoweaver. A fall into nothingness is not likely, for Pater, to be a pleasure—despite instincts to penetrate surfaces. At least, an unsupportable logocentricity has supported. What is "below" is viewed with a certain fear. Again, it is as there were echoes beneath. That grounding is as certain as the potentially disintegrating vantage-as-vanishing-point of Heraclitus, whose stream is in some respects like Homer's "Oceanus," where there are, we recall, the "masterful currents of universal change," as well as those no less important "undercurrents of darkness and horror." This, we cannot actively forget. It is a fact of the unforgettable "*déjà là*," everywhere apparent but most obvious in Pater's nightmare-essay on Pascal in *Miscellaneous Studies*—a focal point that we shall examine before it too disappears "below," as though slipping beneath the surface of an already subterranean surface.

If Marius has "white-nights" of semi-insomnia at "White-nights," he does not have to dream himself home, where one may for a while assume that for a home-body like Pater the earth beneath one's feet will not be "giddy." Presumably, "giddy" ground is circumferential, perhaps of the Sublime Below. But as Pater would have it, in his remarkable essay on Pascal, there are, in his "Thoughts," "cries of obscure pain" as from an insomniac whose immediate grounding is, at best, tentative:

> . . . we shall not rightly measure [Pascal's "Thoughts"] but as the out-come, the utterance, of a soul diseased, a soul permanently ill at ease. We find in their constant tension something of insomnia, of that sleep-lessness which can never be a quite healthful condition of mind in a human body. Sometimes they are cries, cries of obscure pain rather than thoughts—those great fine sayings which seem to betray by their depth of sound the vast unseen hollow places of nature, of humanity, just beneath one's feet or at one's side.
>
> (MS, 82)

If Pascal, with his "vast unseen hollow places . . . just beneath one's feet or at one's side," were more artist than philosopher, he might be like Pater's ironic Merimee, who is as sympathetically, if conflicted in that sympathy, described as one of Pater's argumentative Voices ("What Meri-mee gets around his singularly sculpturesque creations is neither more nor less than empty space" [MS, 15]). But it is, in this Pascalian world of ruptured topography which is that of the Jansenist skeptic who holds a certain abyssal fascination for the Pater who pretends to see himself, of necessity, as something of the reluctant highwire artist, as if, after Heraclitus, one could be a good deal less certain about foundations in general, falling, perhaps, into depths (or ground "ungrounded") that has, in fact, already withdrawn—a groundlessness that is the "*déjà là*" of vertiginous terror. Despite bravado, Pascal speaks to Pater, as Merimee cannot.

This world of Pater's Pascal is, as a world of awesome verticality, "a scene of harsh precipices, of threatening heights and depths—the depths of his own nothingness" (MS, 86). Pascal's thoughts, his very diction, reflects the serious business of this void: "Vanity: nothingness: these are his catchwords . . ." (MS 86–87). Emptiness is the result of a God not so much in exile, as simply in hiding: "*Ce qui y paraît*" (i.e., what we see in the world) "*ne marque ni une exclusion totale ni une présence manifeste de divinité, mais la présence d'un Dieu qui se cache:*" (*Deus absconditus*, that is a recurrent thought of his) "*tout port de caractère*" (MS, 87). Despite Pater's doubly-bound almost highwire fascination for the "below," for one never-theless reluctant "mettre en abîme," his is decidedly not the amateurish (or oddly "playful") act of a professional free-fall artist; rather, what he understands are the desperate requirements for substantial grounding; the very essence and function of *place*, mnemonic or otherwise. Still, Pater's somewhat heterodox Sebastian, whose only "play" would be Russian roulette, might find himself happily (and obliviously) situated in the abyss of *space*, as the quintessential Pater, affiliated with Pascal's sense of the dread below, without enough redeeming desire, would not.

The world of Pater's Pascal is one of "abysmal dilemmas" (MS, 87). If the act of reading his "Thoughts" is like witnessing the "mental seed-sowing of the next two centuries" (MS, 82), there is also, at least as compared with the skepticism of Montaigne, something almost eschato-logical about Pascal's world. In the world of Pater's Pascal, it is as if there would *only* be a tomorrow. It seems likely that a catastrophe will occur. Pascal, as if anticipating Derrida's double-bind, might be erasing his thoughts, his "history," in his abyssal location, as well as actively, as with the "Will of [Un]Vision," forgetting the immediate future:

> It is the *world* on the morrow of a great catastrophe, the casual forces of which have by means spent themselves. Yes! this *world* we see, of which we are a part, with its thousand dislocations, is precisely what we might expect as resultant from the Fall of Man, with consequences in full working still. It presents the appropriate aspect of a lost world. . . .
>
> (MS, 86)

Pascal, with his "soul permanently ill at ease," is no more at home, unless one can become nostalgic about the abyss, than any of Pater's exiles. And like Pater's circumferential, perhaps "siderealized," personae of "distanced intimacy," and his Amielian Voices of plural vocality, of interruption (often rude), of *queries, conjectures* and the like, which may be merely "vain puerilities," so-called by Serres' demon, his Third Man of static, who would interrupt the flow of both information and energy, Pascal's footing would appear to be dependent upon that bridge (the Seven Bridges of Koenigsberg, one imagines for a moment)—though not the highwire for the highwire artist of both pragmatic and (free) play, whose wire is tight and doubly-bound (a security precaution for those interested in security). As with the catastrophe-quake of Marius, Pascal's ground is at least "giddy."

Pater is Pascalian, though one could hardly imagine the inclusion of the Pascal essay in a volume entitled "Appreciations." Obsessed with the problem of "footing," what Pater will in fact attempt, as he would attempt to gain even precarious support, what Pater, in fact, will attempt, as he would gain support, as of past and future repetitions with only minimal differences, is entirely different from the use that an early, particularly superstitious people, even then recognizing the problems of transport/topology in a primitive form, put to a child in "Denys l'Auxerrois." Certain workmen, digging around Roman ruins, look for "security"—a "similar pledge of security"—even as they see indications that their predecessors required the same "reassuring certitude," the same sense of a filled, safe ground, even if it is not Apollo's or Derrida's entirely problematic Center but rather the filling of ground in a curious way:

> It was as if the disturbing of that time-worn masonry let out the dark spectres of departed times. Deep down, at the core of the central pile, a painful object was exposed—the skeleton of a child, placed there alive, it was rightly surmised, in the superstitious belief that, by way of vicarious substitution, its death would secure the safety of all who should pass over. There were some who found themselves, with a little surprise, looking round as if for a similar pledge of security in their new undertaking.

Pater's own method of dealing with "abysmal dilemmas," or creating a *place* of temporary security, is closer to filling *in* or *over* than either burial or excavation. As an "embodied paradox," he would employ the antithetical integration of a kind of weaving process, Penelope who might be "recrossing" threads of return—a weaving process, as of palimpsestic tapestries, that must cover, as best a texture can that erases even as it superimposes the often transparent, those hollow "undercurrent[s]" below, as with a *locus standi* of presumably woven safety over an abyss of false origins and false "first sights" that may be successfully "willed" into authentic "first vision," before either the un-"vision" of *"oubliance"* or the time of the "after-thought" when priority is authenticated in regressive visitation.

Voice of Assurance (how did the speaker come by this rare commodity? Did he earn it? [doubtful!]): indeterminacy, white if you must, the relative, the Heraclitean present tense of duration/flux, the delight in phenomena—all of which arrive with a dismantled metaphysics of presence, whose accomplices (unwitting) are those "abysmal dilemmas"—are supported, given that "reassuring certitude" of the "staking" of Derrida, as of an "effective centre," by a network of weaving pattern between what is first and final. The present achieves what unwithdrawing it has by attention paid precisely to those framing tenses of "longing," or "regret and desire," what is "deferred" and "belated," and the repetitions and substitutions that are "between"—if not, as supplements, "beyond."

Voice of Query (more or less in earnest, but becoming increasingly quiet, as if exhausted): do the Seven Bridges of Koenigsberg, which must be crossed and recrossed (forever?) by the vertiginous explorer who would, but cannot, find a single, uncrossed path for the negotiation of the seven bridges, represent an analogue for the crossed and recrossed palimpsestic texture of Pater's language? Are they, those bridges of necessary crossing that would nevertheless be crossed-out, like Pater himself until, with the ultimate irreversibility of his energy, he runs, out of steam, "downhill"—as of the second law of thermodynamics? The entropaic Pater as narcissistic homebody turned home-corpse, with only the echoes of the echoes remaining . . . the dying out, slow, if inevitable, the running *down*. . . .

One suspects that the support of even a second grounding after the necessary dismantling of the logocentric is not enough. There is an increasing need for support, on ground level—more than an Architecture of the Abyss can support. Whether or not Pater can turn a *"chez soi"* into a *chez moi* that will accommodate him is, at this point, problematic—a *chez moi* of Janusian antithetical inclusion. Such concerns are for later. But for now, one can say that, with Pater, there will always be the necessary circumferential voices that threaten a "metaphysical security" that has been lost—or purposefully dismantled. "Abysmal dilemmas" are a part of the Paterian psyche that are *"déjà là."* His is a search for the *locus standi*. Perhaps there is, in fact, no *locus standi* for the "no one" that Pater at times appears to be.

Chronology

1839 Born August 4 in Shadwell, East London. Was moved soon after to Enfield, near London, the scene of "The Child in the House."

1842 Death on January 28 of father, Richard Pater.

1853–58 Student at the King's School, Canterbury.

1854 Death on February 25 of mother, Maria Pater.

1858 Entered Queen's College, Oxford, to read Classics.

1862 Graduated Queen's College; remained in Oxford tutoring private pupils.

1864 Became Fellow of Brasenose College, Oxford, where until 1885 he taught.

1865 Travels in Italy, particularly to Florence.

1866 Prints early version of his essay "Coleridge."

1869 Moves to house in Oxford with his sisters, Hester and Clara. Begins close association with Swinburne, Dante Gabriel Rossetti and Burne-Jones.

1873 Publication of *Studies in the History of the Renaissance*. Public fame begins.

1885 Publication of *Marius the Epicurean*. Moves to London, in August, with his sisters.

1887 Publication of *Imaginary Portraits*.

1889 Publication of *Appreciations*.

1893 Publication of *Plato and Platonism*. Moves back to Oxford with his sisters.

1894 Death in Oxford on July 30.

Contributors

HAROLD BLOOM, Sterling Professor of the Humanities at Yale University, is the author of *The Anxiety of Influence, Poetry and Repression*, and many other volumes of literary criticism. His forthcoming study, *Freud: Transference and Authority*, attempts a full-scale reading of all of Freud's major writings. A MacArthur Prize Fellow, he is general editor of five series of literary criticism published by Chelsea House.

GRAHAM HOUGH is Emeritus Professor of English at Cambridge University. His best known book remains *The Last Romantics*.

IAN FLETCHER, formerly of the University of Reading, is now Professor of English at the University of Arizona. He is the foremost authority on the English literature of the period 1880–1914, and is widely known for his writings on Pater, Swinburne, Lionel Johnson, and W. B. Yeats.

J. HILLIS MILLER is Frederick W. Hilles Professor of English and Comparative Literature at Yale University. He is the best known spokesman both for the Geneva school of criticism of Georges Poulet, and for the deconstruction of Jacques Derrida and the late Paul de Man. His studies of Victorian and modern literature include *The Disappearance of God, Poets of Reality*, and important books on Charles Dickens and Thomas Hardy. He has also written extensively on William Carlos Williams and Wallace Stevens.

GERALD MONSMAN has written extensively upon every aspect of Pater's work. He is Professor of English at Duke University.

PERRY MEISEL is Professor of English at New York University. Besides his book on Pater and Virginia Woolf, he has written on Thomas Hardy and on Freud.

BILLIE ANDREW INMAN is Professor of English at the University of Arizona. She is the author of *Walter Pater's Reading*.

JAY FELLOWS is Mellon Professor of Literary Theory at the Cooper Union School of Architecture. He is the author of *The Failing Distance* and *Ruskin's Maze*, two remarkable studies of John Ruskin, and of two equally distinguished forthcoming books on Pater entitled *Paterian "Under-Textures"* and *White Indeterminacy in Walter Pater*.

Bibliography

Aldington, Richard, ed. *The Selected Works of Walter Pater.* New York: Duell, Sloan and Pearce, 1948.

Benson, Arthur Christopher. *Walter Pater.* London: Macmillan, 1906.

Bloom, Harold, ed. *The Selected Writings of Walter Pater.* New York: Columbia University Press, 1974.

Child, Ruth C. *The Aesthetic of Walter Pater.* New York: Macmillan, 1940.

Crinkley, Richmond. *Walter Pater: Humanist.* Lexington: The University of Kentucky Press, 1970.

Currie, Robert. "Pater's Rational Cosmos." *Philological Quarterly* 59, no. 1 (Winter 1980).

DeLaura, David J. *Hebrew and Hellene in Victorian England.* Austin: The University of Texas Press, 1969.

Dellamora, Richard. "Pater's Modernism: The Leonardo Essay." *The University of Toronto Quarterly* 47 (1977–78).

Evans, Lawrence, ed. *The Letters of Walter Pater.* Oxford: Clarendon Press, 1970.

Fletcher, Ian. *Walter Pater.* London: Longmans Green, 1959.

Hough, Graham. *The Last Romantics.* London: Gerald Duckworth, 1949.

Johnson, R. V. *Walter Pater: A Study of his Critical Outlook and Achievement.* Melbourne: Melbourne University Press, 1961.

Lenaghan, R. T. "Pattern in Pater's Fiction." *Studies in Philology* 18 (1961).

Levy, Michael. *The Case of Walter Pater.* London: Thames and Hudson, 1978.

Meisel, Perry. *The Absent Father: Virginia Woolf and Walter Pater.* New Haven: Yale University Press, 1980.

Monsman, Gerald Cornelius. *Walter Pater.* Boston: Twayne Publishing Co., 1977.

———. *Pater's Portraits: Mythic Pattern in the Fiction of Walter Pater.* Baltimore: Johns Hopkins University Press, 1980.

———. *Walter Pater's Act of Autobiography.* New Haven: Yale University Press, 1980.

———, ed. "Walter Pater: An Imaginative Sense of Fact." *Prose Studies* 4, no. 1 (May 1981).

Peters, Robert. "The Cult of the Returned Apollo: Walter Pater's 'Renaissance' and 'Imaginary Portraits.' " *Journal of Pre-Raphaelite Studies* 2, no. 1 (November 1981).

Seiler, R. M., ed. *Walter Pater: The Critical Heritage.* London: Routledge and Kegan Paul, 1980.

Sharp, William. *Papers Critical and Reminiscent.* London: Heinemann, 1912.
Stein, Richard L. *The Ritual of Interpretation: The Fine Arts as Literature in Ruskin, Rossetti and Pater.* Cambridge: Harvard University Press, 1975.
Wright, Thomas. *The Life of Walter Pater.* 2 vols. London: Everett, 1907.

Acknowledgments

"Introduction" by Harold Bloom from *Selected Writings of Walter Pater*, edited by Harold Bloom, copyright © 1974 by Harold Bloom. Reprinted by permission of New American Library, New York.

"The Paterian Temperament" by Graham Hough from *The Last Romantics* by Graham Hough, copyright © 1947 by Methuen & Co., Inc. Reprinted by permission.

"The Place of Pater: *Marius the Epicurean*" by Harold Bloom from *The Ringers in the Tower* by Harold Bloom, copyright © 1971 by The University of Chicago Press. Reprinted by permission.

"Walter Pater" by Ian Fletcher from *Walter Pater* by Ian Fletcher, copyright © 1959, 1971 by Ian Fletcher. Reprinted by permission.

"Walter Pater: A Partial Portrait" by J. Hillis Miller from *Daedalus* 105, no. 1 (Winter 1976), copyright © 1976 by J. Hillis Miller. Reprinted by permission of *Daedalus*, Boston, MA.

"The Abandoned Text: *Gaston de Latour*" by Gerald Monsman from *Walter Pater's Art of Autobiography* by Gerald Monsman, copyright © 1980 by Yale University. Reprinted by permission of Yale University Press.

"The Chemistry of the Crystal" by Perry Meisel from *The Absent Father: Virginia Woolf and Walter Pater* by Perry Meisel, copyright © 1980 by Yale University. Reprinted by permission of Yale University Press.

"The Intellectual Context of Walter Pater's 'Conclusion' " by Billie Andrew Inman from *Journal of Prose Studies* 4, no. 1 (May 1981), copyright © 1981 by Frank Cass & Co., Ltd. Reprinted by permission.

" 'Abysmal Dilemmas' : Pater's Withdrawing Ground" by Jay Fellows from *Abysmal Dilemmas* by Jay Fellows, copyright © 1986 by Stanford University Press. Reprinted by permission of Jay Fellows.

Index